CHALLENGE

THE SOUTH DAKOTA STORY

By Robert F. Karolevitz

BREVET PRESS, INC.
Sioux Falls, South Dakota

PINE HILL PRESS, INC.
Freeman, S. Dak. 57029

Dedicated to
South Dakotans of All Eras
— Indian and non-Indian, men and women —
and especially to those
who have faced and conquered
the challenges in anonymity.

A FOREWORD

South Dakota is unique among the 50 in its capacity to test the timbre and temperament of those who have called it home.

Other states may possess greater wealth, have more natural attractions, boast of teeming populations and beckon job-seekers with massive, depersonalizing industries.

But South Dakota's uniqueness comes from less definable characteristics relating mostly to her people. If there are any general traits which seem to epitomize a majority of South Dakotans — Indian and non-Indian, from pre-territorial days to the present — they include a fierce but quiet pride in an independent spirit, an intense insistence upon "elbow room," and a sense of personal conquest under geographical conditions and climate which have not always been favorable to the faint-hearted or the unenduring.

The purpose of this book (besides telling the story of the land and those who have lived upon it) is to instill a sense of pride among natives of and sojourners in the United States commonwealth which measures up to the galvanic title of *The Challenge State*.

In the past, South Dakota has been semiofficially nicknamed for the coyote, the environmentally adaptable but not universally appreciated official state animal which inhabits all 67 counties. It has also been known as the Sunshine State, a title it shares with Florida, but not always in the same positive context since solar intensity (especially in July and August) has often afforded mixed blessings to farmers and ranchers in an agriculturally dominated area. Another popular reference has been the "Land of Infinite Variety," but that slogan, too, is more promotional than properly descriptive since many other states have as much or more physical diversity.

Unlike the previous nicknames, the *challenge* concept is appropriate to both the land and the people. It is a word which has a positive, inspiring tone. It pointedly describes and dramatizes the continuing struggle for a free-spirit life by Indians, homesteaders, farmers and entrepreneurs who have pitted themselves against nature on the prairie arena.

Success against odds is always more gratifying than unearned reward, and in that regard South Dakotans can stand tall knowing that what they have achieved has not come easy.

A determined effort has been made to face reality in this book. Not every chapter in the state's history sparkles with virtue nor have all the characters in the drama been faultless and honorable. Recognition of these shortcomings is mandatory to the truth. For instance, we cannot excuse what ultimately occurred when two peoples from two unlike cultures (Indian and white) came into conflict on the land to which each, for their own reasons, honestly felt entitled to possess.

We can, however, seek to understand the conditions which brought about the unhappy results without resorting to emotional generalizations which enflame and perpetuate the problem rather than guiding it to solution. Truth is usually found between the extremes, and in almost any uncolored reporting of historical conflict, that truth often must be faced remorsefully and apologetically by one or both sides of any given issue.

Use of the expression "white" to describe in general the region's non-Indian pioneers is not meant to discredit blacks or Orientals who also came to the Territory in the early days. The facts are, however, that their numbers were few and their influence limited by the practices and prejudices of the post-Civil War period.

Portraying the state's rich but occasionally rustic heritage posed two basic decisions:

First, because this volume was commissioned originally for use as a textbook at the junior high school level, it was necessary to choose between tailoring the narrative strictly for the educational process or developing the story for an all-age audience. It is a recognized precept that by demanding more from students, greater results will be achieved. For that reason, the second course has been followed; and, as a consequence, a few vocabulary challenges have been presented to the young people. However, not only does this permit the book to fill a general readership void, but such important elements of the South Dakota epic as the white-and-Indian relationships cannot be explained adequately in limited terms.

Secondly a choice of presentation had to be made from among the traditional year-by-year, event-by-event chronological approach; the use of unrelated chapters, each devoted to a specific topic; or a somewhat innovative tack of developing the text around a series of major challenges which were responsible for the way in which the state and its people emerged socially, politically and economically.

In the end, the latter format was selected because it permitted greater opportunity to emphasize and expand the *why* as well as the *what* of the unfolding saga. Though a continuing effort was made to tie the challenge sections together to maintain the flow of the story through the years, rigid chronology was interrupted whenever necessary to avoid a litany of dates, names and places.

There were other considerations, too.

Obviously, it was not possible to trace or even mention the development (and in some cases the demise) of all the towns and cities in the state. The same was true of the long roster of political, religious, educational, cultural, business and tribal leaders who left their impressions in varying degrees on the South Dakota scene. The omissions were made largely by subjective choice; but to assist those who may want to fill in the voids, an extensive bibliography has been included.

This book, understandably, cannot be all things to all people, so its principal job is to provide historic highlights and to serve as a springboard for further reading elsewhere. Serious students and others interested in greater depth can turn to the somewhat ponderous, disjointed (and occasionally inaccurate) five-volume *History of Dakota Territory* by George W. Kingsbury; Dr. Herbert S. Schell's excellent *History of South Dakota;* the various *History Collections* of the South Dakota State Historical Society; *Dakota Territory 1861-1889: A Study of Frontier Politics* by Howard Roberts Lamar; and *Dakota Panorama,* edited by J. Leonard Jennewin and Jane Boorman for the Dakota Territory Centennial Commission, which contains an outstanding bibliography and a series of informative though unrelated essays about the region's past.

Finally, it must be pointed out that this is a book of history and not of current events. Consequently, the story is not brought completely up-to-date for one primary reason: the long-range effects of legislative action, dramatic happenings, the contributions of individuals, and the seemingly wondrous achievements of science and technology require an aging period of a decade or more before accurate assessments and valid judgments can be made. Therefore, the most recent developments have either been limited to brief mention or left to the reader to keep personally informed through the news media or other contemporary publications.

With those introductory remarks, this "labor of love" is offered with the hope that it will generate native pride in *The Challenge State* and provide a realistic textbook for studying the heritage of a bountiful land — where the bounty is seldom attained without a struggle.

— Robert F. Karolevitz

PRONUNCIATION GUIDE

The names of some of the people, tribes, places and geographic features involved in South Dakota's history may be unfamiliar because they have been derived from Indian or foreign sources or are pronounced unusually by local tradition. For that reason, the following guide is included:

Arikara	A-*rick*-a-rah
Belle Fourche:	Bell *Foosh*
Bijou Hills:	*Bee*-jew Hills
Bon Homme:	*Bon*-um
Brule or Brulé:	Brool (the popular usage) or Brew-*lay* (the original French used in reference to the subtribe)
Burleigh:	*Burr*-lee
Chouteau:	*Shoo*-toe
Flandreau:	*Flan*-droo
Kadoka:	Ka-*dough*-ka
Kneip:	Ka-*nipe*
La Verendrye:	Lah Va-*ron*-dray
Lead:	Leed
Mdewakanton	Mehday-*wah*-con-tahn
Medary:	Meh-*dare*-ee
Mellette:	Meh-*let*
Minneconjou:	Min-neh-*con*-jew
Moreau:	Mah-*roe*
Oahe:	Oh-*ah*-hee
Oglala:	Oh-*glah*-lah
Picotte:	*Pee*-cot
Pierre:	Peer
Sans Arcs	Sahnz Arks
Sica Hollow:	*Shee*-cha Hollow
Sioux:	Soo
Trudeau:	*True*-dough
Volin:	*Vah*-lin
Wahpekute:	Wah-peh-*cue*-tay
Wakonda:	Wa-*kon*-da
Yanktonnais:	*Yank*-tone-nay

CONTENTS

A PROLOGUE

SETTING THE HISTORICAL STAGE

Mountain, plain or prairie fields,
Summer heat or snows,
South Dakota's people are
The grandest crop she grows.

— *Badger Clark*

South Dakota lies in the very heartland of North America. A total of 77,047 square miles of diverse land area — approximately 370 miles long by 210 miles wide — constitutes the mid-continental commonwealth which is 16th among the 50 United States in size, 45th in population (1970 census: 666,257), first in the production of gold, 39th or 40th (with its twin, North Dakota) in admission to the Union.

The dam-harnessed Missouri River — which has been known popularly through the years as the "Big Muddy" or the "Old Mizzou" — divides the state into two distinct sections, geographically and philosophically.

It has been called a "land of savage extremes," with temperatures ranging from 40 degrees below zero to 116 above, although these low and high points are relatively infrequent. It offsets its eerie

(Clyde Goin collection)

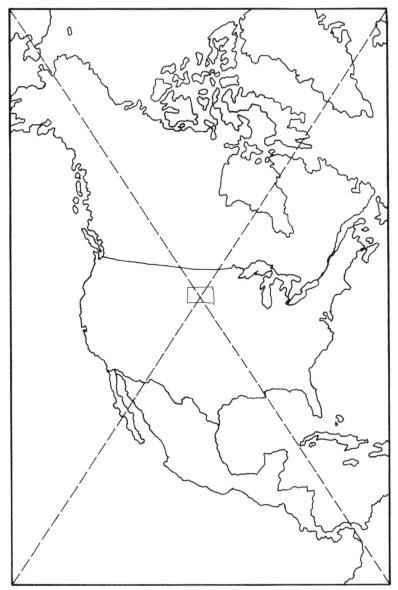

South Dakota is located in the heart of the North American continent. Similarly, the center point of the United States — including Alaska and Hawaii — has been calculated to lie 17 miles west of Castle Rock in Butte County. Within the state's 77,047 square miles, it would be possible to include the European nations of Albania, Belgium, Denmark, The Netherlands, Switzerland and Luxembourg, with enough room remaining for Israel.

Badlands — called "hell with the fires burned out" by George Armstrong Custer — with the richly productive black loam of the southeastern corner of the state. It has known blizzards, floods, dust storms and drouth — but one day of a South Dakota springtime or its matchless Indian summer makes one forget immediately the rigors of a chilling winter or a scorching July.

It is an expansive country with soaring eagles and darting prairie dogs. Beneath the earth are the splendors of Jewel Cave, and above it stand gnarled cottonwoods old enough to have witnessed the total period of organized government in the region. In April and May each year, the lavender-hued pasque — the official state flower — bursts from untilled sod on pastures and hillsides to signal a new planting season on farmlands lying under open skies in the center of the nation.

While its food and fiber production affects all the states, it physically adjoins six neighbors: North Dakota, which separates it from Canada; Minnesota and Iowa on the east; Montana and Wyoming on the west; and Nebraska to the south. Before 1889 it was part of the vast Dakota Territory. Earlier it was an undefined portion of the Louisiana Purchase from France in 1803 — and before that the Spanish claimed the prairie expanse.

Boundaries are important, of course, because they establish specific political land units and make the application of laws possible, but it must be remembered, too, that a state also means the people living within the particular borders. In other words, the geographic features of South Dakota are like a skeleton: to give it life, the flesh and blood of the citizenry must be added.

Both the land and the people will be discussed in this volume, with the greater emphasis placed on the human element. Without people there would have been no progress, no problems, no challenges, no achievement nor failures, no sorrow nor joy — the stuff of which history is made. Consequently, in Book One which follows, the collective cast of characters who participated in South Dakota's past will be introduced.

The parade of people — beginning with the Asiatic ancestors of the American Indians — has both brightened and bloodied the land, but viewed in proper context, the abrasions created by successive waves of newcomers (red and white included) are explainable and understandable — if not always defendable.

By knowing what lured or impelled various groups to migrate to the region which ultimately became South Dakota, one can grasp more readily the substance of the collision of cultures rather than belaboring the surface sore spots. The story is exciting and dramatic, often lighthearted and occasionally tragic. It is, after all, a continuing saga of people of many different backgrounds and the challenges they faced on a specific portion of the earth's real estate.

Let us begin, then, as far back in the shadows of time as we can to set the stage for this unending pageant. . . .

5

BOOK ONE

THE CHALLENGE OF CONFLICTING CULTURES

*"There are many humorous things
in the world, among them the white
man's notion that he is less savage than the other savages."*
— *Mark Twain*

We really don't know very much about the first South Dakotans.
Undoubtedly they were people of the Late Stone Age who —
more than 20,000 years before Jesus of Nazareth walked the earth —
were part of unknown numbers of migrations from Asia across the
ice-and-land bridge which then existed between Siberia and Alaska.

Who they were or by what route they finally came to the center
of the North American continent will probably never be completely
known.

But the fact remains that they did survive what must have been
one of man's most arduous journeys, and once they arrived, it is
questionable whether or not their life style was much improved in
their new surroundings.

They shared the terrain with animals no longer in existence. To-
day it seems incredible that giant earth sloths, lumbering
rhinoceroses, saber-toothed tigers, boulder-size land turtles and
woolly mammoths once roamed over the site of Rapid City; and that
tiny three-toed horses and four-horned antelopes galloped along
what is now the right-of-way of Interstate 90 west of Chamberlain.

It's true, however; and the first South Dakotans lived by hunting those unusual beasts, especially the prehistoric elephant and an
oversized cousin of the present-day bison or buffalo. With their crude
stone and wooden weapons, they also had to protect themselves
against the same animals, while they found shelter in caves or primitive huts of branches and earth when they weren't foraging for food.

Whether the people emigrated elsewhere or were wiped out by
the ravages of nature has not been accurately determined. They —
and the strange animals which existed with them in the swamplands
which rimmed the Black Hills — disappeared, however, and virtually no record of their life pattern remained.

(South Dakota Department of Tourism & Economic Development)

Meanwhile, other migratory groups were establishing themselves elsewhere on the continent, and from them a race of people (now called Indians) began to emerge. These early Indians left no written records, so their movements and tribal development have been difficult, if not impossible, to reconstruct with precise detail.

Relentlessly the years slipped away — five, ten, fifteen thousand of them — and in the region which was to become South Dakota, another group of people appeared on the scene. These ancient prairie dwellers came to be known as the Mound Builders because of the man-made hillocks which revealed their village sites to later generations. The mounds — most numerous in the Big Sioux and James River Valleys and in the vicinity of Big Stone Lake — were primarily burial grounds, but archaeological siftings have uncovered other traces of the bygone culture — bits of pottery, shell beads, stone tools and weapons. (A village of 45 identifiable lodge sites on the shore of Lake Mitchell in Davison County may well have housed tribal descendants of those earlier residents.)

Elsewhere in the world, the Egyptian pyramids were already centuries old when the Mound Builders began establishing themselves on the Dakota Plains. Obviously they lagged far behind the Iron Age which was emerging in Europe, northeast Africa and the Middle East; and in 332 B.C., when Alexander the Great conquered Egypt, they were gathering berries along the prairie streams and probably stalking deer and buffalo with their still primitive clubs and lances.

These people also faded from their Dakota domain, undoubtedly before the arrival of Columbus and again with no record of the cause of their disappearance. It could have been drouth and starvation, a harsh and bitter winter or the forceful eviction or annihilation by more powerful, marauding nomads.

Whatever the reason, the Mound Builders, too, became part of the region's mysterious past which anthropologists and archaeologists continue to explore for additional clues about the unknown South Dakotans of another era.

In truth, America was really discovered by those prehistoric Asiatics who had no calendar to mark the date nor a writing system to boast of their accomplishment. Most likely they were merely in pursuit of food or a more livable climate and did not even consider that they had come upon a "new land."

However, by the time Christopher Columbus made his famed landing in 1492, the much earlier arrivals of Mongolian strain had had many centuries to spread across both American continents and literally thousands of generations of interbreeding to develop varied physical characteristics which were later to distinguish one tribal group from another.

Social scientists have estimated that there were some 900,000 inhabitants in the area which now comprises the continental United

"SEVEN COUNCIL FIRES"

DAKOTA or SIOUX

Dialects   *Tribes*

D
A   *Santee*
K   "People   *Wahpeton* "People of the Leaves"
O   Who Use   *Sisseton* "Marsh Dwellers"
T   Knives"   *Mdewakanton* "Spirit Lake People"
A   *Wahpekute* "Shooters Among the Leaves"

N
A
K   *Yankton* "End Village People"
O   *Yanktonnais* "Little End Village People"
T
A

   Oglala "To Scatter One's Own People"
L   *Brule* (Sicangu) "Burned Thigh People"
A   *Teton*   *Two Kettle* (Oohenumpa)
K   "People
O   of the   *Sans Arc* (Itazipo) "Have No Bows"
T   Prairie"   *Blackfeet* or Black Mocassin (Sihasapa)
A   *Hunkpapa* "People Who Camp by Themselves"
   Minneconjou "People Who Plant Near the Water"

States when Columbus first planted the Spanish banner in the sands of the Bahamas. At least 200 mutually unintelligible languages — not to mention numerous dialects — reportedly were spoken in the region north of Mexico. Strangely enough, it was Columbus who mistakenly called them "people of the Indies" because he thought he had landed on the Asiatic islands still almost half a world away. The name Indians (though at first an incorrect designation) was universally adopted and became the accepted term to describe the descendants of the first Americans.

More than 400 years earlier Nordic explorers had told of encountering dark-skinned natives on the northeast corner of North America, and the Vikings referred to these people as *Skrellings*. Somehow *Indians* seems more appropriate.

It is difficult to grasp the idea of gradual changes in people and geography over thousands of years when modern civilization has been so comparatively short in time span. Consequently, reconstructing the exact details of early human involvement in the territory which was to become the future state of South Dakota is a little like trying to work a giant jigsaw puzzle for which a majority of the pieces are missing.

Through the centuries it can be assumed that numerous hunting parties or even whole tribal migrations passed across the land, but clues are rare and scattered, and the study has been further complicated by conflicting information, faulty research and unusual theories.

Among the varied unproved concepts advanced are that the Mandan Indians — who undoubtedly crossed South Dakota in their early wanderings — were directly descended from the Mound Builders or possibly from Welsh explorers who supposedly preceded Columbus to America by more than two hundred years.

Sometime prior to the first Columbus expedition, a branch of the Pawnee Indians, known as the Arikaras or Rees, began a gradual northward movement from their previous locations on the plains of Kansas and Nebraska. They were primarily agricultural Indians who raised corn, beans, squash and a narrow-leaf native tobacco. It has been conjectured that an extended drouth period may well have been the cause of their search for a new home.

Ultimately they arrived in South Dakota (no one has yet pinpointed the exact time), and at various sites on the Missouri River — notably in the vicinity of present-day Pierre — they established their permanent villages. Unlike nomadic tribes which never remained at one place long enough for a crop to grow, the Arikaras built igloo-like huts of poles and branches covered with clay and enclosed them within a log stockade surrounded by a moat or ditch.

The village itself was strategically located on a hill to improve further the defensive position against attacking enemies; and within the walls, the mud houses were systematically arranged in rows. Gardens were tilled outside the compounds and were planted and maintained by women. The men, meanwhile, hunted, fished and went on trading expeditions with furs, tobacco and other agricultural commodities. Much of the commerce was carried on to the westward with Cheyenne, Crow, Arapaho and Kiowa Indians who roamed in the area adjacent to the Black Hills. In later years — after the Spaniards had introduced the horse to the New World — the Arikaras traded for much cherished ponies.

For many decades the Arikaras — the first truly identifiable South Dakotans — lived comfortably and well in their riverside villages. Then, beginning some time during the mid-1700s, their seemingly pleasant existence was disrupted and finally destroyed by a combination of factors: the introduction of the dreaded smallpox disease by white fur traders and the westward movement of the Dakota or Sioux.Indians against whom the Arikaras were unable to defend themselves. The end result was that the seriously weakened Rees — ultimately reduced to less than 500 people — were driven up the Missouri where they were later to associate themselves with the Mandans in what was to become North Dakota.

The exodus of the Arikaras marked the beginning of a changing pattern of life on the prairie expanse. The "permanent" villages of the Mound Builders, possibly other successors to them and later the Rees, were superseded by the temporary camping grounds of a new, nomadic people — the Sioux or Dakota Indians — who moved into the South Dakota area from the east and northeast.

The "Seven Council Fires" of the Sioux or Dakota Nation represented seven major tribal units speaking one basic language with three distinct dialect divisions. In their own tongue, they referred to themselves as *Dakota* or *Lakota* Indians, the name being derived from the word *ko-dah* or *ko-lah* for "friend." Paradoxically, the word *Sioux* originally had an almost opposite meaning, being a French corruption of a Chippewa expression for "snake" or "enemy." However, because the term Sioux has lost its earlier derisive meaning, both Sioux and Dakota will be used interchangeably throughout this book.

In preceding years the tribes making up the "Alliance of Friends" apparently were located in the Ohio River Valley before the more dominant Iroquois Indians forced them out of that region. In Wisconsin and Minnesota — generally between the headwaters of the Mississippi and Lake Superior — they again were pressured heavily, this time by the Chippewas (an Algonquin branch) who had a decided advantage because of firearms procured from the French.

Exactly when the various Dakota tribes and subtribes became separate entities has not been specifically documented, but as the Dakotas were driven out of choice hunting grounds by other Indians, various groups splintered away to seek new food sources, which was then the primary concern of every social unit.

The English colonies were well established on America's eastern seaboard when the Dakotas began to emerge from the forested regions onto the open plains where — in their new environment and with the acquisition of guns and horses — they were to develop into a formidable power.

The tribes of the "Seven Council Fires" were the Wahpetons, Sissetons, Mdewakantons and Wahpekutes, known collectively as the Santees; the Yanktons and Yanktonnais, who were related closely by dialect; and the Tetons, who, in turn, were divided into seven subtribes: the Oglalas, Brules, Two Kettles, Sans Arcs, the Blackfoot band (not to be confused with a larger tribe with the same name in western Montana), the Hunkpapas and Minneconjous (see chart on page 9).

There was, of course, no mass movement of the Dakotas into what is now South Dakota. They came gradually over a period of years and by various routes, usually in pursuit of the animal most important to their survival, the buffalo. The various tribes and subtribes migrated to general geographic locations. The Yanktons, for instance, established themselves along the Missouri on both sides of the James River (also known as the Jacques or Dakota). The Yanktonnais moved to the northward between the James and Big Sioux Valleys as far as Devils Lake. The four Santee tribes encamped in the country around Big Stone Lake. Because of the nomadic character of their existence, however, it was impossible to pin them down to anything remotely resembling boundaries. They were free-spirited people, and they moved whenever and to wherever the hunting or trading called them.

The various Teton bands were especially mobile, spreading out over central South Dakota, deposing the Arikaras and ultimately crossing the Missouri to begin a century-long reign over their prairie domain. One available record, a tribal history or "winter count" consisting of pictographic drawings on a buffalo skin, gives evidence that an Oglala band "discovered" the Black Hills about the same time that American colonists were signing the Declaration of Independence from Great Britain. Other Indians — notably the Cheyennes, Crows and Kiowas — had preceded them to the vicinity of the hallowed mountains.

During this period, the Dakotas not only broadened their occupation of the land which would soon be named for them, but they systematically improved their weaponry and increased their horse herds. At periodic trading assemblies they bartered buffalo skins, an-

The migrations of Indians, (right), into the region which was to become South Dakota cannot be pinpointed to exact time or route. Some of the western and northward movements occurred gradually over a period of years, often led by a vanguard of small hunting parties. In some cases, however, rapid shiftings took place, brought on by intertribal battles, lack of food supply or epidemics.

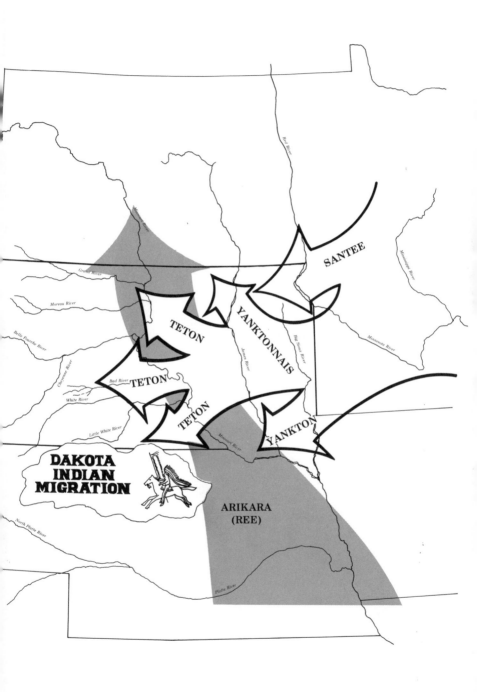

SANTEE

TETON

YANKTONNAIS

TETON

Bad River TETON

White River

TETON

Little White River

YANKTON

DAKOTA INDIAN MIGRATION

ARIKARA (REE)

Grand River

Moreau River

Belle Fourche River

Cheyenne River

Missouri River

Jones River

Big Sioux River

Minnesota River

Mississippi River

Red River

Missouri River

North Platte River

Platte River

telope hides and assorted furs for steel arrow points, short-barreled flintlocks, iron kettles, Hudson Bay blankets, needles and other goods which came primarily from French voyageurs.

The Buffalo: Foundation of the Indian Economy

At this point it would be well to consider the most influential factor involved in the western migration of the Dakota people. The American bison — known more popularly as the buffalo — was a supermarket-on-the-hoof for the tribes of the "Seven Council Fires."

Buffalo hides sewn together provided the covering for the Dakotas' conical tepees; bones became such various implements as awls, knives and scrapers; the heavily furred winter coat of the animal was expertly tanned (using buffalo brains as a softening agent) to make a warm, pliable robe; sinews were used for bowstrings; glue from the hooves made skin-covered shields almost impregnable to arrowhead or lance point; horns and other parts of the beast were utilized by medicine men in tribal ceremonials. And always, of course, came the first consideration: food supply!

Raw livers and small intestines were delicacies to be consumed immediately after a kill. Tongues, marrow bones and a strip of fat running along either side of the backbone just under the hide were favored morsels. Choice cuts of freshly slain buffalo were cooked over an open fire or stewed in kettles acquired from traders; but because there were often weeks and months between successful hunts, the preservation of meat was of major importance.

Thin strips of flesh were cut by the Indian women and dried, either under the hot sun alone or with the help of a fire beneath the pole racks. This "jerky" or *pah-pah* would keep indefinitely and was easily portable. For variety, the dried meat was pounded into a flaky mass over which hot buffalo tallow was poured. Alternate layers of meat and fat were packed in buffalo skin bags, and this nutritious pemmican *(wah-s'nah)* became a vital winter ration.

The buffalo dominated the lifestyle of the Dakota Indians, especially the Teton bands. The tribes were nomadic, not necessarily because they wanted to be, but because the buffalo herds were also nomadic and had to be followed. In general, the animals followed the ripening grass northward in the spring from the southern plains into Canada. The process was repeated in a southerly direction in the fall along rather definite migratory routes, two significant trails passing through South Dakota, one between the Badlands and the Black Hills and another which crossed the Missouri near the Bijou Hills where the river bottom offered a shale ford.

During their seasonal movements, the buffalo traveled in vast herds numbering in the tens of thousands. They then separated into smaller units which wandered somewhat unpredictably throughout the land of the Dakotas during the summer grazing period. Though there were many, many of them, the buffalo was not an easily claim-

The Dakota Indians did not have a written language, but the history of individuals and tribal units occasionally was preserved in pictographs on animal skins which were called "winter counts." The one above by a Sioux warrior named Lone Dog has been interpreted to cover a span of years from 1800 to 1871, reading from the center of the spiral outward. It includes seven references to trade with the whites, four of epidemics of white men's diseases but no indication of battles with them. On the other hand, 24 symbols depict intertribal conflicts. (South Dakota State Historical Society)

ed victim of the hunt. Bulls, measuring almost six feet tall at the shoulders, sometimes weighed more than a ton; cows were smaller, but they, too, were horned and could be particularly ferocious when they had their calves at side. As slow and cumbersome as they looked, buffalo were surprisingly agile and fast, and — especially when wounded — they would attack man, beast or railroad car in a suicidal rage.

Needless to say, the Dakota hunters — before they had guns or horses — were pitted against a formidable adversary. It is believed that the ancestors of the Indians drove the prehistoric bison into a swamp where it could be drowned or slain more easily with spears and clubs. Later generations stampeded herds over a cliff where the animals killed themselves or were so severely injured that they could be slaughtered by hand weapons. At that time the buffalo were so plentiful (as many as sixty million were estimated to exist in North America at their peak) and the Indian hunting methods were so primitive that the supply was apparently unlimited.

Then, several factors changed that seemingly endless, uninterruptible larder!

With the arrival of European explorers and exploiters came knives, arrowheads and lance points made of steel, but even more revolutionary to the Indian way of life was the introduction of horses and firearms. The so-called Indian pony was descended from the animals brought to America by Spanish conquistadors in the sixteenth century. Over a period of many years, wild herds of mustangs grew from the few mounts which escaped from or were turned loose by the expeditions of Hernando Cortes, Francisco Vasquez de Coronado and others in Mexico or the southwestern section of the future United States.

Prior to the coming of the white man, the Indian bands tediously followed the buffalo herds on foot. Their only help came from domesticated dogs which hauled some of the camp equipment on a wheel-less trailer called a *travois* which consisted of two long poles lashed together over the dogs' back and dragged behind them on the ground. The horse — as an item of trade or the prize of warfare — was gradually introduced to the Great Plains where the Dakota Indians, especially the Teton subtribes, welcomed it as a cherished addition to their culture.

The American bison — popularly known as the buffalo — was the foundation of the Sioux economy. Hardy and prolific, the giant beast was almost exterminated in the mid-1800s by wasteful, unrestricted hunting, a fact which aggravated the conflict of cultures between Indians and whites. (South Dakota Department of Economic and Tourism Development)

Strangely enough, it is one of the great contradictions of history that the Indian, in adopting the white man's steed and weapons, improved his living standard in one sense while at the same time participating unknowingly in the progression of events which ultimately would accentuate the conflict of Indian and white cultures and result almost in the extermination of the buffalo.

The White Man: Stranger from Afar

More than 150 years before South Dakota became a state, the first European explorers made their way across the rolling prairies.

By the early 1700s, French fur traders had extended their interests west of the Great Lakes to the Upper Mississippi. There are unconfirmed hints in the fragmentary records of history that small parties of intrepid voyageurs may have reached or gone beyond Big Stone Lake and the Big Sioux River even before the turn of the century. It has been conjectured, for instance, that Daniel Greysolon (the Sieur Dulhut after whom the Minnesota city of Duluth was named) may have been the first white man to enter South Dakota as early as 1679. Pierre Charles Le Sueur, another peripatetic seeker of adventure and furs, may also have reached the state, as may other unknown traders who followed a map published in 1701 by William De L'Isle which showed a trail leading from the Mississippi to the falls of the Big Sioux River.

No definite proof of any of these visits has been uncovered at this time, so until better evidence can be found (if indeed such evidence actually exists), an unusual documented event which occurred in 1743 stands out notably as a milestone episode in the region's somewhat hazy past.

On March 30 of that year two brothers, Louis Joseph and Francois la Verendrye — together with two employees of their family trading enterprise, Edouard La Londette and Jean Baptiste Amiotte — achieved a small measure of immortality when they buried an inscribed lead plate on a hill overlooking the Missouri River near the present site of Fort Pierre. The metal tablet — eight and one half inches wide by six and one half inches high — memorialized the fact that they had visited the promontory and claimed the land for France.

The explorers — then in their late twenties — had not told the Arikara Indians, with whom they had encamped, that the plate had been interred, but they did explain that the pile of rocks which they erected on the site was in honor of their king in a far-away place.

All of their efforts would have gone for naught, however, had not a group of schoolchildren walking in the hills 170 years later (on February 16, 1913, to be exact) stumbled upon the plate, a corner of which had been uncovered by erosion long after the rocks had been scattered or hauled away. George O'Reilly, one of the young finders, suggested that the heavy object might be sold for type metal to the local print shop, but before he and his companions — who included Harriet Foster and Ethel Parrish — could carry out their plan, they luckily met George W. White and Elmer W. Anderson, state legislators from Vivian and Willow Lake, respectively. The older men convinced the youngsters that the unusual plaque should be taken to State Historian Doane Robinson for possible identification. The result, of course, was that Robinson had the plate translated, and the information it contained helped explain the sketchy diaries of the La Verendryes which up until that time had baffled researchers who had attempted to trace the route of the explorations. The children who made the discovery were given a cash reward of more than $700, and the valuable memento became the property of the South Dakota State Historical Society.

One side of the plate carried a formal inscription to attest that in the twenty-sixth year of the reign of Louis XV of France, 1741, the lead tablet had been placed by Pierre Gaultier de Varennes de la Verendrye. This was an obvious error, of course. Pierre, who was then 57 years old and ailing, had been frustrated in an earlier effort to find the "river to the Western Sea," and in the spring of 1742 he sent two of his four sons — Francois and Louis Joseph — on another unsuccessful attempt. It was this journey which resulted finally in their arrival at the Missouri River in central South Dakota. Before they buried the lead plate, a message was crudely scratched into the soft metal on the unengraved side to indicate the exact day of the historic event and the witnesses thereto.

Whether the La Verendryes and their companions were the first, sixth or twelfth white men in what was to become South Dakota is relatively insignificant, but their expedition — which apparently took them within sight of the Black Hills — marked the beginning of increased white traffic into the region. Ironically, the advent of European traders and explorers generally paralleled the migrations of the Dakota Indians into the area. It would be more than a century, however, before the numbers of Caucasians would grow sufficiently to create an abrasive effect of serious proportions between peoples of unlike backgrounds.

In the years which followed, French-Canadians were periodic visitors to the region, and the first of numerous intermarriages with Indian women began to occur. France herself, however, was too busily engaged in military conflict with England to be concerned about any westward expansion on the American frontier. As a matter of fact, when the fortunes of the French and Indian War began to favor the British, the king of France ceded the territory west of the Mississippi to his cousin, the king of Spain, so that England could not claim it as she later did numerous other French possessions.

The secret Treaty of Fontainebleau which accomplished the transfer in 1762 created much furor among officials and citizens in New Orleans and St. Louis when its provisions were announced many months later. For this narrative, though, the one important fact to remember is that sovereignty over the so-called Louisiana Territory — which included South Dakota — was shifted to Charles II of Spain.

A small lead tablet eight and one half inches wide documented the visitation of Louis Joseph and Francois La Verendrye with two companions to the site of present-day Fort Pierre in 1743. The plate was discovered 170 years later by schoolchildren on the gumbo bluffs overlooking the Missouri River. A chance meeting with two legislators deterred the youngsters from selling the valuable discovery for scrap metal. (South Dakota State Historical Society)

A Spanish Interlude: The Traffic Increases

All of the international dealing and double-dealing meant little or nothing to the Indians on the Great Plains — but at this point it must be clearly understood that a precedent was being established which, in later years, would lead to contradiction and conflict.

First of all, the two European powers — France and Spain — gave little thought at the time to any ownership rights of Indians to the land. The French king assumed full possession of the territory and deeded it to Spain, apparently on the basis that there were no other parties to be considered in the transaction.

Secondly, none of the involved tribes remotely understood the concept of "legal ownership" at that time, nor was it likely that they cared since such a philosophy was foreign to their life style and value system. They recognized the reality of "possession by force" since they were subject to it in their own intertribal clashes, but they could not be expected to grasp the fact that long before there was a United States government, the land on which they camped and hunted so freely was being bargained for and exchanged between European nations, and they obviously were included in the package along with the trees, mountains, buffalo and prairie flowers.

The 34 years of Spanish rule were marked by gradually increasing fur trade on the Missouri, the activity moving slowly northward as the availability of pelts near St. Louis was unable to supply the demand. The traders themselves were predominantly Frenchmen, many of Canadian birth who were peculiarly adapted, it seemed, to the rugged existence which characterized the occupation. Various expeditions, including those of the Missouri Company headed by Jean Baptiste Trudeau (in some references also spelled Truteau) and an independent entrepreneur, Jacques D'Eglise, passed through South Dakota or remained to barter with the Arikaras. D'Eglise spent the winter of 1794-95 with the latter Indians, and Trudeau built a cabin (known later as the Pawnee House) on the Missouri above the site where Fort Randall would be built in present-day Charles Mix County. Trudeau's party also wintered there that same year (1794-95) while members gathered furs from various tribes, including Dakotas, Omahas and Poncas.

There were other evidences of white infiltration, too. Pierre Dorion (who was mentioned later in the Lewis and Clark diaries) had preceded the American explorers by at least 20 years, married a Yankton Indian and lived along the Missouri River in the general vicinity of the future city which would adopt the name of his wife's tribe. He is conceded by most sources to be the first permanent white settler in the region which would become South Dakota. Dorion was followed shortly thereafter by Joseph Gerreau, who lived with and married into the Arikara tribe, and was also contacted by Lewis and Clark on their first expedition in 1804.

None of these early journeys or residences among the Indians had particular long-range importance except that they signified a growing movement of white merchants and opportunists into the area. However, the Spanish officials were concerned about encroachments on the Upper Missouri by British firms, notably the Hudson's Bay and Northwest Companies, and in 1796 John Evans led a party from St. Louis to the Mandan villages where he took over the British trading post there and raised the Spanish flag as a symbol of possession.

It is interesting to note that the British interests were also represented largely by men of French derivation, a fact which later was to be reflected in the surnames of French-Indian families. Mixed-bloods — a number of whom, like Colin Campbell, had Scottish names — were also evident.

In 1800 Registre Loisel of St. Louis, who was involved in the firm which succeeded the original Missouri Company, received Spanish approval to establish a trading operation on the Upper Missouri. When he attempted to proceed up the river, he was stopped by a Dakota band some 35 miles below the site where the La Verendrye brothers had buried their plate, and there he promptly built Fort Aux Cedres on Cedar Island, which for a decade was to be a welcome stop-over point for traders before it was destroyed by fire in 1810.

Meanwhile, France as a nation had recuperated from her defeats by the British in America, and with Napoleon Bonaparte rising to power, had begun negotiations with Spain to reclaim the Louisiana Territory (named by Cavelier de La Salle for King Louis XIV of France). This fact became known to President Thomas Jefferson of the fledgling United States, and the international parlaying took on a third dimension.

Louisiana: The Biggest Bargain in American History

Little recognition has been given the fact that Napoleon I played an indirect but important role in the history of South Dakota. The First Consul drove a hard bargain with Spain, and just as the vast Louisiana wilderness had been ceded away by France more than three decades earlier, he got it back through the terms of the Treaty of San Ildefonso which the Spanish king finally signed on October 15, 1802.

President Jefferson's view of the retrocession was one of deep concern. With Spain, then a relatively weak nation, in control of the western lands and the vital port of New Orleans, the United States did not have to worry too seriously about her frontier defense or the unhampered use of the Mississippi River. France, on the other hand, was a power to be feared if the unpredictable Napoleon were to use Louisiana in some way to retaliate against the British in Canada.

Accordingly, Jefferson instructed the United States minister in Paris, Robert R. Livingston, to try to stop the reacquisition by the French if possible; or, if that could not be done, to make an offer for the purchase of New Orleans. The first attempt was futile, but the second bore unexpected fruit. After months of delay and indecision, Napoleon not only agreed to sell the Mississippi port city but he also included the entire territory in the deal. A threat by Livingston, of an alliance between the United States and Great Britain if a solution to Louisiana could not be found, may have been a deciding factor.

At any rate, Napoleon opened the way to serious negotiations which ultimately resulted in a completed sale. The treaty concluding the action was dated April 30, 1803. For $11,250,000 outright and the assumption of $3,750,000 in citizens' claims, the United States bought the immense domain in the exact form that France received it from Spain. The new nation had doubled its size at an estimated cost of three cents an acre for land which would one day include all or part of 13 states. With interest payments, the final bill came to $27,267,622, which in later years would be far less than the value of just one annual wheat crop in South Dakota.

It should be noted here, of course, that throughout the bargaining with France or in the deliberations of the United States Senate before ratifying the treaty, little consideration was apparently given to the concept of Indian ownership of the land. Their hunting grounds were included, it seems, in the section which transferred "all public lots and squares, vacant lands and all public buildings, fortifications, barracks and other edifices which are not private property."

William Clark (left) and Meriwether Lewis traveled up the Missouri River in 1804 to explore the Louisiana Purchase acquired from France the previous year. Lewis, the private secretary of President Thomas Jefferson, was chosen to lead the expedition which crossed the future state of South Dakota on both the outbound and return trips. Portions of the journals of the two men provide significant pre-territorial views of the region. (Yankton County Historical Society)

Lewis and Clark: Across South Dakota and Beyond

Even before Napoleon had approved details of the sale of Louisiana to the United States, President Jefferson was already making plans to explore the land he confidently hoped to acquire. He appointed Meriwether Lewis, his private secretary, to lead the proposed expedition; and Lewis, in turn, selected his friend, William Clark, to be his second in command. Congress ultimately voted $2,500 to finance the venture, and the two young officers were instructed to explore the Missouri River from mouth to source and to seek a waterway to the Pacific Ocean which could be developed for commercial purposes.

After many months of preparation, the party of 45 young men — including Clark's black slave known as York — headed up the meandering stream on May 14, 1804, in three boats, the largest being 55 feet long. Two horses were led or ridden along the river bank.

The importance of the Lewis and Clark expedition to South Dakota specifically was largely indirect. The journey dramatized the acquisition of the land by the United States and served to spur greater traffic into the area following its completion. Moreover, the journals of the explorers — which were far more detailed than the La Verendrye diaries — documented earlier historical events and achievements; authenticated the presence in the region of Pierre Dorion as well as the existence of Trudeau's Pawnee House and Loisel's "cedar fort;" and made specific notation of various Indian tribes and their location at that particular time.

The expedition crossed South Dakota on both the outbound and return phases of the 25-month trip. The men first sighted the future

Sacajawea, the teenage Indian girl who aided Lewis and Clark in their exploratory trip across the Louisiana Territory, has been the subject of much historical controversy. One group of researchers has argued that she is buried in what is now South Dakota at one of Manuel Lisa's trading posts. Another has insisted she lived to be an elderly woman and died among her Shoshoni people in the Wind River country of Wyoming. Adding to the confusion is the fact that her name is spelled more than a dozen ways in various references. (State Historical Society of North Dakota)

state on August 21, 1804, when they passed the mouth of the Big Sioux River. It took them 54 days to reach the North Dakota line (not yet established, of course), and during that period their journals revealed that they had set up 42 different campsites, seven of which were probably on the Nebraska side of the river. On the way back to St. Louis, they crossed into South Dakota on August 21, 1806, exactly two years to the day after first entering the state. Their downstream journey was considerably speedier as they passed the Big Sioux on September 4, after having spent just two weeks traveling from border to border.

The South Dakota portion of the Lewis and Clark expedition was highlighted by such diverse episodes as a visit to Spirit Mound near Vermillion; parlays with various Indian bands; the worrisome 12 days during which 17-year-old George Shannon was lost from the group after he had gone in search of the two horses which had wandered away; an arrangement with Pierre Dorion and his son for guide services; and the great curiosity of the Indians when they saw their first black man, York.

It is often mistakenly assumed that Sacajawea, the young and somewhat controversial Indian maiden who guided the expedition across the Rocky Mountains with a baby on her back, was with the party in South Dakota. This is erroneous, of course, since her services were not acquired until Lewis and Clark wintered at the Mandan villages in northern Dakota. The "Bird Woman" — as she was called — traveled across South Dakota later on the way to St. Louis, according to one group of historians; others have argued that she died and was buried in northern South Dakota at the trading post called Fort Manuel. Undoubtedly the lives of two different Indian women — both wives of Toussaint Charbonneau, the Lewis and Clark guide — have become involved in the historical controversy. (Sacajawea's name, incidentally, is spelled more than a dozen different ways in various references.)

The Lure of Furs and Fortune: "Fire Water" Introduced

During the first half of the 1800s, furs were in great demand in Europe, China and the populated centers of the United States. Even before the Lewis and Clark expedition cast a national spotlight on the region and its rich natural resources, French and British trading firms had begun to capitalize on what then seemed to be an endless supply of buffalo robes, antelope and deer skins and, to a lesser degree, the pelts of wolves, otter, beaver, muskrat, mink, raccoon, badger and other available species.

The most lucrative approach, of course, was to motivate the Indian people to do the work of harvesting the animals through the lure of trade goods — beads, blankets, knives, kettles and a variety of other trinkets and tools. The barter system was not new to the Indians because they had long participated in intertribal trading fairs, exchanging furs, hides and food commodities for redstone pipes, flint for arrowheads, walnut bows, horses and guns. The native needs were not especially great because of the limited numbers of people and their nomadic lifestyle which did not permit the amassing of hard-to-transport personal possessions. On the other hand, the white man's markets — in the eastern United States, Europe and Asia — were insatiable, as a result, another element in the conflict of cultures was imposed.

Simultaneously, the introduction of whiskey to the trade system was to have unfortunate, long-range effects. Many of the Indians proved susceptible to it, and because they could drink it immediately and not have to carry it around, the problem of transportation was automatically solved. Because they had no knowledge of alcoholism at the time, they simply could not understand its ultimate consequences.

For the trader, liquor was an ideal exchange premium. It was relatively cheap in the first place, and even more so when it was watered down. In addition, a tin cupful of the so-called "firewater" quickly reduced the Indians' trading capabilities, and the dealer almost immediately got the upper hand. The magnetic attraction of the whiskey barrel was later to become a contributing factor in the development of animosities between the races in the era of agreements and treaties. Even more despicable, of course, was the addition to the whiskey of laudanum, an opium-based drug, which added to the debilitating effects upon the unsuspecting victims.

From the beginning, the United States government tried to stop illegal liquor traffic and to assure honest trade practices with the Indians by licensing various companies to operate in specific areas. These organizations were policed as well as they could be under the circumstances, but the lack of government troops or inspectors and the vast distances involved made enforcement virtually impossible. However, to protect their licenses, the companies in general were not as flagrant in their violation of trading laws and regulations as were many independent trappers and traders who roamed the region acquiring furs by fair means and foul.

Meanwhile, the traffic up the Missouri River began to increase year by year following the Lewis and Clark visitation. The skins of prairie animals — plus a much coveted food delicacy, the tongues of buffalo — were the objectives of hardy individuals and organized companies seeking to capitalize on the natural bounties. Two names were particularly prominent in the South Dakota region: Manuel Lisa and Pierre Chouteau, Jr.

Lisa was a Spanish entrepreneur who recognized the potential wealth on the Upper Missouri. As a young man he had learned the rudiments of the trading business when Spain owned the territory, and shortly after Lewis and Clark returned to St. Louis, he organized a keelboat expedition which traveled through South Dakota all the way to the mouth of the Big Horn River in Montana. The trip was highly profitable, and the 36-year-old Lisa began to think in grander terms. His St. Louis Fur Company (which later became the Missouri Fur Company) was one of the first such American firms to operate in South Dakota and beyond.

Lisa himself made numerous trips up the river. In his dealings with the tribes, he did not operate strictly on the basis of cheap trinkets and beads. Instead he provided seeds, agricultural equipment and breeding stock as he taught Indian women to raise vegetables, chickens and domestic cattle. To the men he gave steel traps in an effort to get them interested in taking smaller furbearing animals. (They preferred to pursue the buffalo and other large game, so at first the traders had to rely on white trappers for beaver, mink, muskrat and other pelts.) At his various posts — including two Fort Lisas, one at the mouth of the Big Horn and the other near Council Bluffs — he fed old and ailing Indians, and his humane practices were apparently respected enough by most Dakotas and Arikaras with whom he dealt that he was considered an important factor in maintaining their neutrality during the War of 1812 against Great Britain.

In a contradictory note, however, according to the diary of John C. Luttig, one of Lisa's employees, Fort Manuel was burned by hostile Yanktonnais in 1813, and 15 Americans were killed before the post was abandoned. Nonetheless, the undaunted operator continued to maintain other facilities along the Missouri, and until his early death in 1820 at the age of 48, he was a dominant force in the development of the fur trade in middle America. Lisa's company persisted for ten years under other leadership before it was finally dissolved in 1830.

Associated with Lisa for a time was Pierre Chouteau, Jr., whose grandfather was one of the French founders of St. Louis and who himself was still a teenager when Lewis and Clark returned from their western odyssey. Chouteau, like Lisa, combined a spirit of adventure with keen business sense. In 1831, as an official with a branch of John Jacob Astor's powerful American Fur Company, he added a new element to trade on the Upper Missouri when he dispatched the steamboat *Yellowstone* to Fort Tecumseh, a ramshackle trading post built of driftwood near the mouth of the Teton or Bad River in South Dakota. The larger and speedier sidewheeler proved far superior to the old oar-and-pole-powered keelboats, and on its return trip to St. Louis, the *Yellowstone* brought back a valuable cargo which included ten thousand pounds of buffalo tongues.

The following year Chouteau himself accompanied the steamer which bucked the Missouri currents all the way to Fort Union on the North Dakota-Montana border. He stopped midway through South Dakota during the expedition where a new installation, named in his honor, was built to replace the dilapidated Fort Tecumseh. The improved facility soon came to be known popularly by its abbreviated title, Fort Pierre, and it has since been credited with being the first permanent white settlement within the future state. By 1838 Pierre Chouteau, Jr., and Company was the surviving successor to Astor's

Missouri operations, and for the next two decades, his firm was in virtual control of trading on the upper river.

Throughout the first half of the nineteenth century, the fur business flourished along the Missouri and its tributaries. It brought the first steamboat up the muddy river; it was a factor of great economic importance to the young United States which had incurred new debts in the War of 1812; and it delivered considerable wealth to whites and Indians alike, in the latter case particularly to the Teton tribes of Dakotas.

But the results were not all positive.

The trading gave the Indians material rewards, and a vicious circle began to develop. The more buffalo robes, humps and tongues which they were able to deliver to the traders, the more rifles, horses and steel knives they obtained. The weapons and mounts, in turn, permitted increased slaughter of buffalo over a much wider range, and in a matter of a few short years, the vast herds began to reflect the added hunting pressure. The Indians, meanwhile, became more and more dependent upon the system because even when they had acquired a large number of guns, the latter were worthless unless trade for gunpowder continued.

At the same time the greed of some of the barterers manifested itself in the cheap quality of trade goods, the bribing of governmental agents, the increased flow of whiskey and a total disregard of conservation of the source of supply by both Indians and whites. Under the circumstances, it was almost inevitable that a confrontation had to come between the tribesmen and the growing numbers of profit-motivated traders who sought opportunities for wealth on the new frontier.

The Military Makes Its Appearance: Prelude to Conflict

The early trading posts on the American frontier were often referred to as forts, though they were usually little more than crude huts or cabins and no soldiers were involved in their operation or defense. Prior to the War of 1812 there had been occasional clashes between Indians and whites in the Upper Missouri country, but they had been scattered and unrelated. The activities of British agents in attempting to incite various tribes against the Americans (apparently successful in the case of Fort Manuel), not to mention a number of post-war incidents, caused the United States government to reappraise the situation.

Secretary of War John C. Calhoun — probably influenced more by British settlement in the Red River Valley than by possible Indian aggression — proposed the establishment of military fortifications in the region. As a result, in 1819 Fort Atkinson was built on the Nebraska side of the Missouri opposite Council Bluffs and Fort Snelling on the Mississippi at the mouth of the Minnesota River. Troops were stationed at both installations, but for almost four years their activities were mostly routine and boring.

Then, on June 2, 1823, Arikara Indians suddenly attacked a trading party headed by General William H. Ashley, killing 13 American employees of the expedition and wounding almost a dozen. The attackers' losses were negligible. The assault came without warning after a seemingly friendly trading session the previous day at the Arikara villages near the mouth of the Grand River. A smoldering resentment had been building among the Rees because of a number of incidents between traders and tribesmen which, in several cases, had resulted in deaths.

News of the episode reached Fort Atkinson when the party's keelboat arrived with the wounded. Colonel Henry Leavenworth, then in command, decided to ascend the Missouri with all his troops — 250 of them — to punish the Arikaras and to demonstrate the readiness of the United States to maintain peace, by force if necessary. Enroute up the river, his expedition snowballed. Five days after leaving the fort on June 22, he was joined by a force of 50 men and two boats in charge of Joshua Pilcher, then head of the late Manuel Lisa's Missouri Fur Company. Pilcher was intent on revenge because the Arikaras had attacked and robbed several of his posts.

Between the Big Sioux and James Rivers one of Leavenworth's boats was wrecked with the loss of eight men, 70 muskets and a large quantity of supplies. Farther upstream he added to his force a small band of Yankton warriors who were eager to fight their traditional enemies, the Arikaras. Not long afterwards about 200 Hunkpapas offered their services. Meanwhile, the survivors from General Ashley's party and the men from an earlier expedition he had sent north under Major Andrew Henry became part of the growing army, and early in August when Leavenworth arrived at the Arikara villages, he was leading a force which numbered more than a thousand men, including regular troops, voyageurs and Indians. The Arikaras probably had less than 800 armed braves to face him.

On August 9 the attackers besieged the Indians in their fortified villages in a battle which lasted through the 11th. Reports of casualties varied, but apparently no whites were killed and only two slightly wounded. Leavenworth's Dakota allies lost two dead and seven wounded, while the Arikaras had between 30 and 50 killed, including some women and children. The Yanktons and Hunkpapas bore the brunt of the attack supported by army artillery, and in time the Rees gave up the fight and asked for terms. They agreed to repay Ashley for the property taken from him and not to interfere with trading activities in the future.

The hurriedly dictated treaty satisfied Colonel Leavenworth that the purposes of the United States troops had been served, but his

---

The term "fort" was used to designate a variety of installations in South Dakota's past, (right), ranging from crude log-cabin trading posts to highly developed troop cantonments like Fort Meade. Fort Sod, Fort Brule and the Yankton stockade existed for only a brief time during and after the Santee outbreak in 1862. Others like Fort Pierre served more than one purpose.

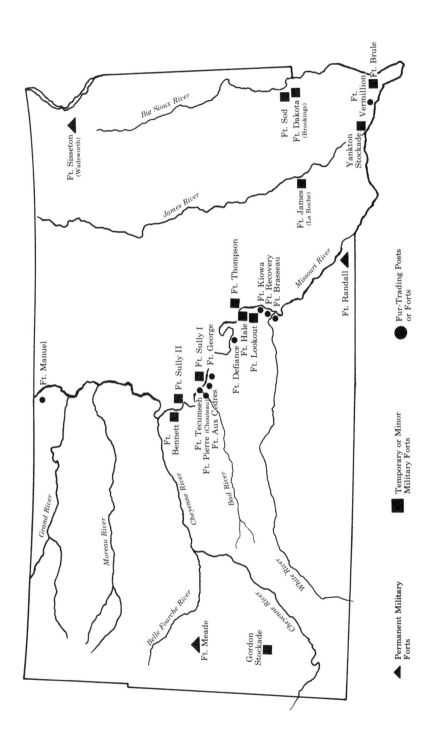

Big Sioux River

Ft. Sisseton
(Wadsworth)

James River

Ft. Sod

Ft. Dakota
(Brookings)

Yankton
Stockade

Ft.
Vermillion

Ft. Brule

Ft. James
(La Roche)

Ft. Thompson

Ft. Kiowa
Ft. Recovery
Ft. Brasseau

Missouri River

Ft. Randall

Ft. Manuel

Ft. Sully II

Ft. Sully I

Ft. George

Ft. Defiance
Ft. Hale
Ft. Lookout

Ft.
Bennett

Ft. Tecumseh
Ft. Pierre (Chouteau)
Ft. Aux Cedres

Grand River

Moreau River

Cheyenne River

Bad River

Belle Fourche River

White River

Ft. Meade

Gordon
Stockade

Cheyenne River

● Fur-Trading Posts
  or Forts

■ Temporary or Minor
  Military Forts

▲ Permanent Military
  Forts

allies were not as pleased with the agreement as he was. Pilcher was angry because the attack had not been more aggressively pursued. The Dakota Indians also thought the Americans had taken weak measures — so they promptly stole six army mules and seven of Ashley's horses. To make matters worse, Leavenworth failed to heed a warning that the Arikaras would flee during the night — which they did — and in the morning only the vacant villages remained, save for one old woman. Fires, which the colonel accused Pilcher of setting, then destroyed most of the lodges and primitive fortifications.

While the battle at Grand River receives little attention in historical annals, it marked the first and only consequential employment of United States military forces in combat with Indians in South Dakota — including the so-called Battle of Slim Buttes — until the fateful encounter at Wounded Knee 67 years later. Also it underscored the pressures which then and afterwards were placed on army commanders by third parties calling for vengeance and punishment of the tribes. In that instance the Sioux allies were involved on the side of the whites (and they pressured Leavenworth, too); in ensuing years they were to become the victims of similar pleas for retaliation.

The troopers themselves gained some field experience in Indian country during their 75 days away from the fort, but generally the brief campaign was to be labeled by historians as feeble and ineffective. Despite its outcome, however, it was in truth the beginning of the gradual involvement of force which ultimately would reach its bloody climax at Little Big Horn more than a half century into the future.

Word of Leavenworth's actions and the seemingly growing restlessness of the Indians caused Congress to authorize a commission to secure treaties of peace with the various tribes along the Missouri and Mississippi Rivers. A total of $10,000 was appropriated — four times more than for the Lewis and Clark expedition — and General Henry Atkinson, after whom the fort at Council Bluffs had been named, was put in charge of the Missouri phase of the project. The second commissioner was Major Benjamin O'Fallon, who served as an agent under his uncle, William Clark, then superintendent of all Indian affairs within the Louisiana Territory.

The two men organized the Yellowstone Expedition of 1825 (named for its ultimate destination), and on May 16 they left Fort Atkinson in nine keelboats with an escort of 476 men. The cargo included guns, blankets and tobacco as presents for the Indians; and an interesting feature of the shallow-bottomed vessels were hand-operated paddlewheels invented by General Atkinson.

In South Dakota the commissioners sent runners to bring in the tribes, and at various locations along the river treaties of friendship were signed with Yanktons; Yanktonnais; Oglala, Hunkpapa and Blackfeet subtribes of the Tetons; the Arikaras still in the area; and a band of Cheyennes who happened to be available. Similar pacts were made with other tribes in North Dakota and Montana, with chiefs receiving gifts of guns while their followers were given lesser tokens.

The expedition was concluded in late October without incident or problem. It was largely a show of force, a repeat of which General Atkinson recommended "every three or four years" rather than the greater expense of erecting and maintaining forts along the river. The twelve treaties which the commissioners brought back with them to St. Louis were the first such formal documents entered into with the Indians of the Upper Missouri by the United States government. They were, of course, primarily non-controversial expressions of mutual good will and did not involve concessions or the question of land ownership.

New Faces on the Frontier: Curiosity and Christianity

Fur traders, trappers, explorers and soldiers were not the only white men to enter South Dakota during the presettlement years. Scientists, artists, map-makers, inquisitive European observers and missionaries were among the vanguard of visitors attracted to the Great Plains.

Curiosity about the region, its flora and fauna, the Indian inhabitants and the potential wealth of the unexplored wilderness beckoned British botanists John Bradbury and Thomas Nuttall; Henry M. Brackenridge, a Pennsylvania lawyer with an intense interest in natural history and geography; and Duke Paul Wilhelm of Wuerttemberg, who forsook the comforts of royal living in Europe to satisfy his burning thirst for knowledge. They were all in the Upper Missouri country prior to 1830, and their experiences and observations were carefully recorded for future generations. In his journals — which later were translated from German into English — Duke Paul confirmed details of Colonel Leavenworth's siege of the Arikara villages, and though he was a guest of Joshua Pilcher and appreciative of the latter's courtesies, the duke defended Leavenworth's handling of a situation which could very well have resulted in a wholesale massacre of the Arikaras.

In 1832 Pierre Chouteau, Jr., invited George Catlin, an attorney and self-taught artist, to travel up-river on the *Yellowstone* to pursue his interest in sketching and writing about American Indians. Catlin spent more than two weeks at Fort Pierre where he recorded his observations of Teton life in words and pictures. Later his published paintings and descriptions (not always totally accurate but not purposely misleading) revealed to eager eastern audiences the details of Indian culture on the Great Plains.

In 1833 Prince Maximilian of Wied traveled through South Dakota, accompanied by the Swiss artist, Charles Bodmer. Subsequently, they collaborated on a German-language book, *Travels in the Interior of North America,* which was a comprehensive, illustrated account of their visitation to the region. A decade later John

James Audubon, the famed artist-naturalist, crossed the future state, sketching and taking notes which were recorded for posterity in his unique style.

Other prominent visitors to pre-territorial South Dakota included Joseph Nicolas Nicollet, who mapped the northeastern sector of the state; Lieutenant John C. Fremont, who served his exploring apprenticeship with Nicollet and who was later to win lasting notoriety as "the Pathfinder" of America's West; Jim Bridger and Jedediah Strong Smith, each of whom gained historical notoriety elsewhere as frontier heroes; and Hugh Glass, a legendary figure who was attacked and badly mauled by a grizzly bear about 15 miles south of the present town of Lemmon. Glass, according to the adventurous story, then crawled and staggered some 200 miles cross-country to the Missouri River where, after several other dramatic escapes from hostile Indians, he finally made his way to safety.

The important fact, of course, is that, following the Lewis and Clark adventure, the plains land destined to become the state of South Dakota was crossed and recrossed by men of varied motivations. Among those who had other interests besides the profits of trapping and trading were Christian missionaries anxious to spread their faith to the Indians. Catholic priests were the first clerics to arrive on the frontier primarily because of the early French and Spanish influence. During the fur trading era, an estimated 1,000 white men (100 or more trappers and boatmen for every trader) were active on the Upper Missouri, with a majority of them having some Catholic heritage. Many were French-Canadians who lived with the tribes and married Indian women. Though they were not always devoutly religious themselves, these voyageurs sent appeals for priests to baptize their children and to acquaint their wives with Christian doctrine.

If not the first, certainly the most prominent "black robe" to visit the South Dakota region was Father Pierre Jean De Smet, a Belgian-born Jesuit, who ascended the Missouri in the spring of 1839 on a steamboat appropriately named the *St. Peter.* On May 11 he debarked near the mouth of the Vermillion River where he began a missionary career which continued until his death in 1873 at the age of 72. The Yanktons to whom he first ministered on that brief visit apparently were fascinated by him and his message. He had to turn down their request that he remain with them, but before he left, he baptized several children and presumably offered Mass, a ritual which was to impress many spiritually conscious Indians during the ensuing years.

Other Catholic priests to enter the bounds of the future state were Fathers Christian Hoecken and Augustine Ravoux. Father Hoecken was a Hollander whose records of baptisms in 1840 at Fort Pierre, Fort Lookout, the "village of the Yanktons" and at the confluence of the Vermillion and Missouri Rivers are still preserved. The Dutch cleric died of cholera 11 years later on another trip up the

Father Pierre Jean De Smet, a Belgian-born Jesuit priest, traveled up the Missouri in 1839, ministering primarily to French traders and trappers and their Indian families. During more than three decades he ranged widely across the frontier, and though he died three years before the Black Hills gold rush, he apparently had envisioned the consequences when he warned the Sioux not to reveal the presence of the yellow metal if they wanted to preserve the tranquility of the Hills. The Kingsbury County seat of De Smet was named for him. (South Dakota State Historical Society)

Missouri. Father De Smet, himself gravely ill with malaria (called ague on the frontier), administered the last rites of the Catholic Church and then prepared his fellow priest for burial in a tarred coffin. Father Ravoux, who was sent out by the Bishop of Dubuque whose jurisdiction extended into the Louisiana Territory beyond Minnesota and Iowa, traveled westward from Big Stone Lake in 1845, crossed the James River and held services at Sand Lake in present-day Brown County.

Some historians have credited Jedediah Smith, the Bible-carrying Methodist frontiersman, with delivering the first public prayer by a non-Indian in South Dakota aboard the steamboat *Yellowstone* in 1823. It was 17 years later before the first Protestant minister, Rev. Stephen Return Riggs, a Presbyterian, visited Fort Pierre and conducted services.

By 1843 — one hundred years after the La Verendrye brothers had buried their historic plate — the Great Plains of Dakota were on the threshold of a gigantic social change. All of a sudden the excessive profits in the fur trade began to drop, primarily because men of wealth switched from beaver hats to silk stovepipe models. In the United States itself a serious economic depression which began in 1837 was in its sixth year. The great migrations to California and Oregon had begun, and the Cherokee Indians had been forcibly removed from Georgia and sent on the long "trail of tears" to a territory set aside for them in Oklahoma.

On the Upper Missouri the increasing appearance of more and more white men began to effect relationships between them and the Indians. Tribe-destroying plagues — such as the devastating smallpox epidemic among the Mandans, Arikaras and Hidatsas in North Dakota in 1837 — were blamed on the intruders (and rightfully so). The competition to secure furs for gradually dwindling prices put more emphasis on liquor traffic and aggravated the incidence of cheating. Steamboats on the river and the sound of gunfire at an ever-growing rate shattered the quiet of a wilderness in transition.

For Better or Worse: An Indian Policy Begins to Evolve

To better understand what ultimately befell the various Indian tribes in South Dakota and how a conflict of cultures developed, it is best to look back to colonial days to trace the factors, events and official documents involved in the relationship of Indians and whites long before the Louisiana Purchase became a reality.

From the dawn of recorded history, it has been the practice of dominant individuals, tribes and nations to acquire land held by weaker neighbors through force or by unchallenged occupation with no recourse nor compensation. Uniquely enough, the discovery and ultimate settlement of the New World did not follow completely the age-old concept of conquest and subjugation. Instead, in that portion of the North American continent which was to make up the 13 original colonies of the United States, the land was claimed and colonized — but the recognition of some form of ownership by Indian inhabitants and the need to pay them for abandonment of their wilderness domain became an accepted philosophy which was to prevail despite wars, enmity and violent contrary opinions. The justice and validity of such an approach cannot be challenged, but its practical application was seriously complicated by the backgrounds of the peoples involved.

The Indian, first of all, had no knowledge of such confining terms as acres, square miles or surveyors' lines. His "ownership" of land was based entirely on the simple fact that he lived and hunted there. Deeds and land titles were completely foreign to him, not only because he had no written language, but because the idea of parceling out land and protecting it by recorded document was a concept which at that time he couldn't grasp. The only borders or boundaries he understood were streams, mountains or other geographic features which limited movement, but they were not applied to ownership except if a stronger tribe was beyond those streams and mountains to prohibit free access to the land. The Indian in his religious beliefs felt a unique closeness to the earth, not as something to possess but to be part of, in both a spiritual and physical sense.

The white man, on the other hand, had an almost opposite view, based on centuries of organized civilization in which real property, defined and protected by law, was a basic cornerstone. When he came to the New World — which was "discovered" and not conquered as such — he automatically applied his system to the vast unknown territory, assuming as a matter of course that the Indian inhabitants also understood that philosophy.

To the honor of the various European nations and such independent colonizing groups as the Plymouth party, the Indian tribes were deemed to have title to the land (whether the natives realized the significance of such legalities or not) and that all aboriginal ownership had to be purchased or otherwise bargained for in order to establish unrestricted claim to settlements, town sites or personal holdings. In other words, the white man quite properly granted to the Indian a right the latter only hazily understood. The trouble came later, of course, when the recognized Indian land titles were progressively extinguished by purchase, treaty and law. The process, in most cases, may have been legal, but the manner in which Indian ownership was chipped and sliced away could not always be morally defended.

Because this point is so important to South Dakota history and relationships between Indians and whites, further backgrounding is appropriate.

Fifty years after Columbus landed in the New World, Spanish Laws of the Indies decreed that Indians were free persons, that they should not be taken as slaves and that property should not be taken from them except in fair trade. Though the Spaniards themselves did not always live up to that particular legislation, the idea behind it became a prevailing view in international law. As an application of that philosophy, a popular American legend recalls the purchase in 1626 of Manhattan Island (the heart of New York City) from the Canarsee Indians by the Dutch for trinkets and cloth valued then at 24 dollars.

In 1643 the Dutch government became the first European nation to enter into a formal treaty with an Indian tribe, the Mohawks. This was not merely an isolated case, however. The Plymouth settlers, Lord Baltimore in Maryland and William Penn in Pennsylvania all completed purchase or occupancy agreements with Indians residing on their claims or grants. Later, when England became the dominant force in colonial America, the Royal Proclamation of 1763 formalized for the first time the concept of Indian land titles and prohibited issuance of patents to any lands claimed by Indian tribes until the Indian title had been extinguished by purchase or treaty cession.

Twenty four years later, after the Revolutionary War and the creation of the United States, the Northwest Ordinance of 1787 was proclaimed, and included in its third article was the statement:

> . . . The utmost good faith shall always be observed towards the Indians; their lands and property shall never be taken from them without their consent; and, in their property, rights, and liberty, they shall never be invaded or disturbed, unless in just and lawful wars authorized by Congress; but laws founded in justice and humanity, shall from time to time be made for preventing wrongs being done to them, and for preserving peace and friendship with them.

That tenet became the basis for future relationships between the United States and Indian tribes, and it was enacted into law by Congress shortly after ratification of the United States Constitution.

What was written and what actually occurred in practice did not always harmonize, however. It is a simple axiom that the man on the mountain does not fear the flood. Conversely, wherever white settlement developed within or near Indian-dominated lands, the settlers were continually suspicious and occasionally lived in terror of the natives. Though the Indians were misunderstood, they did participate in enough incidents — including killings and torture — to aggravate the nervousness of the whites. As the tribes were forced westward, the pressures and animosities in the old colonial area faded, and while frontier-dwellers referred to tribal members as "barbaric savages," the people in the heavily populated east — who were no longer faced with the problems of direct confrontation — began to think of the Indians as "the Nobel Red Men."

This all too human attitude must be kept in mind when one attempts to analyze why there were conflicts between whites and Indians in the back-country, but also why there were considerable disagreements among white Americans over the formulation and application of an Indian policy. Those who were on the scene often reacted emotionally and violently out of fear; those who were far removed from possible danger were able to contemplate possible solutions on a moral and ethical basis. This situation was to persist in South Dakota longer than in most other areas of the United States.

In 1831 — during the height of the fur-trading era on the Upper Missouri — the United States Supreme Court ruled that the Cherokee Nation in Georgia was not a "foreign" state but a "domestic independent nation" not altogether free from local and federal laws. This opinion established the philosophy that Indians were, in effect, wards of the government and set the stage for the forced removal of the Five Civilized Tribes to the Indian Territory in Oklahoma beginning in 1835. Subsequently, it was also the basis for development of the reservation policy elsewhere.

So when the region which was to become South Dakota began to feel demands for settlement at the mid-point of the 1800s, the first requirement — from a legal point of view — was to eliminate whatever title the various tribes held to the desired land.

At that juncture, the Wilderness Age was rapidly approaching its end. Needless to say, there were many, many challenges — for both Indians and white men — lying ahead.

BOOK TWO

THE CHALLENGE OF THE NEW FRONTIER

*"Behind the scared squaw's birch canoe
The steamer smokes and raves;
And city lots are staked for sale
Above old Indian graves."*
— *Anonymous*

With the decline of the fur business and the mounting destruction of buffalo herds, the Dakota Indians on the Upper Missouri faced an inevitability which other tribesmen had already experienced east of the Mississippi. The white man's relentless quest for land on which to build towns and establish farms would certainly not stop in Minnesota and Iowa, nor would the South Dakota prairies be bypassed entirely by the flood of immigrants heading for California and Oregon in the 1840s.

The failure of Lewis and Clark and others to find a waterway directly to the Pacific slowed to some degree the development of commerce on the Missouri above Council Bluffs; and the giant overland routes westward — the Oregon, California, Mormon and Pony Trails — kept most of the wagon traffic confined to Nebraska and Kansas. But South Dakota was not completely overlooked.

In 1845 a small advance party of Mormons led by James Emmett arrived at Fort Vermillion, one of the posts of Pierre Chouteau, Jr., on the Missouri River which consisted of four or five crude cabins occupied by French traders. Presumably the first white women and children to enter the state's limits were included in the hardy band which was one of several sent out from Nauvoo, Illinois, as the vanguard of a larger migration to follow. Despite warnings of potential danger from the Indians, Emmett and his people decided to remain at the site for the winter. Not only did they go unmolested by the Dakotas, but they took advantage of the time to impart their religious message to some of the willing natives.

While the Latter-Day Saints left Fort Vermillion the following spring to join the march to Utah, the isolated, unsung Emmett party was a harbinger of things to come. The United States was caught up in an emotional binge called Manifest Destiny, an almost evangelistic fervor to grow and expand. The westward movement was a major symptom of that national disease.

(South Dakota Department of Tourism & Economic Development)

The federal policy of clearing the title to Indian lands and opening them to settlement had its first direct effect on South Dakota in 1851 when the Santee Indians ceded 30 million acres in Iowa and Minnesota, including all the territory east of the Big Sioux River from the Missouri northward beyond Lake Traverse. The Sisseton and Wahpeton bands signed the Treaty of Traverse des Sioux on July 23 after a five-day council, while the M'dewakantons and Wahpekutes approved a similar agreement at Mendota on August 5. (Chieftains "signed" by touching a pen held by a clerk who did the actual writing.)

Almost from the beginning the two pacts were a source of trouble as the Indians were confined to a narrow reservation straddling the Minnesota River which white settlers encroached upon even before the treaties were ratified. The promised annuities were held up, and, according to some sources, the chiefs had been tricked into signing a power of attorney (by merely touching another pen) through which traders were able to siphon off a considerable portion of the $1,665,000 paid to the tribes.

The bumbling start was to have unfortunate repercussions in South Dakota during the decade which followed. First of all, Yankton and Yanktonnais Indians occupying part of the ceded area did not agree to the terms and, as a result, frustrated earliest attempts at settlement in the state. Later the Santees themselves, growing more and more unhappy with post-treaty developments, launched a bloody campaign to seek revenge and redress.

While the Santees were relinquishing their lands in 1851, another council was being held that same year at Fort Laramie, Wyoming, which resulted in a further treaty which also had an important bearing on the future of South Dakota. As one of eight different tribes who participated in the 18-day meeting, the Teton Dakotas agreed to permit unhampered passage of immigrants through Indian lands, to allow the United States government to build roads, military posts and other installations within unceded lands, to cease intertribal warfare, to make restitution for wrongs committed against United States citizens in exchange for the protection of the federal government against depredations upon them, and to accept from the United States an annual payment — in provisions, merchandise, domestic animals and agricultural implements worth $50,000 — for a period of 15 years as a consideration for past grievances and concessions made.

More far-reaching, however, was the allocation of distinct tribal territories by the terms of the hallmark document. As a result, Teton land was stipulated to lie between the Black Hills and the Missouri from the north fork of the Platte River to a northern border along the Heart River from its headwaters to its mouth. Before ratifying the treaty, the United States Senate increased the time period for annuity payments to 50 years (at the discretion of the President) and to make the pact binding for ten years with renewable options every five years.

The Fort Laramie Treaty of 1851, though it provided for no land cession, was destined to become a major bone of contention between the tribes and the federal government. In South Dakota, meanwhile, townsite planners and promoters appeared on the scene for the first time, intent upon taking advantage of the Santee land relinquishment.

Squatter Government: A False Start

Settlement of new territory was usually accomplished by two very different kinds of people. First, there were the opportunists and entrepreneurs (some good, some bad) who recognized the profit potential in western lands. Then came the ordinary land-seekers — farmers, family men, freedom-craving aliens — who, as a general rule, were much less greed-motivated and were interested primarily in personal homesteads. This difference must be kept in mind during any analysis of why men acted as they did or why conflicts developed.

After the Santee treaties were ratified, the narrow strip of ceded land beyond the western boundary of the proposed new state of Minnesota offered a chance for alert operators to get in on the ground floor of another territorial development. Consequently, two rival organizations — the Western Town Company of Dubuque, Iowa, and the Dakota Land Company of St. Paul, Minnesota — each sent out agents to select townsites at or near the falls of the Big Sioux River. The Iowa party arrived in May of 1857, selected a 320-acre tract and made plans to establish a settlement called Sioux Falls.

The St. Paul group made its appearance the following month, and although members were chagrined to find another company already on the scene, they chose an adjoining townsite which they named Sioux Falls City. At the same time other Dakota Land Company representatives had located favorable plats on the Big Sioux north of the falls and took the necessary action to establish the villages of Medary (named for the governor of Minnesota Territory who was a partner in the land company) and Flandreau (for Judge Charles E. Flandrau of St. Paul, despite the spelling discrepancy).

Unfortunately for the land companies, other Dakota Indians — notably the Yanktonnais — did not appreciate the eagerness of the developers. They rejected the Treaty of Traverse des Sioux because they argued that the Santees had no right to give up the particular tract along the lower Big Sioux. Consequently, warrior parties appeared at the settlements of Medary and Flandreau, and before they could get a good start, the townsites were abandoned.

[Much of the fear among whites on the Dakota frontier at that time was caused by a small band of Sioux renegades under Scarlet Point (Inkpaduta) who had participated in the Spirit Lake massacre in Iowa in early March of 1857 during which 42 settlers were killed and four women carried away. Later, two were murdered and two rescued, one at Lake Herman and the other (a 13-year-old girl named Abigail Gardner) near Ashton in Spink County. Four heroic Christian Sioux — Greyfoot, Sounding Heavens, John Otherday and Paul Mazakutamani — played leading roles in securing the freedom of the captives.]

At the combined townsite claims of Sioux Falls and Sioux Falls City, meanwhile, a crude redoubt of logs and earth called Fort Sod was erected as a defensive measure. The stockade was approximately 100 feet square and had walls three feet thick and eight feet high with portholes for weapons. Mrs. Goodwin, wife of one of the settlers, made a United States flag out of old flannel shirts to fly over the fort.

Fortunately, the Indians did not force a confrontation at that time, but the threat of violence in the area was a strong deterrent to a quick population increase. The presence of armed Dakotas and approaching winter did cause the temporary withdrawal of some of the Dubuque contingent to Sioux City. A few members of both groups stayed on, however, and Samuel J. Albright, South Dakota's first newspaper editor, described one of the dramatic occasions of their sojourn:

> Ten colonists of the Western Town Company and six of the Dakota Land Company spent the winter of 1857-58 at Sioux Falls, amid many privations and hardships. They were extremely fortunate in one thing, however. Among the Iowa party was a young but very intelligent physician, Dr. J. L. Phillips, fresh from his eastern studies; and upon his knowledge of surgery and medicine depended a most valuable life. The circumstances are these: early in February, 1858, Mr. W. W. Brookings, the head of the Iowa colony, had the misfortune to have both his feet badly frozen while returning from an attempted journey to secure the site on which the city of Yankton now stands. From want of attention, or through lack of the necessaries for prompt treatment, mortification resulted; and, as a last resort, in order, if possible, to save his life, amputation of both legs below the knees was resorted to. This operation was successfully performed by Dr. Phillips, with no further implements at hand than a large butcher's knife and a small tenon-saw. Marvelous as it may appear, the patient, lying upon a bed of "buffalo robes" in his floorless cabin, with none of the surroundings and comforts deemed indispensable to a sickroom, not only survived the shock incident to the harsh surgery, but entirely regained his health.

The founders of Sioux Falls were mostly young politically-minded promoters of different professional and business callings who visualized a bright, profitable future for what ultimately turned out to be a premature townsite. The Big Sioux could be made navigable to the falls, they envisioned. A railroad line would be forthcoming, and, if they played their cards right, the new settlement would certainly have the inside track to be named the territorial capital.

Accordingly, the young men began immediately to set up a "squatter's government." First they got the Minnesota Assembly to establish Big Sioux County around their townsite (a questionable move because the area was distinctly outside the bounds of the new state of Minnesota and therefore out of its jurisdiction). They sent a delegate to Congress (Alpheus G. Fuller) to petition for territorial status, and in the fall of 1858 they conducted a false election in which a small handful of men produced a vote total which ran into the hundreds.

In the end their extralegal efforts, though ambitious and nervy, were doomed to failure. They had attempted to establish a government *before* the arrival of a permanent citizenry; and politicially, they had depended upon the continuation of a Democratic administration at the national level. When Abraham Lincoln, a Republican, was elected in 1860, they lost their connections in Washington, D.C., and the "squatter government" collapsed without accomplishing any lasting results.

The Yankton Cession: A True Beginning

In the meantime, there was activity on the Missouri River which was destined to have a more permanent outcome.

With the fading of the fur trade business, United States military forces moved into the area, not only to protect the passage of settlers heading farther westward but to establish government authority over the region. In 1855 army officials agreed to buy Chouteau's dilapidated Fort Pierre for $45,000, and six infantry companies arrived by steamboat that summer to begin rejuvenation of the post in preparation for the coming of cavalry units.

Simultaneously, General William Selby Harney (after whom Harney Peak in the Black Hills was later named) led an expedition from St. Louis through Nebraska enroute to Fort Laramie. On the way he attacked a camp of Brule Indians near a place called Ash Hollow on Blue Water Creek. In the one-sided conflict which followed, the Brules lost 86 killed (including some women and children) and the army four. The assault, undoubtedly aggravated by trigger-happy young soldiers in their first encounter with an enemy they knew little about, was defended as a retaliatory measure for the earlier annihilation of a patrol of troopers under Lieutenant J. L. Grattan.

Regardless of right or wrong, the Ash Hollow affair emphasized an obvious trend: the large-scale entry of the military into the affairs of the prairie frontier, an involvement which was to last for more than three decades. When the bloody engagement ended, General Harney and his command proceeded to Fort Laramie. After a show of force and a parlay with Indians gathered there, the general — known popularly as "White Whiskers" — ordered his troops onto the trail again. They marched on eastward into South Dakota, along the White River through the edge of the Badlands, crossing over to the Cheyenne and finally following the Bad River to Fort Pierre.

Harney's reaction when he saw the post was decidedly negative, but with winter coming on, it was too late to establish a new headquarters. When spring came, however, he made arrangements for the construction of Fort Randall some 185 river-miles downstream, and ultimately Fort Pierre was abandoned by the army. Subsequently the stockade and buildings were torn down, with portions of the material being used in the construction of Fort Randall. The contractor in charge of the dismantling apparently held out some of the best cedar logs which were rafted down the river to be used in building a trading post at the Yankton Sioux village.

Although Fort Randall was one of the so-called permanent army installations on the prairie frontier, there was nothing particularly significant to South Dakota's history in Harney's occupation of the state's first true military base, but the presence of one particular officer on his roster — Captain John Blair Smith Todd — was to have important bearing on the area's future.

Dissatisfied with conditions at Fort Pierre and Fort Lookout (near present-day Chamberlain), General William Harney selected a site on the west bank of the Missouri 30 miles above the mouth of the Niobrara for a permanent military installation. Fort Randall — named for Colonel Daniel W. Randall — was erected in 1856 and remained active until 1892. All vestiges of the post then disappeared except the ruins of a combination chapel, library and lodge hall for soldier-members of the Independent Order of Odd Fellows built of chalkstone in 1874-75. (Yankton Daily Press & Dakotan)

Captain Todd, a West Point graduate from Kentucky and cousin of Mary Todd Lincoln, was 41 years old in 1855 when he decided to resign his army commission to capitalize if he could on the development potential of the Dakota country. Todd allied himself with Daniel Marsh Frost, a wealthy St. Louis merchant, and also secured for himself the position of sutler (storekeeper) when Fort Randall was activated.

The Frost-Todd company combined the long frontier experience of the ex-captain with the capital and cunning of the St. Louis investor. Their plan in the beginning was to develop fur trading posts and frontier stores along the Missouri, but the reduced quantities of pelts and an ebbing market caused them to turn quickly to the more promising field of land speculation and townsite development. The one holdup, of course, was the need to extinguish the title to the land held by the Indians, whose ownership rights were officially guaranteed by the United States.

Captain Todd — distinguished-looking, forceful and shrewd — began at once to develop a strategy for treaty negotiations. Two people figured prominently in his plan. The first was Charles F. Picotte, born of a French father and a Dakota mother, and Strike-the-Ree, a leading chief of the Yankton Indians.

Old Strike — as the chieftain was popularly known — was the subject of several historical controversies. For instance, when Lewis and Clark arrived at or near the ultimate site of the territorial capital in the fall of 1804, they supposedly wrapped a small Indian child in an American flag as a gesture of friendship — and according to the legend (for which there is no specific documentation), the youngster grew up to become chief of the Yanktons.

His Americanized name was either Strike-the-Ree or Struck-by-the-Ree, depending upon which tradition one chooses to believe. The latter title reputedly grew out of an intertribal battle in which the then young brave was defeated in personal combat by an Arikara (Ree) opponent. As a result, Old Strike was said to have worn a kerchief or other covering over his head for the rest of his life to hide the scars of a partial scalping. The second story reverses the victor and victim, with the Yankton warrior avenging an earlier murder of his brother by plunging a spear through his Arikara adversary. For the achievement, he won the name Strike-the-Ree.

Historians disagree on the subject, but George W. Kingsbury — who was at Yankton during its village years and who knew Old Strike — always used the latter name. Similarly, the Frost-Todd trading post ledger, kept by George D. Fiske at the Indian camp in 1859 listed the Sioux leader's account under the heading "Strike the Rhee." On the premise that the proud chieftain would most likely have borne a title signifying victory rather than defeat, this history will follow Fiske's and Kingsbury's lead. Adding another element of confusion, Kingsbury included a photograph of the Yankton leader in his history with a notation that the latter was then in his 93rd year. Other sources say he died at 84 on July 28, 1888.

At his Missouri River village, Strike-the-Ree was generally resigned to the inevitability of settlement. To his fellow tribesmen he said:

> The white men are coming in like maggots. It is useless to resist them. They are many more than we are. We could not hope to stop them. Many of our brave warriors would be killed, our women and children left in sorrow, and still we would not stop them. We must accept it, get the best terms we can get and try to adopt their ways.

Strike-the-Ree, known also as Struck-by-the-Ree, was chief of the Yankton Sioux, one of the Seven Council Fires of the Dakotas. Resigned to the inevitability of settlement by whites, Old Strike agreed to the cession treaty of 1858 which opened a large portion of eastern South Dakota to settlement. Approximately 14 million acres of land were involved. (South Dakota State Historical Society)

Todd, of course, hoped to use the chieftain's influence to win a cession pact. He also planned to take advantage of Picotte's relationship with the tribe by utilizing him as an interpreter and, to some degree, as a salesman for the Frost-Todd proposal. For his participation, Picotte was promised a sizable grant of land.

Despite some resistance, principally by another chieftain named Smutty Bear, a delegation of Indian leaders — 14 in all — was taken to Washington, D.C., where they were wined, dined and whiskeyed sufficiently enough to weaken the strongest objections. The ultimate result was that on April 19, 1858, a treaty was signed by all parties, relinquishing ownership to approximately 14 million acres of land between the Missouri and Big Sioux Rivers south of a line running generally from Fort Pierre to Lake Kampeska.

For their part, the Yanktons were to remove themselves to a reservation of some 400,000 acres on the east bank of the Missouri in present-day Charles Mix County where they were to be paid $1,600,000 in annuities over a 50-year period. They were also to have free use of the Red Pipestone Quarry for "so long as they shall desire." Included were specific provisions to educate the Indians "in letters, agriculture and mechanic arts, and housewifery;" a resident agent was to be appointed; and Article VII recognized Charles Picotte's valuable services and liberality to the Yanktons" for which he was granted 640 acres of land outside the reservation. He subsequently selected a tract encompassing much of the original townsite of Yankton.

The most interesting element of the treaty, however, was a clause which stated that "all persons (other than Indians or mixed bloods) who are now residing within said ceded country, by authority of law, shall have the privilege of entering one hundred and sixty acres thereof, to include each of their residences and improvements, at the rate of one dollar and twenty-five cents per acre." With little question, Captain Todd was responsible for that particular article because it permitted him and his partner to get first choice of key townsite locations where they already had trading posts in operation. Their priority selection, of course, was adjacent to Picotte's land at Strike-the-Ree's village, soon to be known as Yankton and for which Todd and Frost has other ambitious plans.

Similar to the aftermath of the Santee treaties, not all Dakota Indians were in accord with the cession, and a number of Yanktons were included among the antitreaty remonstrators. It was claimed by some Tetons that the Yanktons were merely living on the land by permission of the Tetons and therefore had no right to sign it away. Strike-the-Ree and Picotte were viewed as traitors by more militant Indians, and seeds of future conflict were planted. While the tribal feuds were being waged, however, the United States government prepared to carry out the terms of what it considered a binding document after it was ratified by the Senate on February 17, 1859.

Almost five months after that date, the river steamboat *Carrier* arrived at Strike-the-Ree's camp on July 10 with the newly appointed Indian agent Alexander H. Redfield and a cargo of annuity goods, including food, calico, blankets, agricultural implements and a considerable amount of gold and silver coins. Redfield merely dangled this bounty before the Indians like a carrot on a stick, and several hours later the *Carrier* moved upstream again, this time bound for the agency beyond Chouteau Creek some 65 miles farther west. The Yanktons — estimated variously by eye-witnesses and historians as from two to three thousand people — followed the boat on shore shortly afterwards.

Meanwhile, just several hundred yards away, across the swirling stream in Nebraska Territory, a small group of white opportunists had waited for the departure of the Indians so that they could stake their claims on the land relinquished by Old Strike and his followers, as well as on the ceded territory being abandoned by the tribal units

Three major participants in the negotiations for the Yankton land cession treaty of 1858 were (left to right): Smutty Bear, who was opposed to the pact; Charles F. Picotte, half-breed interpreter who profited from the signing; and Strike-the-Ree, the dominant Yankton chief whose observations of the white man's numbers and affluence during a trip to Washington, D.C., convinced him it was impossible to prevent settlement of his people's hunting grounds. (South Dakota State Historical Society)

under Crazy Bull on the James River, Smutty Bear six miles or so west of the main village and smaller camps all the way to the mouth of the Big Sioux. Shortly before the arrival of the annuity boat there had been a threatened revolt of Indians not favorably disposed to the treaty. Again the authority of Old Strike was upheld, and a second possible uprising was averted by a council meeting, a peace pipe ritual and a great feast featuring two roast oxen.

The Indian exodus which followed on July 10, 1859, marked a milestone day in South Dakota history. No proclamations or official signal opened the territory to land-seekers, but as the trail poles of travois carriers and hooves of Indian ponies kicked up acrid dust on the warm, mid-summer day, the Yanktons filed silently and solemnly out of their village clearing. The old native domain had ended; a new settlement era had dawned.

First Settlements: More for Profit Than Posterity

There was not a great flood of settlers into the ceded land. The people of the United States were generally more preoccupied with the crisis developing over the question of slavery; and California and Oregon were still primary goals of most western migrants.

Prior to the arrival of Major Redfield and the annuity boat, however, there had been several incidents involving premature settlement. Troopers from Fort Randall ranged up and down the Missouri, driving over-eager whites ("sooners") out of the territory, while the Indians — especially the defiant ones — guarded the stream banks against intruders. Charles Picotte later wrote:

> . . . . . we came pretty near having a fight before the treaty was ratified. The whites would come over from Nebraska, put up houses — sometimes in the night — at Yankton, Vermillion and Smutty Bear Bottom. I had about forty Indians go with me on one occasion to explain to them that the treaty was not ratified and that they had no right there and must take their effects away, for we should certainly burn their houses.

When the time of legal entry arrived, the first men on the scene — generally young adventurers in their twenties or early thirties — came, not necessarily to build homes, but to vie for the potential profits of a new land. Control of townsites generated the greatest competition, especially if the territorial capital or a county seat designation were later to be attained. And there was the element of politics, too. Ambitious young lawyers and others motivated by the possibilities of elected or appointed positions made their appearance within the South Dakota borders ahead of farmers and ranchers and families.

Men like Frost and Todd knew, too, that providing annuity goods for Indians on reservations offered lucrative contracts, especially if some of the provisions could be grown or manufactured within the region. The same was true of army supply orders. Still other advantages to be gained by early domination included such government-related needs as legal printing, postal services, road construction and land offices.

Needless to say, the stakes were attractive, and it became evident quite quickly that the developers on the Big Sioux and Missouri Rivers were in a race to control the political and economic future of the still unorganized Dakota Territory (a title which already was being freely used in 1858). The previously mentioned attempt of the Sioux Falls land companies to rush the territory into existence as a "squatter's government" was a notable phase of the competition; and at Yankton, shortly after the Indians departed, the Upper Missouri Land Company — dominated by Frost and Todd but including prominent pioneers of Sioux City — also began to agitate for official territorial status.

The political intrigue and maneuvering by the various factions (which included the settlement of Pembina on the Red River near the Canadian border) is a story all its own, but stripped of the details and generally insignificant complexities, the ultimate result was victory for Frost and Todd. Not only did they have stronger political connections than their opponents, but their gamble that the Missouri River would be Dakota's first important artery of commerce and magnet for settlement paid off handsomely.

Meanwhile, the flow of newcomers increased gradually as surveyors began the tedious task of dividing the once unbounded Indian land into permanent legally definable parcels according to the white man's system of measurements. The circumstances placed early historic emphasis on Yankton and Sioux Falls, but there was activity elsewhere, too. All along the Missouri from Sioux City past Yankton to the new reservation the evidences of settlement became more prevalent.

A party headed by John H. Shober, enroute from Minnesota to the Colorado gold fields in 1858, was impressed with what they saw in the vicinity of Bon Homme Island and decided to stay. Unfortunately, they were among the "sooners" driven out by Fort Randall soldiers who destroyed their cabins and chased them across the Missouri. Later, when entry was legalized, the colony returned and established the village of Bon Homme.

Near the mouth of the Vermillion River a community began to grow around the old trading post of Fort Vermillion and the rope ferry operated by A. C. Van Meter, who was also the mail carrier between Sioux City and Fort Randall. "Sooners" were also evicted from that area, and in the summer of 1859, other claim-seekers appeared, including at least one party of Norwegian immigrants of whom there would be many in ensuing years.

Closer to Sioux City a French settlement developed between the Big Sioux and a geographic feature on the Missouri known by the Indians in literal translation as "Elk Point," a name which was in turn adopted for a new townsite. Eli B. Wixson, who built a log cabin hotel there in 1859, said he selected the location because he had observed an extensive flooding of the region in the spring two years earlier and only the passageway used by the once plentiful elk herds remained above water.

Typical of most frontier expansion movements, the first arrivals were almost all men. The rigors of the experience were considered inappropriate for the "weaker sex," according to the customs of the time. When the first non-Indian wives did appear in pre-territorial South Dakota, however, they proved themselves equally capable of enduring the heat, the cold, the discomfort and the strain of rolling back the wilderness as the men.

Mrs. Paul Pacquette, wife of the Big Sioux ferry operator near Sioux City; Mrs. Aaron Hammond, wife of one of the Bon Homme "sooners;" Mrs. John Goodwin and Mrs. Charles S. White, both of whom had accompanied their husbands to the original Sioux Falls settlement; Mrs. J. B. Greenway, whose spouse became the James River ferry contractor east of Yankton; and Mrs. John Stanage, wife of an ex-soldier and member of the first territorial legislature, were all in South Dakota during or before 1858.

The Dakota Territory: First Step to Statehood

For a variety of reasons, the newcomers to the Dakota country were extremely anxious for official governmental recognition at the federal level, not only for the protection of incoming families but because of the political largesse offered by a new territory or state, such as supply contracts, office plums and real estate manipulations.

The "squatter government" at Sioux Falls was a premature effort based on fictionalized population figures which obviously didn't impress Congress. (As an example of the fraud, the unofficial county of Midway of which Medary was the seat was represented to have a thousand voters *after* the area had been evacuated because of the Indian scare.) The appearance in Washington, D.C., of Alpheus G. Fuller and Jefferson P. Kidder as "elected" delegates to Congress in 1857 and 1858, respectively, gave the region some exposure in the nation's capital but not enough to generate serious consideration of territorial status. Southern Democrats especially were not interested in any action which might result in future non-slave states, and Republicans similarly were not favorable to a "squatter government" which was clearly under control of the opposite party.

Meanwhile, following withdrawal of the Indians, the Yankton-based promoters headed by Captain Todd had also entered into the campaign for organized status. In November of 1859 a meeting was held in the village at Strike-the-Ree's old camp at which time a memorial to Congress was drafted and Todd was commissioned to deliver it to Washington. Like the Sioux Falls delegates, he too failed to overcome the reticence of the national politicians who were wrestling with the slavery question and trying to overcome the effects of the Panic of 1857 which in less than three years had resulted in the known failures of more than 13,000 businesses throughout the country.

But the new Dakotans — or '59ers as many of them called themselves — were persistent!

In January of 1861 they again sent Captain Todd back to Washington, D.C., this time with a petition signed by 578 settlers in the Missouri River Valley. By then Abraham Lincoln had been elected President and was soon to be inaugurated. That, of course, assured Republicans of control of territorial appointees, which may have been one reason why they dropped their insistence on a no-slavery clause in the measure to create Dakota Territory. All of a sudden, without debate or even a tally vote, the legislation was rushed through, and on March 2, 1861 — two days before his term ended — President Buchanan signed the bill into law.

Dakota Territory, as created by Congress, was a mammoth entity. Encompassing all the future states of North and South Dakota and Montana, in addition to parts of Wyoming and Idaho, the new political subdivision of the United States contained some 350,000 square miles and a very scanty non-Indian population. Almost immediately the responsibility to name the first governing officials of the vast western country about which relatively little was known fell to President Lincoln. Less than a month earlier, however, Jefferson Davis had been elected provisional head of the Confederacy, and the threatening clouds of rebellion overshadowed all other domestic considerations. Undoubtedly territorial patronage — so important to political hacks and greedy speculators — was of far less concern to the new President than the firing on Fort Sumter on April 12. Three days later he declared that a state of insurrection existed, and the terrible Civil War was underway.

Dakota Territory, as organized in 1861, included all or part of the future states of North and South Dakota, Montana, Wyoming and Idaho. By 1868 only the two Dakotas remained, a condition which continued for 21 years until statehood was achieved in 1889.

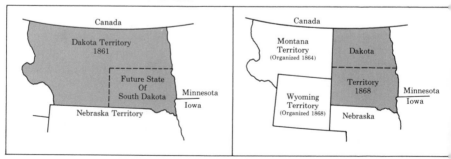

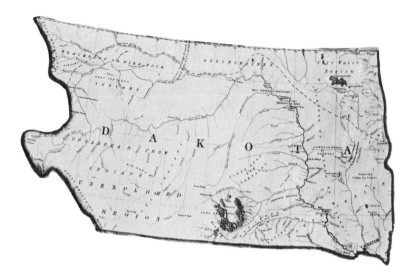

The original Dakota Territory was a vast land encompassing both the future states of North and South Dakota, much of Montana and parts of Idaho and Wyoming. Attempts to govern the area from the tiny village of Yankton in the southeastern corner were frustrated by great distances and lack of communications. (Yankton Daily Press & Dakotan)

The fact that Dakota Territory came into existence at such a dramatic period in the nation's history had a substantial effect on the developments in the region. It was far removed from the overriding problems of survival, so in contemplating the activities which occurred on the frontier, one must always relate them to what was happening on the national scene in order to assure proper perspective.

The war, for instance, had a direct bearing on the Frost and Todd domination of Dakota politics. Because of his relationship to Mrs. Lincoln and his personal role in bringing the Territory into being, Todd was waiting patiently in the wings in hopes of being named first governor. It was expected that he could overcome the objection that he was a Democrat, but just when the Dakota appointments were being considered, Daniel Frost led a brazen attempt to sieze the United States arsenal in St. Louis for the Confederacy, after which he joined the secessionist army and ultimately became a brigadier general.

Because of the close association between the two men, that act eliminated Todd from further consideration; and under the circumstances, the President turned to a loyal friend and neighbor for the governorship — 36-year-old William Jayne, a physician who had served the Lincoln family in Springfield, Illinois.

Other recipients of territorial patronage appointed at the same time included Chief Justice Philemon Bliss, a former abolitionist congressman from Ohio; Secretary John Hutchinson, a Minnesota attorney who had also been an anti-slave activist in Kansas; Attorney General William E. Gleason, a fastidious gentleman from Maryland; Surveyor General George D. Hill, a large, jovial political opportunist from Michigan who was described as having an "overwhelming affection for alcohol and an unfailing instinct for speculation;" and as marshal, William Shaffer, a young Missourian who served for a time and then left to join the Union army. Named agent for the Yankton Indians was Walter A. Burleigh, a physician and attorney from Kittaning, Pennsylvania, who was to play a prominent role in the formative period of the territory.

A New Capital: A New Government

Being handed a political plum was one thing, but being assigned to establish a government in the unpopulated hinterlands was a somewhat dubious reward. As the newly appointed officials made plans to go to Dakota, they were not altogether sure just where the temporary capital would be located. There was competition among Sioux Falls, then the most flourishing village; Vermillion, second in size and growing rapidly with the influx of land-seekers; and upstart Yankton, just beginning to take shape as a legitimate townsite. John Todd had failed in his solicitation of the governorship, but apparently he was more successful in his second quest. In later years State Historian Doane Robinson credited Mrs. Lincoln's intercession as the deciding factor in Governor Jayne's selection of Yankton as the first seat of government, although no actual documentation of that conjecture has ever been found.

When Jayne and Secretary Hutchinson arrived at the capital on May 26, 1861, they could hardly have been less impressed. What they

In 1866, seven years after the Indian exodus, Yankton was a treeless village on the Missouri River and seat of government for a vast territory. The largest building at left was the Ash Hotel and directly above it to the east was the original capitol or legislative hall. The dark building slightly to the right was the newly erected Episcopal church built by the Reverend Melancthon Hoyt, pioneer missionary and chaplain of the Dakota militia. Little evidence of the stockade of 1862 remained. (Yankton County Historical Society)

saw was a motley cluster of log cabins and rough-board shacks, populated mostly by rugged, ill-clad young adventurers in their twenties and thirties, all anxious to profit from the new status of their infant village. Lots had been surveyed but titles were questionable; streets were vaguely located, mud-bound or dusty depending on the weather; and even the crudest accommodations for government — not to mention living quarters and eating facilities — were virtually nonexistent. The choice had been made, however, and if it were true that the President's wife was behind the selection, no new appointee would want to challenge the decision. As it was, the alternate possibilities had no more to offer.

After he had established the executive office of the Territory in a log cabin, Governor Jayne in his first official act called for a complete census to find out just whom he had been sent out to govern. Six enumerators covered the vast region as best they could and arrived at a total population of 2,376, including mixed bloods but not Indians. Undoubtedly the figure was only approximate because a short count was returned from the Pembina district in the north where many of the residents (mostly of French-Indian derivation) were out hunting buffalo.

Bringing government to such a sparse, scattered population with little or no communications between settlements was a distinct challenge, to say the least. The Western Union Telegraph Company had been organized in 1856 but its services didn't reach Dakota until 1870. Roads were merely prairie trails, with rivers and creeks still without bridges. So it was that when Governor Jayne set the first general election for September 16, 1861, the complications of campaigning and getting out a legal vote were unique, but they certainly didn't deter the eager participants.

Although most of the territorial officials were presidential appointees, the settlers themselves had the responsibility for selecting a delegate to the federal Congress and to choose the members of the two-house legislature provided by the Organic Act — nine councilmen and 13 representatives. The impending election not only gen-

erated interest because of its importance to the future of the area, but because it was a most welcome diversion from the boredom of frontier existence.

In keeping with the custom of the times, of course, women were excluded from the entire electoral process. Only "free white male" residents of the Territory at the time of the passage of the Organic Act — provided they were United States citizens or had taken the proper oaths to become such — were eligible to vote or hold office. The concept of the equality of the sexes was not even remotely considered, and while the few ladies at hand spent "many a lonely hour of tears and trials . . . in their jail-like cabins of logs and dirt" (as a contemporary newspaper report described their situation), the men launched a campaign which for them was one giant, festive stag party.

Pioneers of Dakota held a reunion in 1911 on the 50th anniversary of the Territory's creation. Among those attending were (front row from left): Horace T. Bailey, John H. Shober, Governor William Jayne and John R. Hanson; (back row): historian and editor George W. Kingsbury and C. J. Holman. Shober was president of the first territorial council, while Bailey, Hanson and Holman were at Strike-the-Ree's camp before the 1858 cession. Kingsbury and Hanson later had South Dakota counties named for them. (Yankton County Historical Society)

Moses Kimball Armstrong, surveyor, journalist and politician, described the first Dakota election as "wide open, red-hot and mighty interesting." In his book *Early History of Dakota Territory* he wrote of candidates and campaign speakers assembling in Sioux City from which point they would "charge across the Sioux to attack the bewildered voters with spread-eagle speeches, torch-light parades, fife and drum and bottles labeled 'fire water'." Armstrong's report continued:

> These campaign parties traveled in cavalcades made up of men on foot, on horseback and with a band wagon. The musicians were to furnish the music and do the fighting at the meetings, the law-yers were to make the speeches and do the lying, the voters were to furnish the cheers and do the drink-ing, while the candidates were to do their bragging during the campaign and to pay the bills and do the swearing after election.

Much of the political activity was centered at Yankton, Vermillion and Bon Homme, each of which had a candidate for congressional delegate. Captain Todd was Yankton's man, of course, and he ran as an independent (no doubt so his past history as a Democrat wouldn't be too obvious to the Republican administration in Washington). Charles P. Booge, a sutler at the Yankton Indian agency, was chosen by a Peoples' Party convention in Bon Homme, and A. J. Bell of Vermillion was nominated by the Union Party, which, in effect, made him the Republican candidate.

While a territorial delegate did not have the same voting privileges as a United States Representative, the office was not an insignificant one. The delegate not only was the spokesman for his constituents in Congress, but he was the pipeline through which flowed much of the governmental patronage — job appointments, contracts and other benefits. The built-in capability to "pay off" politically made the position a lucrative and powerful one, and so the Booge-Todd-Bell campaign had some valuable stakes involved.

A notable feature of the pre-election activity was the establishment of two of the area's earliest newspapers, *The Dakota Republican* at Vermillion which backed Bell's candidacy, and *The Weekly Dakotian* (spelled *Dakotaian* and *Dakotan* at various times in its continuing existence) at Yankton in support of Todd. Neither qualified as South Dakota's first journalistic endeavor, however. Preceding them was *The Dakota Democrat,* which made its initial appearance in Sioux Falls on July 2, 1859. Samuel J. Albright, the publisher, admitted that he had brought his press and type to the village on the Big Sioux because he was after the territorial printing. He left when it appeared that Sioux Falls was out of the running for

In the early territorial and statehood period, politics was an all-male activity. Custom forbade the inclusion of women in such election-day gatherings as the above assembly at the legislative hall in Yankton in 1866. Lack of other diversion was partly responsible for the broad interest and involvement in governmental affairs by the rough-clad, generally ill-educated frontiersmen. (Yankton County Historical Society)

the capital location, and the newspaper was continued as *The Northwestern Independent* until 1862 when the Indian uprising of that year forced the abandonment of the settlement. South Dakota's first printing press was thrown into the Big Sioux, and — according to legend — Albright's type metal showed up later as lead inlays in decorative peace pipes.

To the Dakota Indian, the Sacred Pipe is an instrument of deep religious significance. This particular redstone pipe reputedly was inlaid with type metal taken by Sioux warriors in 1862 when they destroyed the shop of *The Democrat,* South Dakota's first newspaper, in Sioux Falls. Like other historic legends, this story has been disputed by various researchers. Many of the pipes used by Indians in their tribal rituals were made in large quantities by white manufacturers who traded them to the Sioux in a highly profitable exchange for buffalo robes or other furs. (South Dakota State Historical Society)

The first interest of the Yankton and Vermillion journals was the election of their respective candidates, but they served a broader purpose, too. As crude and limited as they were, they brought entertainment, diversion and belated word from the "outside" to the isolated Dakotans. Moreover, they generated a spirit of local pride and boomerism, often to an exaggerated degree. Depending upon the editor — who might be extremely talented or have just enough education to permit him to spell a little better than most of his readers — the frontier papers ranged from dull to bombastic. Some of them were filled with caustic comments and invectives which in later years would surely have sent a victim running to a libel lawyer. The first Dakota papers tended to fit somewhere between the extremes, although the editors were not averse to an occasional use of the acid pen. For instance, when the election was over and John Todd was declared the winner (getting 397 of the 585 votes cast), *The Dakotian* indicated lingering ill will in rather forthright language:

> C. P. Booge, his wet nurse, and purse-holder, were in town since election. Booge looks melancholy, and his two bowers seem somewhat out of wind. We are not, however, disposed to exult over a prostrate foe — we are therefore willing to let bygones be bygones, so far as some of Booge's friends are concerned; but Charley's insane ambition has caused us to doubt him, and while we shall treat him civilly, we shall never feel toward him as we did in the better days of yore.

With a delegate chosen and legislators named, the Territory of Dakota was ready to pursue its own destiny, at least to the extent that the federal tethers permitted. As winter approached, however, most of the appointed officials left Yankton for more comfortable quarters elsewhere. They had heard about the blizzard of the previous February when George Fiske, one of the town's first residents, froze to death not far from his cabin. There were rumors of Indian unrest, too, so the political carpet-baggers decided it was better not to remain in such a cold, precarious place if it weren't absolutely necessary.

The Pony Congress: With Horseplay and Horse Sense

Monday, March 17, 1862, was a pleasant, cloudless day in Yankton, Dakota Territory, when the members of the first territorial legislature gathered in the frontier capital which, according to a pioneer's diary of that date, boasted 19 varied structures, "comprising one hotel, two boarding houses, one saloon, one store, two Legislative halls, a Secretary's office, one Surveyor General's and Governor's office, and seven log buildings, six of which are occupied."

The men who came to Old Strike's camp by pony, stage and wagon were a young lot — nine councilmen and 13 representatives who averaged just over 32 years of age. Representative John L. Tiernon, an ex-soldier from Fort Randall, was the youngest at 22, and Representative Reuben Wallace of Bon Homme, at 50, was not only the senior legislator but was considered to be the oldest white man in the Territory. Their formal education beyond the school of experience was scanty, but in general the frontier lawmakers were aware of their responsibilities, and they came to the bleak little capital intent upon providing some workable, horse-sense government. Everybody was present except Representative Hugh Donaldson of Pembina who arrived on the fifth day of the session after a long, slow winter trip across both the future states of North and South Dakota.

When the Pony Congress (as the first legislature came to be known) convened for business, the Council was located in a new frame building on Broadway, then Yankton's only street of consequence. The House was brought to order in a large cottonwood log cabin which had been serving as a church for the Reverend Melancthon Hoyt's small Episcopalian congregation. On the third day a joint session was held in the House chamber at which time Governor Jayne's 7,054-word opening message was read by a secretary (since the chief executive had not yet returned to the capital). It instructed the rough-clad legislators to provide adequate civil and criminal law; to devise financial, educational, electoral and military systems; to build roads; to prohibit slavery and [contradictorily] to confine the Indian; to institute a geographical survey and a transcontinental railroad through the Territory; to support the Union in the "infamous rebellion"; and to urge passage of The Homestead Law.

When the speech was concluded, the combined bodies ordered it printed and distributed to the populace: 2,000 copies in English, 600 in Norwegian, 400 in German and 200 in French. The language breakdown indicated, to some degree, the proportions of the various nationalities then coming into the Territory in its first year of official existence.

After the subdued beginning, the lesgislative session quickly burst into a heated, factional shouting match over the permanent location of the capital. The Yankton members felt they had been betrayed when House Speaker George M. Pinney of Bon Homme (whom they helped choose in exchange for support of their town) tried first to get his own village named, and when that failed, he switched his support to Vermillion. Before it was all over (Yankton finally won on the 20th day), the newly formed territorial militia was called in to keep the peace, Pinney was replaced by 22-year-old John Tiernon and at least two physical confrontations were reported. Francis M. (Frank) Ziebach, who had edited *The Dakotian* during the campaign and was later foreman in charge of public printing, wrote:

The Ash Hotel (shown as it appeared in 1866) was the scene of much political activity during legislative sessions at the territorial capital. Innkeeper Henry Ash and his wife provided lodging and meals for lawmakers in the two-story structure built primarily of native cottonwood lumber. The horseplay of the so-called Third House occasionally erupted within its walls. (Yankton County Historical Society)

Shortly after the Pinney episode in the house I saw the ex-speaker enter a saloon on Broadway a short distance from my printing office. I knew that a party of legislators were congregated there and I expected a demonstration, and kept an eye out from the window, beside the case where I was working. Pinney had barely had time to walk from the door to the bar when a crash came, and I saw the former speaker come forcibly through the window of the saloon, bearing the sash with him. The sardonic countenance of Jim Somers [the 23-year-old sergeant-at-arms of the House] appeared through the opening behind him.

Council members were not above the show of temper either, and during a meal at the new two-story Ash Hotel, John Boyle and Enos Stutsman, representing Vermillion and Yankton factions, reputedly got into such a violent argument that they started throwing condiment bottles, cups, glasses and even the skeleton of the fowl they were eating at one another. Stutsman was a small man with a massive head and, in addition, he had been born with just one leg and that somewhat shorter than normal. But he was a noted scrapper with or without his crutches, and he flung himself across the table at his equally enraged fellow attorney. Fortunately, on-lookers separated them before any serious damage was done, and they lived to carry on their conflict verbally in the less dangerous confines of the Council chamber.

Despite the occasional flareups, the Pony Congress accomplished a surprising amount of business, developing basic laws which in time were to influence the new state of South Dakota 27 years later. The boundaries of 18 counties were defined, and — to offset the awarding of the capital to Yankton — Vermillion was named site of the territorial university and the penitentiary went to Bon Homme. Among other items approved during the 60-day session, the pioneer lawmakers prohibited swine and stallions from running free, banned Indians from roaming from their reservation without a pass, granted citizenship to Charles Picotte, provided for ferries across the various territorial rivers, outlawed gambling and bawdy houses [which never really occurred in practice], upheld the sanctity of the Sabbath and organized the Dakota militia to protect the settlers against Confederate or Indian attacks.

It was a small but legal beginning to grow on and, in the minds of the people involved, worthy of a celebration. The legislators apparently enjoyed a mixture of horseplay along with their serious deliberations, and much of the hilarity revolved around the so-called Third House, mock sessions of which were held at Antoine Robeare's saloon or Henry Ash's hotel. Frank Ziebach presided over these lighthearted meetings as "the squatter governor," delivering fanciful speeches and enacting satiric legislation for laughs only. Ziebach was so widely addressed as governor during the early territorial period that a few unsuspecting writers in later years embarrassingly mistook him for the real thing.

Even before official adjournment came on May 16, the members took advantage of a pleasant springtime to enjoy themselves despite Yankton's limited accommodations. Moses Armstrong in one of his popular dispatches to the *Sioux City Register,* printed anonymously although most everyone knew who wrote them, described the legislative carousals from the vantage point of a participant:

> For three nights before the adjournment, campfires could be seen in the streets from dark to daylight, around which were seated, wigwam style, electioneering parties of councilmen and representatives, all happily drinking, smoking, eating, singing, snoring, speechmaking and milking cows. I happened to cross the street one morning at the peep of day, and there I beheld beside a smouldering campfire, two lusty legislators [Chris Maloney and John McBride] holding a kicking cow by the horns, and a third [John Stanage] pulling his full weight at the cow's tail. On each side of the milkless heifer sat two councilmen [Downer Bramble and Enos Stutsman] flat upon their unfailing foundations, with pails in hand, making sorrowful attempts and vain, at teasing milk enough from the farrow quadruped for their final pitcher of eggnog. Off on one side lay a cor-

pulent representative [Hugh Donaldson] sprawled upon his belly and convulsed with laughter. And there in front of the scene stood another eloquent law-maker [John Boyle] with hat, coat and boots off, making a military speech and appealing to the cow to give down in behalf of her country.

The Homestead Act: An Indian Outbreak

Shortly after the Pony Congress disbanded, two important events occurred, each of which had a direct and significant effect on the Territory. The first was the passage of the Homestead Act on May 20, 1862, which ultimately was to bring thousands of settlers to Dakota in quest of free land. The second was a precipitous uprising of the Santee Indians in Minnesota which quickly spread to the new Territory, driving many frightened residents from the region and delaying — for a while, at least — a large migration to the potentially dangerous prairies.

No one who can look without bias on the depradations made by unscrupulous traders on the Santees can deny the justification of their complaints. While many Indians had conformed to the provisions of the Treaty of 1851, others maintained a festering resentment of the pact and toward the growing numbers of settlers who moved into the Minnesota River country during the decade.

News of the Civil War, and especially the early setbacks suffered by Union forces, reached the Indians. The more militant ones among them believed that the ideal opportunity for retaliation had arrived. Not only had many of the able-bodied men been called away from their frontier homes or had volunteered for service in the fratricidal conflict, but the Santees speculated that the demands of the greater war would prohibit the diversion of any large military campaign to challenge them. When the regular annuity payment due in June was not delivered according to schedule, the situation became more aggravated and it was only a matter of time before the seething cauldron would bubble over on the contested land.

The first incident came on August 17, 1862, twelve miles west of Litchfield, Minnesota, when four young Santees attacked and killed three white men and two women, presumably following a quarrel over a stolen nest of chicken eggs. When the quartet returned to the tribe for protection, a decision was made not to turn the perpetrators over to the authorities. Meanwhile, another band under Little Crow, hungry because rations had not been issued and the cession gold had not arrived, apparently tried to obtain credit from an agency storekeeper who — according to one report of the episode — refused and replied: "Let them eat grass." On August 18 the sutler was found dead with his mouth full of grass.

Almost immediately thereafter, the long pent-up animosities burst out in wholesale rebellion. Raiding parties swarmed over the area, killing and mutilating isolated settlers in a campaign of revenge. Women and children were included among the hundreds of victims, as the Santees departed from Dakota warrior tradition. But the attacks did occur, and probably no event or confrontation did more to instill a lasting enmity between the two peoples throughout the area than the so-called War of the Outbreak.

In the end the Indians had underestimated the ability and willingness of the government and frontier residents to respond; and within four months the revolt was quelled and 38 Santees were hanged at Mankato in a mass execution on the day after Christmas in 1862 as a gruesome climax to a gruesome episode. How many other Indians died during the widespread "war" has never been determined, while the number of settlers who were killed ranged from 490 to 800, depending upon historical source.

Following the revolt, the imprisonment of hundreds of Santees in Minnesota and Iowa and their shipment by rail and boat to Crow Creek is sadly reminiscent of the Trail of Tears of the Five Civilized Tribes a quarter of a century earlier. It was a further indictment of the system which caused Judge Charles Flandrau, who was himself involved in the defense against the outbreak, to say: "Had I been an Indian, I would have rebelled, too."

Although the bloody drama was centered mostly in Minnesota, it quickly spilled over into the adjoining Territory and had a direct bearing on the history of South Dakota. It came just when the pace of settlement was picking up and the excitement of a new territorial government was spreading across the frontier.

Rumors of the numbers of raiders and their purpose swept like a crackling prairie fire from settlement to settlement. Then, on August 25 — just eight days after the first incident near Litchfield — one of the small bands of insurgents killed Judge J. B. Amidon and his son, William, as they were working in a hay field less than a mile from the village of Sioux Falls. News of these slayings reached Yankton shortly thereafter, and the mounting excitement finally spurred Governor Jayne to action. On August 30 he issued a proclamation calling for the enrollment of every male citizen between 18 and 50 into home defense units in all the counties.

That same night the citizens of Yankton gathered at the Episcopal log chapel to sign up, and on the next day plans were made for a stockade big enough and strong enough to withstand a major Indian attack. Of considerable worry, of course, was the possibility that the Yankton tribe would join the Santees on the warpath. The fortification was built at the capital, and fleeing residents from Sioux Falls, Bon Homme and other isolated homesteads came to Yankton for protection. Settlers from Vermillion and elsewhere along the Big Sioux Valley fled to the temporary Fort Brule at Elk Point, to Sioux City or across the Missouri River southward.

As it turned out, the Santees did not press their campaign in South Dakota except for scattered raids by renegade patrols; and Strike-the-Ree's Yanktons maintained their neutrality. However,

A sketch of Fort Pierre, lower, taken from an original depiction by Alexander H. Murray in 1844 and one of the Yankton stockade, upper, drawn years later by Ben C. Ash, who had been a child in the hastily erected redoubt in 1862, were slightly more fanciful than accurate. Neither was built with such precise neatness. The capital city fortification was taken down as soon as the Santee scare had passed, and in 1855 General William S. Harney considered Fort Pierre too dilapidated for extended use. (South Dakota State Historical Society)

everyone was so keyed up emotionally that two or three Indians showing up on horseback without warning — regardless of their mission or intent — was enough to spread panic throughout any particular vicinity.

The student of history must recognize that this powder-keg atmosphere created situations and crystallized opinions which were to resound through the years. The oppressed Indians had struck out at all white people; and the settlers, in turn, responded with harsh anti-Indian sentiments. It is little wonder that long-time bitternesses were generated as a result. The frontier newspapers were especially outspoken in their demands for retribution. "Now in God's name let the columns of vengeance move on," insisted the *St. Paul Press;* and *The Yankton Dakotian* echoed the call for crushing the insurgents in the name of all settlers who had "seen their wives and husbands, fathers, mothers and children, butchered before their eyes . . ."

An inspiring story which emerged from the War of the Outbreak was the episode in which eleven young Teton Sioux (none of them more than 20 years old) obtained the release of two white women and seven children from a band of Santees near the present town of Mobridge in November of 1862. Martin Charger, Kills Game and Comes Home, Four Bear, Mad Bear, Pretty Bear, Sitting Bear, Swift Bird, One Rib, Strikes Fire, Red Dog and Charging Dog bargained away most of their personal possessions to ransom the captives who had been carried to the Missouri from Minnesota. Apparently the gallant Tetons were never repaid for their losses. Martin Charger, according to the legend, even gave up his moccasins to one of the barefooted women, and because they were unrewarded for their services, they became known as the Fool Soldiers.

Peace Restored: A Second Try at Settlement

Without question, the Santee uprising caused a slowup in the development of Dakota Territory. Not only did the news of armed Indians on the prowl keep land-seeking families out of the region, but some of the earlier more fainthearted arrivals decided to return to the less dangerous states to the east. Those who remained, however, were generally tough, tenacious people who could accept the challenge of the unpredictable frontier. They returned to their homesteads even before the scare was over; and less than a month after the Amidon killings at Sioux Falls, Moses Armstrong was to write from Yankton:

> Nearly all the farmers in this country have left the fortification and removed back on their premises, and they now complain, not so much of the Indians, as of the depredations of the roaming squads of cavalry scouts committed on their fields and gardens, and pigs and chickens and fences. Rails are used for firewood, chickens are bagged by the sackfull; corn, potatoes and vegetables are confiscated for Uncle Sam's use as freely as though the Dakota farmers were considered rebels against the government.

That commentary underscored another problem which was to crop up periodically throughout Dakota Territory and other western backlands. The army did not always send its most exemplary troopers into Indian country, especially with the personnel demands of the Civil War taking precedence. Consequently, men of marginal character — in uniform and as deserters — precipitated further white-Indian abrasions, not to mention the contentions between settlers and soldiers as indicated in Armstrong's dispatch. "Galvanized Yankees" — Confederate captives who agreed to put on the despised uniform of the North to fight Indians rather than remain in Union prison camps — added to the disciplinary problem. It was part of the

Martin Charger was one of eleven Teton Dakotas participating in the release of two white women and seven children captured by a Santee band in 1862. They bargained away personal possessions to affect the exchange, and afterwards, instead of being lauded for their noteworthy achievement, they became known legendarily as the Fool Soldiers. (South Dakota State Historical Society)

age-old and continuing story of human behavior; a few unprincipled traders, agents, land speculators, military castoffs, riverboat rowdies and renegade Indians created most of the trouble; and everybody else — regardless of race — suffered for it.

Meanwhile, just when the Santee uprising was at its heighth, the general territorial election called by the first legislature was held on September 1, 1862. It was a badly mismanaged affair with fraudulent votes and questionable results. There was no balloting at all in Sioux Falls because the village had been abandoned; at Fort Randall a company of Iowa soldiers given leave on election day (supposedly to pick wild plums) went instead to vote for Governor Jayne who was running against Todd for delegate to Congress; at "the lakes" (near present-day Gayville) there were willful efforts to mislead the Norwegian settlers regarding their right of franchise; and when Jayne was "officially" declared the winner by a vote of 237 to 221, the returns from the Red River Valley precincts had not yet come in.

Todd ultimately regained his seat after a congressional investigation. The recount vote was recorded as 344 to 256, with 80 ballots thrown out. Discrepancies like that caused even the most naive frontiersmen to question the honesty and legitimacy of the entire election, but after the revised results were announced, Doctor Jayne stepped down and returned to his medical practice in Illinois. Meanwhile, Secretary John Hutchinson had become acting governor until a new chief executive could be appointed. The second legislature convened at the capital in the new two-story frame building erected for it by the inveterate promoters, Moses Armstrong and Charles Picotte.

It took more than local spirit and editorial promotion to revive the dwindling flow of immigrants into the Territory, however. Despite the hangings at Mankato, occasional Indian assaults continued in the spring of 1863. A white freighter was killed at Greenway's ferry crossing on the James River within four miles of the territorial capital, but the optimistic *Weekly Dakotian* announced on July 7 that such attacks were overblown and should not deter new settlers.

Three weeks later the paper carried the sad and disturbing news that the five children of Phoebe Ann and Henson Wiseman — ranging in age from four to 16 — had been murdered by Indians in the family cabin near St. James, Nebraska, hardly more than a dozen miles southeast of Yankton. The father was absent as a member of General Alfred Sully's expedition against the Santees in northern Dakota, while the mother had gone to Yankton for provisions. The Indians (four or five of them) escaped across the Missouri and up the James River Valley.

While this attack did not actually occur in South Dakota, its repercussions were felt throughout the Missouri River settlement

John Nairn sketched Fort Thompson for the October 28, 1865, edition of *Harper's Weekly,* providing an interesting comparison between an artist's conception and a camera's view (opposite page). The agency located there also served Winnebago Indians as well as Santees. The Winnebagoes had ceded their land in Minnesota, and ultimately they moved again to a Nebraska location. After the Santees received their own reservation in northeastern South Dakota, the Lower Yanktonnais headquartered at Fort Thompson. (United States Army Corps of Engineers)

area. Also affecting immigration was a crop-destroying drouth in the summer of '63, a natural phenomenon which Dakotans then and in the future would learn to expect and to overcome. With the Territory less than three years old officially, there seemed almost to be a conspiracy against its survival and success. But, yet, the magnetic attraction of free land, the spirit of adventure and the thrill of flirting with danger, which has compelled certain men and women through the ages to leave the places of familiarity and plunge into the unknown, prevailed. Dakota had a good measure of that magic appeal; and prodded by a little bit of salesmanship, there were people ready and willing to be lured to the prairie — Indians, drouth or not.

The Territory at the time had two dedicated promoters: Surveyor General George D. Hill and Dr. Walter A. Burleigh, Indian agent for the Yankton tribe. Hill was a man with a dual reputation; he was appreciated for his agricultural knowledge and his enthusiasm for Dakota, but he was widely spurned for his personal habits and his apparent willingness to manipulate surveying contracts. Burleigh, like Governor Jayne, was a physician who had left a medical practice in Pennsylvania to pursue political plums on the frontier. Unlike the governor, however, Burleigh was also an attorney and gave early indication that he was in Dakota, not only to do the job he was sent to do, but to make a personal profit in the process, if he could.

Burleigh and Hill teamed up indirectly to do a major selling job in behalf of their adopted land. Hill had learned of the formation of a Free Homestead Association at Syracuse, New York, organized to migrate en masse to the West. The surveyor general got in touch with James S. Foster, secretary of the organization, and began immediately to promote the virtues of Dakota. The competition was tough, however. All states and territories with available public land were interested in luring immigrants, and when word got out that almost 500 men, women and children might be attracted in a single

In 1863 a detachment of soldiers from Fort Randall built a stockade on Crow Creek where Colonel Clark W. Thompson had laid out a reservation principally for Santee Sioux banished from Minnesota after the outbreak of the previous year. The post near the so-called big bend of the Missouri was named Fort Thompson. (Yankton County Historical Society)

The first capitol of Dakota Territory was an unimpressive two-story frame structure at Yankton built by Moses Armstrong and Charles Picotte in time for the second legislative session in 1863. The lumber they had planned to use for such a building the previous year had been commandeered for a stockade during the Santee uprising. (Yankton County Historical Society)

group, the Syracuse colony became the target of relentless promotion. Hill met with representatives of the association when they visited the Territory in the late summer of 1863, and Burleigh went to New York to try to complete the selling job.

In the end the Dakota appeal was successful, and the New Yorkers started the long trek westward by rail and wagon. Enroute they were bedeviled by Iowa promoters — anxious to add to that state's population — with reports of Indian massacres and terrible drouth conditions in the new Territory. Several families succumbed to the stories and remained at Marshalltown, the railhead. Others grew tired of the long, tedious overland journey and dropped off along the way. By mid-May the main body of colonists had crossed the Big Sioux into Dakota, and by that time the original concept of the entire group locating around a single town (the capital) had faded away under the strain of the trip. Some 25 families separated from the wagon train and selected individual farm sites at various locations between the Iowa border and Yankton. A similar number proceeded to the capital and a few others went farther westward to the village of Bon Homme.

The New York colony, though somewhat unusual, typified the hardy souls willing to risk the challenges of the prairie in exchange for free land. However, despite the availability of seemingly endless farm acres, Dakota did not get off to a stampeding start. Created as it was on the eve of the Civil War, its new official existence was overshadowed on the national scene by the more crucial issue. Then, just when the first substantial flow of settlers could have been expected, the Santee uprising occurred. When the Indian threat began to ease up in 1863, the first of two serious consecutive drouth years plagued the region, coupled with another natural disaster which the *Weekly Dakota Union,* a second Yankton newspaper, described on August 2, 1864:

> A terrible army of grasshoppers have [sic] swept through this whole valley . . . Cornfields are stripped of leaves, tassels and ears, leaving nothing but the plant and naked stalk standing . . . Potatoes are actually eaten into the ground. Cabbages, tomatoes and all garden vegetables are mowed flat to the earth, all in the space of two days. They came down the valley from the northwest, and kept a southeasterly course. Whole groves of young willows, in the skirts of the forests, were literally loaded down or cut to pieces . . . the products of the season have vanished before us like the dew of the morning.

While all these negative conditions existed, the Territory was further handicapped by the efforts of Minnesota and Iowa land merchants to divert westward-bound families long before they reached the Big Sioux or Red Rivers. At the same time Dakota's feeble hope for a transcontinental railroad across its flatlands disappeared when the Union Pacific right-of-way was established in Nebraska. Once railroad construction began in earnest following the Civil War, the massive promotion efforts by the railroad company in the eastern United States and in Europe focused attention on available land along its trackage. As a result, Dakota was bypassed again as it had been earlier by the great overland migrations to Oregon and California.

James S. Foster, a leader of the New York Colony, was appointed territorial superintendent of public instruction in 1864 at which time the latent school system began to develop. The village of Bon Homme had a log schoolhouse in 1860, generally recognized as the first in the Territory though its use was limited. Vermillion claimed the first "permanent" building, also of logs. In the ensuing years teachers welcomed pupils to classes in sod houses, clapboard shacks and other structures of marginal comfort. (South Dakota State Historical Society)

"A decade of uncertainty" was the way Historian Herbert S. Schell described the 1860s. Somehow avid Dakota boosters like Burleigh, Hill, Moses Armstrong, Governor Newton Edmunds (appointed by President Lincoln to replace Jayne) and George W. Kingsbury, publisher of the combined Yankton papers, were not disheartened by the slow start or the adversities of nature. Others were, however, and after a crop failure or two they pulled up stakes and left. There were those who professed that the plains region would never be suitable for agriculture. As Kingsbury related, they believed firmly that the land had been intended by the Creator for the Indians and buffalo and that "the whites were only flying in the face of the Almighty's great purpose in wresting the country from them."

Gold! From the Earth and from Uncle Sam

Interestingly enough, two natural attributes and the direct economic return from the government's intervention in the Indian problem helped maintain enthusiasm for Dakota's future when the prospects for a quick expansion of farm settlements were dimmed.

The first factor was the discovery of gold in the Salmon River area of Idaho. While the diggings were far removed from the settlement sector of Dakota Territory, the second natural boon was the Missouri River which provided the most ideal transportation artery to the mining camps via Fort Benton in Montana. During the summer of 1863, 18 steamboats journeyed up the river, giving promise of

The so-called forts of early Dakota were often just a grouping of nondescript log cabins and stables used for troop accommodations or as trading posts. They were anything but luxurious, as an inspection report of Old Fort Sully indicated: "The officers' and men's quarters are not fit to live in ... The roofs and floors are made of mud; the houses are filled with bed-bugs, fleas and rats." The first Fort Sully east of Pierre was abandoned in 1866 and a second built some 30 miles north on the Missouri River. Ultimately, the logs of the original encampment were used for steamboat fuel. (Yankton County Historical Society)

greater activity to come. The gold-rush traffic — both ways — supplemented the somewhat skimpy income of the river towns and individual citizens who cut fuel for the paddlewheelers or sold what little produce they could spare over and above their personal needs. It was, in effect, a preview of a relatively brief but profitable era which was soon to follow and during which traffic on the "Old Mizzou" became a dominant feature of commerce in the Territory.

Meanwhile, the supply and labor demands at the Yankton Indian agency and the various forts — Randall and Sully on the Missouri and Wadsworth (later renamed Fort Sisseton) in the northeast corner of the future state of South Dakota — provided employment for Dakota settlers as carpenters, freighters, wood-cutters, hay-foragers and similar work assignments. Three times during the first half of the decade — in 1863, 64 and 65 — General Alfred Sully led expeditions from Sioux City up the Missouri to do battle with the Indians in North Dakota; and the hard-pressed territorial residents benefited to some degree from the military traffic in terms of supply and services.

Under the best of circumstances, the settling of a new frontier was never easy, and in the case of pre-statehood South Dakota, the conditions were far less than ideal. The dogged persistence of those who prevailed despite the elements, the insects, the Indians and other discouraging factors began to develop a special kind of Dakota personality — an independent obstinancy; a quiet, almost self-effacing pride in having overcome the adversities when others couldn't. In a way the Dakota tribesmen, who were on the land before the white colonizers and who also had survived frigid winters, scorching summers, drouth, floods, prairie fires and hunting failures, had an outlook much the same.

BOOK THREE

THE CHALLENGE OF THE RIVER

"To me, the Amazon is a basking alli-
gator; the Tiber is a dream of dead
glory; the Rhine is a fantastic fairy-
tale; the Nile, a mummy periodically
resurrected; the Mississippi, a con-
venient boundary line . . . But the
Missouri — my brother — is the eter-
nal Fighting Man!"
                     — John G. Neihardt

South Dakota's major geographical features are the expansive prairies, the Black Hills, the Badlands and the Missouri River. Of the four, the historic stream undoubtedly has had the greatest effect on the most citizens over the longest period of time.

Before the first white men entered the region, the river — brown with sediment and majestically uncontrolled — was a formidable obstacle for Indians and buffalo until the winter cold made it passable over the ice. The Arikaras built their villages on its banks as part of a natural defensive position. It slowed the westward movement of the Dakotas until the first Tetons crossed it some time in the 1700s to begin establishment of their Great Plains domain. Its shorelines provided willows, cottonwood and reeds for multiple uses by the tribespeople; waterfowl, fish and small animal furs were additional bounty from it. Because of the river's treacherous eddies, its depth in some places and great width in others, the Indians did not travel back and forth across it regularly as they did the more fordable streams, nor did they use it a great deal as an artery of transportation. Bull boats — awkward tub-like affairs made by stretching a buffalo hide over a wooden framework — were used when necessary, rather than the romantic birch bark canoe which so many people erroneously associate with all American Indians.

During the extended era — from the La Verendrye expedition in 1743 to the establishment of the Territory in 1861 — the Missouri River was the aquatic highway over which French voyageurs, fur traders and explorers journeyed to and from the prairie wilderness. Trappers harvested rich hoards of beaver, mink, muskrat, marten and other furs from its thicketed banks and those of its numerous tributaries. When the first military commanders came to the region, they recognized immediately the logistical value of the stream for movement and supply as well as its tactical importance.

(Clyde Goin collection)

In terms of miles traveled, the historic Lewis and Clark excursion was predominantly a Missouri River trip from and back to St. Louis, and as the party passed through the land destined to become South Dakota, members of the expedition rarely wandered far from sight of the stream. The two captains — like other explorers of their day — utilized previously mentioned keelboats which were cumbersome wooden vessels of varying length, propelled by oars, poles or tow ropes from shore. Some of the boats had masts but the use of sails for river travel generally proved impractical. Complicating navigation on the Missouri was a forceful current, an ever-changing channel and hidden snags and sandbars which were impossible to see in the mud-brown water. Another limiting factor, of course, was the fact that in most years the river was ice-bound from November till April; and often in the springtime, gorges and floods offered the constant threat of disaster.

As the years passed, the great river — Neihardt's "eternal Fighting Man" — was to prove that it could be friend or foe, changing unpredictably from one to the other with a savage fickleness which Dakota Indians and pioneers learned quickly to fear and respect.

One of South Dakota's most unique geographical features is the Badlands of the White River, a classic example of erosion over a period of a million years or more. Strangely beautiful, the *maco sica* (as the early Sioux called the grotesque landscape) contains fossils of prehistoric camels, saber-toothed tigers, three kinds of rhinoceroses, oreodonts (ruminating pigs) and various other extinct species. A portion of the region was proclaimed the Badlands National Monument by President Franklin D. Roosevelt on January 25, 1939. (Clyde Goin collection)

The Fireboat-That-Walks-on-Water: A Startling Change

When Pierre Chouteau, Jr., revolutionized fur-trading by introducing the steamboat to the Upper Missouri country in 1831, it signalled a major change in the very nature of life on the Great Plains. Guns, steel animal traps, mirrors, telescopes and other mechanical devices had previously convinced the Indians of the white man's unusual capabilities, but smoke-spewing packet boats churning against the stubborn river currents were an awesome sight when beheld for the first time by people who had no forewarning that such monsters even existed. It is one of the marvels of the time, however, that the Indians adapted so quickly to the strange new contrivances thrust so rapidly upon their simple existence. As they accepted the gun for their own use, they also adjusted to the "fire boat," and in time they began to exchange furs for passage or to cut wood which they traded for supplies, weapons or (unfortunately) whiskey.

During the pre-territorial period, the steamboat traffic was understandably limited, and what did occur was almost totally related to the fur business. When the market tapered off and the numbers of buffalo began to diminish, the future of river navigation might have faded had not several other needs for transportation developed in rapid succession. Military posts and expeditions so far from supply sources required the capacity of steamboats to keep their larders full; so did the Indian agencies created by the various treaties. In addition, the annuity goods which were part of the agreements also had to be brought upstream in great quantities. Then the gold camps of Idaho and Montana entered the picture, and the Missouri River became the avenue of supply for the prospectors and the means for them to deliver their valuable dust and nuggets to the markets in St. Louis and beyond.

Meanwhile, the Territory was struggling through its first desperate years of existence, trying to overcome the lagging pace of settlement caused by drouth, grasshoppers, Indian rebellion, the almost total dependency upon federal dollars for economic survival and the many detrimental side effects of the Civil War.

The Union Preserved: Interest in Dakota Revived

Though Dakota Territory was far removed from the battlefield scene, the news that General Robert E. Lee of the Confederacy had surrendered to General Ulysses S. Grant at Appomatox Court House on April 9, 1865, was joyously received on the frontier. Five days after the war-ending victory in Virginia, however, the announcement of President Lincoln's assassination plunged the nation into sorrow. In time Lincoln's death and the succession of Andrew Johnson to the Presidency was to have direct repercussions in the western prairieland.

Two men prominent in the earliest years of Dakota Territory were Captain John B. S. Todd (left), a relative of Mary Todd Lincoln who got the capital located at Yankton where he had land and business interests, and Newton Edmunds, whom Abraham Lincoln appointed as the second territorial governor. Both had South Dakota counties named for them. (Yankton Daily Press & Dakotan)

Newton Edmunds, whose brother was commissioner of the United States Land Office under Lincoln, had been appointed territorial governor by the Great Emancipator to replace Doctor Jayne. Because Democrats in Dakota were accused of being Southern sympathizers (or "Copperheads"), Republicans won overwhelming control during the war, and Doctor Burleigh — the former Indian agent — was elected delegate to Congress, finally ending the political entrenchment of J. B. S. Todd.

At first Edmunds and Burleigh worked harmoniously in behalf of the Territory, both of them supporting a moderate Indian policy in opposition to the War Department's rigid position that further settlement of Dakota should be delayed until *all* Indians were either under complete subjection or dead. There were charges, of course, that military officials wanted to pursue an active campaign against the tribes in order to perpetuate a large standing force which many Americans felt was no longer needed following the collapse of the Confederacy. Edmunds and Burleigh — both equally interested in immediate expansion of the Territory's population — were against the Army's concept of extermination or confinement, with the governor being especially vigorous in his ideas to achieve peace without warfare.

Edmunds had come to Dakota in 1861 from Michigan when his brother in Washington, D.C., got him a minor clerkship in the surveyor general's office, but unlike many other federal employees, he became a permanent resident of Yankton. As a Lincoln appointee to the governorship, he journeyed to the nation's capital to convince the

President that his approach to the Indian dilemma was the most humane and logical. The various military expeditions against the tribes — notably those of General Sully — had proved relatively unsuccessful because the more mobile and scattered Dakota bands were able to maneuver away from the slow-moving troop units. This gave Edmunds additional support for his argument, and as a result, he was granted an appropriation of $20,000 to establish an Indian Commission to sign pacts replacing the Laramie Treaty of 1851 which had a 15-year limitation.

During the fall and winter of 1865-66 the commission concluded agreements with chieftains said to represent an estimated 16,000 Yanktonnais, Brule, Two Kettle, Minneconjou, Sans Arc, Oglala, Hunkpapa and Blackfoot Indians. The individual treaties — with only minor differences in terms — were ratified by the United States Senate in the spring of 1866, and though they were denounced soon after by tribal leaders who had signed them and by others who had not, Governor Edmunds was at least credited with making a valiant attempt to achieve a peaceful settlement in the face of increasing resentment. Many white Dakotans considered him the Territory's savior for his pacific efforts.

As an example of Indian second thoughts following the treaty signings, Moses Armstrong — who was secretary of the Edmunds Commission — reported the speech of a Yanktonnais chief, Bone Necklace, who said in June of 1866:

> This country belongs to me, and this great river [the Missouri] is my own . . . We do not want the whites to travel through our lands on great highways, but they may navigate the river. It would take more than a boat-load of goods every year to pay my

As protection against further Indian outbreaks in the Sioux Falls area, Fort Dakota was established and manned by a small detachment of militia. A similar installation, called Fort James near Rockport, gave added security to nervous settlers. Both posts were short-lived, and Fort Randall on the Missouri remained as the primary deterrent to rebellion in the southeastern sector of the Territory. (South Dakota State Historical Society)

> people for the loss of game . . . What we want our
> Great Father to do for us is to send us guns, powder
> and ball, and let us live unmolested on our own
> plains and hunting-grounds.

The remarks of the Yanktonnais chief emphasized just how far the white culture had already imposed itself upon the red. Bone Necklace probably didn't even realize the contradiction in his request for a return to the hunting grounds of *old* — but with an ample supply of *new* weapons and ammunition for which the Indians had to depend entirely upon their adversaries. Already it was too late for a simple solution to a growing problem.

Moses Armstrong, the commission secretary, recognized the great need for a uniform system of administration for the tribes, even though he wrote that the Indians "are yet a wild and superstitious race of people and should be treated more like children than men." "There are now too many hands at the bellows," he added, "and the Indians become confused and bewildered in the multifarious councils and plans of the Great Father."

Intensifying the confusion at that time was the sudden reversal of Delegate Burleigh's position regarding the Indian question. He loudly denounced Edmunds and his treaties, and started a campaign for the governor's ouster. It has been conjectured that Burleigh's ire was aroused when a congressional committee came to Dakota to investigate charges relative to his conduct as agent on the Yankton reservation during the previous four years. Governor Edmunds, it seems, had cooperated with the inquiry and permitted Indian chiefs to testify publicly against the accused.

Burleigh countered with charges that Edmunds himself was profiting from the treaties he had instigated. Then the territorial delegate took the matter directly to President Johnson who was his personal friend. Shortly thereafter, Governor Edmunds was dismissed from office and replaced by Andrew Jackson Faulk, a printer, lawyer and coal company superintendent, from Kittaning, Pennsylvania — who just happened to be Doctor Burleigh's father-in-law.

There was little question about it: for all his commendable efforts in behalf of the Territory, the physician-lawyer-politician was also an adept manipulator. In describing Burleigh's activities as an Indian agent, author Howard Roberts Lamar wrote:

> . . . he [Burleigh] outdid the average agent in
> fleecing the Indian Bureau and the Indians for all
> they were worth. His daughter was listed on the
> payroll as a teacher to Indian children although no
> school existed on the reservation. His thirteen-year-
> old son drew eighty dollars a month as a clerk. His
> father-in-law [the future governor] appeared in the
> records as a worker.

The first investigator sent to check on Burleigh's activities reported voluminous evidence of questionable practices and called for further research. A few months later a second special agent appeared in the Territory with the delegate himself and publicly exonerated the doctor of all charges. Burleigh was re-elected; Edmunds was deposed; and Faulk moved to Yankton to take over the government. Years later when the facts began to emerge, it was apparent that certain War Department officials and contractors who were well paid to deliver supplies to the military units in Dakota were also involved in applying pressure for Edmunds' removal. After all, his so-called peace policy — if successful — might well have been detrimental to their selfish interests.

The Burleigh-Edmunds feud — which erupted and then disappeared without seemingly significant long-range consequences — did emphasize one fundamental truism: that politics, profit and personalities were all intertwined in the early-day maneuvering for power in the developing land.

The Missouri River Valley: Permanency at Last!

While the spotlight of history is usually focused on the activities — good or bad — of forceful, dynamic or otherwise attention-attracting frontrunners, behind them are the masses of people, quietly going about the business of day-to-day living — and that is precisely what occurred in Dakota Territory in the middle and late 1860s.

It is understandable why the earliest permanent growth took place along the course of the Missouri River where it formed the southeastern boundary of the mammoth Territory. First of all, the locale was accessible to sources of supply and the marketplaces for grain, cattle and other potential products of the new region. The Sioux City-Fort Randall government road, though little more than a wide, well-rutted trail between ferries and fords across Missouri tributaries, was at least an established overland route for wagons and stages. More important, of course, was the gradually increasing steamboat traffic on the river itself.

With the first cession of Indian lands, the creation of the Territory and the location of the capital at Yankton, the politicians and opportunists all gravitated to the seat of government and took claims or invested in town lots in or near Old Strike's former campground. Establishment of the federal land office at Vermillion in April of 1861 gave that community a focal point around which to grow, and though business in land-scrip acquisitions and preemption claims was exceedingly slow for the first few years, the Vermillion office had the distinction of recording what might have been entry number one under the Homestead Act for the entire United States shortly after midnight on January 1, 1863, when the law went into effect. Mahlon S. Gore, editor-printer of the *Dakota Republican* at Vermillion, filed the historic claim on Brule Creek north of Elk Point. Unfortunately for South Dakota, he failed to follow through on his application and another homestead near Beatrice, Nebraska — that of Daniel Freeman, also filed on the first day of 1863 — later became a National

Monument and tourist attraction symbolic of the important milestone in the opening of the American West.

The fertility of the land in the Big Sioux, Vermillion and James River Valleys where the smaller streams emptied into the Missouri from the north was also a vital factor in the selection of land by incoming farmers — many of them Norwegian and Swedish immigrants — to whom a bountiful crop meant more than political involvement. Additionally important to the establishment of permanent settlements and homesteads in the area was the presence of federal troops at Fort Randall and two companies of Dakota militia, whom General Sully had nicknamed the "Kiotes" or "Coyotes". Detachments at Fort James near Rockport and Fort Dakota at Sioux Falls gave the settlers an extra measure of confidence when the fear of Indian attack was still a considerable deterrent to location on remote land claims. This factor, of course, was especially instrumental in delaying the expansion of villages on the upper Big Sioux River, notably Sioux Falls, Flandreau, Commerce City (Canton) and Eminija at the mouth of Split Rock Creek which was to disappear entirely following the Santee outbreak.

Another advantage of nearness to the Missouri River and the capital city was the availability of additional sources of income. Many of the young homesteaders arrived in Dakota virtually devoid of cash, so the opportunities to cut firewood for the steamboats, harvest hay for cavalry horses, hew badly needed lumber and chalkstone block for building materials or to practice other trades or skills learned in the East or the Old Country were not only welcome but necessary for survival. The early newspapers, for instance, pleaded for artisans of all kinds, with the following commentary from the *Weekly Dakotian* of October 6, 1863, being typical:

> A first-class shoemaker would make his everlasting fortune in Yankton. The soles of our people are in a deplorable condition, and demand immediate attention. Who wants to get rich?

"Getting rich" — in one way or another — was the primary reason for almost all of Dakota Territory's population influx in its first decade, and when the census of 1870 was taken, approximately ten thousand non-Indians were recorded as living in the area which would ultimately become South Dakota. The majority of them arrived in 1867 or later, when fear of Indian danger subsided, the drouth cycle passed and, for a time, blackbirds, gulls and other natural phenomena overcame the grasshopper menace. A national spirit of exuberance following the Civil War and the excitement of great railroad expansion also played a prominent part.

Unusual Partners: The Railroad and the River

As the pace of development quickened, Dakotans — especially the land promoters and merchants — increased the clamor for rail service to the region. Steamboats were doing a big business on the Upper Missouri, but much of the advantage of such trade went to the originating ports or terminals like St. Louis or Sioux City. Yankton, Wanari (later Springfield) and Fort Pierre were merely stopover points which produced some revenue for the respective settlements but not the giant profits which a major transportation center could generate. To make better use of the Missouri River, Dakota Territory needed a railroad, and the so-called "Yankton ring" intensified its efforts to accomplish that goal.

Oddly enough, however, the first rail line into South Dakota was a short spur of the Winona & St. Peter Railroad which was built across the territorial border in 1871. A work camp called Headquarters, then State Line, later became the town of Gary. The visionary promoters championed a road extending all the way across the unpopulated prairie to Fort Pierre where a tie-in could be made with steamboats going upriver to Fort Benton. Unfortunately, the Panic of 1873 interrupted the ambitious scheme.

Meanwhile, when 1869 developed as the most prosperous year in the territorial capital's short life, local political leaders concluded that the ideal time had come to push to completion at least one of six possible railroads which various dreamers had predicted for Yankton. The most realistic approach seemed to be the establishment of a 65-mile line generally parallel to the Missouri which would connect the capital with Sioux City and for which some engineering work had already been done.

A serious complication was involved in that particular concept, however. Sioux City was then enjoying the economic benefits of its location at the end of the rail line. The lucrative army and Indian contracts meant extensive profits for merchants of the Iowa border town, so if the railroad were to be extended westward to Yankton,

The steamboat era on the Missouri River was romantic, profitable and relatively brief. Shallow-draft vessels like the *Rosebud* plied northward as far as Fort Benton in Montana during the months when the ice was out. Sandbars, snags and lack of fuel were continuing problems faced by veteran pilots who reputedly could navigate across a "sea of dew." All-season railroads ultimately replaced the riverboat fleet. (Yankton County Historical Society)

the advantages of the territorial trade would go with it. Understandably, Sioux City businessmen vociferously opposed the idea.

Territorial Supreme Court Justice Wilmot W. Brookings (the Dakota pioneer after whom a city and county would be named) was not a man to let obstacles stop him, and he countered the opposition by contacting the Illinois Central Railroad Company. Plans were promptly developed for a line into the Territory from LeMars, Iowa, which would bypass Sioux City altogether. In view of the new strategy, the Sioux Citians did a reluctant about-face and supported the extension of a track from their terminal on the basis that it would be better to have some of the business rather than none at all.

That didn't eliminate all the problems, however. The Dakota Southern Railway Company, founded in a real estate office in Yankton on March 18, 1871, was without finances to lay the proposed trackage. The federal government, by that time, was beginning to withdraw from its earlier policy of generous land-grant aid to railroads, and because the relatively short line through a still meagerly populated area offered little likelihood of quick profits, eastern investors were not particularly eager to become involved. Not enough private money existed in the Territory, so another approach was needed, and someone proposed the idea of Yankton County subscribing construction bonds which could be sold in the East.

A tangled web of legal and financial maneuvers followed, but in the end Governor John A. Burbank (who had succeeded Andrew Faulk) signed the bonding authority and sufficient money was raised to begin construction. On October 1, 1872, a locomotive aptly titled the "Judge Brookings" was the first to cross the Big Sioux River into Dakota Territory. Less than four months later the line was completed through Vermillion to the territorial capital.

The first locomotive to cross the Big Sioux River from Sioux City into Dakota Territory on the Dakota Southern line was appropriately named the *Judge Brookings* for the president of the new railroad company. W. W. Brookings was one of the region's earliest and most active pioneers despite the amputation of both legs which had been frozen in a blizzard. (Yankton County Historical Society)

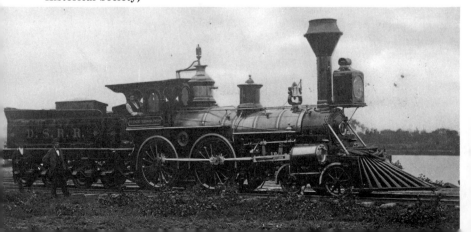

Vermillion started as a trading post and, like Yankton, began to grow after the 1858 cession treaty went into effect. Location of the territorial land office at the Missouri River village helped spur its development. This vintage picture was taken in 1872 not long after the Dakota Southern Railway's tracks were laid. (W. H. Over Museum)

Before 1873 Yankton was a secondary stop-off point for the river boats, debarking passengers and unloading building supplies, machinery and assorted freight of necessity to the young town. When grasshoppers and drouth weren't prevailing, modest amounts of grain were shipped out. Woodhawks sold boiler-length fuel to the boat captains (each steamer requiring approximately 25 cords of hardwood or 30 of dry cottonwood for each 24 hours of running time); but, in general, Yankton's citizens were customers more than profit-takers of the river traffic. Then the railroad changed all that!

The capital city — with a natural shelf-like river frontage to facilitate docking — became a warehousing center and loading terminal for up-river traffic. Sanford B. Coulson, a 33-year-old Pennsylvanian, established the Missouri River Transportation Company (known also as the Coulson Packet Line) with its base of operations in Yankton. The firm won the military shipping contract for the Dakota country in 1873, and as part of the deal, the freight was hauled to the end of the line by the Dakota Southern and then transferred to Coulson boats.

This combination of river and railroad not only brought a wave of prosperity to Yankton but had positive effects throughout the settlement areas from Sioux City westward. A flour mill and brewery were established at the capital along with such other minor industries as a cigar factory, a harness company and a wagon-building firm. These businesses added to the local profits from the steamboat trade; and, as the newspapers indicated, Yankton was on its way to becoming the "new St. Louis." Not all of the freight was sent up-river by any means. On June 11, 1873, for instance, the *Yankton Press* made note of that fact and of the lingering importance of the buffalo:

> The shipments from Yankton over the D.S.R.R.
> last month were five times greater than any previous
> month, consisting of wheat, 10 cars of buffalo robes
> and furs and 5 cars of dry hides, flour to the Chicago
> market and considerable merchandise.

Of major significance, of course, was the realization that Dakota's period of isolation had ended. With the railroad in opera-

Yankton, the capital of Dakota Territory, had a natural shelf-like wharf for Missouri River steamboats, making it easy to load and unload them from the shore. This feature, plus the rail terminal which went into operation in 1873, gave the Mother City an advantageous trading position for a decade or more. (W. H. Over Museum)

tion, no longer would travelers and merchants have to depend upon the unpredictable and uncomfortable stagecoaches and the slow, expensive freight wagons. The telegraph had connected Yankton with the outside world over ash and cottonwood poles in 1870; the first train arrived in 1873; and with a burgeoning steamboat business on the Missouri River, it appeared that the struggling Territory was — as the promoters insisted — destined for a bright, expansive future.

Old Muddy: Too Thin to Plow, Too Thick to Drink

The role played by the Missouri River in the history of the Territory — and later South Dakota — alternated between that of benefactor and villain. More than 500 of its 2,950 meandering miles from St. Louis to the Montana Rockies coursed through the future state; and its continuing impact on the lives of Dakotans, Indian and white, grew rather than diminished as the years went on.

By 1873, of course, the once sprawling Territory had long since been trimmed down to include just the area encompassing the two Dakotas. Idaho and Montana had been separated ten years earlier, and the Wyoming sector was officially detached in 1868. The Dakota legislature had created county governments in the Wyoming district, principally along the Union Pacific right-of-way, but other than that there was virtually no connection or communications between the capital and its outlying precincts.

Even before the dreams of statehood began to emerge in southern Dakota, the fact that the Missouri River cut the region into two almost equal parts was recognized as a geographic boundary line which would certainly affect development. At that time it separated the active settlement lands from the treaty-established Teton domain. The river was an obvious barrier to expansion westward. Then, however, there was little or no interest in the so-called Indian country (still considered by some to be part of the so-called "great American Desert"), not only because there seemed to be unlimited farmstead sites still available to the east but also because the potential of the Black Hills had not yet been widely contemplated.

The divisive effect of the Missouri must be considered in the development period because the evolution of two distinct regional philosophies and life styles — to be labeled ultimately as "east-river" and "west-river" — had its genesis in the earliest settlement days. For a few years the "Big Muddy" offered a sense of security to east-river settlers. After the Santee outbreak had subsided and the threat of Indian violence had decreased, white homesteaders grew confident that the wide, unruly stream would help deter any future attacks in force by nonreservation tribes. This emphasized the river's role as a division line rather than "a tie that binds", and though later events were to see the river communities utilized as jumpoff points for Black Hills expeditions and freight lines, the demarcation aspect of the historic waterway persisted.

Meanwhile, the river benefited the early Dakotans in a variety of ways, not the least of which was its ready supply of victuals. George W. Kingsbury, the pioneer editor, wrote:

> The catfish was an important factor in the settlement of Dakota, and in the opinion of many of the early settlers, the food problem would have been a very serious one had it not been for the abundant supply of this best of all fishes right at the threshold of the settlements . . . The celebrated naturalist Audubon made a very exhaustive investigation of the fishes of the Missouri about the year 1858 and gave his opinion that the catfish was a very valuable article of food . . . For scores of years the early traders subsisted almost exclusively on a diet of buffalo meat and catfish, having vegetables very rarely and small desire for them.

Before adequate wells were dug, the Missouri also provided water for human needs. Most families living in the settlements along its course had their own water barrels which were regularly hauled to the river on stoneboats or in other vehicles for filling. Because the water was excessively murky with silt and sand, each new barrelful had to be allowed time to settle before usuable water could be dipped off the top. At Yankton one enterprising operator built a leak-proof box near the Missouri, and each evening he filled it from the stream. By morning the liquid had cleared sufficiently for him to drain off a supply which he delivered to eager customers in the capital city.

Sawmills, "woodhawk" camps and river-bank trap lines delivered additional bounty from the Missouri's ample storehouse. Ducks, geese, deer and prairie chickens, which were abundant along the streamside, provided variety to the pioneers' larder. Moreover, centuries of springtime floodings had left an easily tilled and fertile valley floor in which settlers — with limited time and tools — were able to plant "sod potatoes" and other crops vital to survival.

Needless to say, the "Old Mizzou" cheered and challenged Dakota inhabitants from prehistoric days onward through the years.

Growth With a European Flavor: An Ethnic Amalgam

While the Territory's first dozen years of official existence was not its most expansive growth period, the settlement pace had begun to pick up sharply during the latter half of that span. Most of the first residents had come to Dakota from neighboring Minnesota, Iowa and Nebraska, or, in the case of the French, from Canada by way of the Red River area. In general they were young individuals or families already experienced in frontier living but lured farther westward by the magnetism of the wilderness. Except for the New York colony in 1864, most of them came alone or in small parties; but even in the earliest year, however, distinct "islands" of nationalities or ethnic groups began to develop. The fact that Governor Jayne's first message to the territorial legislature in 1861 was printed in four languages — English, Norwegian, German and French — was indicative of that pattern of settlement which was to continue for more than half a century.

Among the early arrivals, of course, were numerous Yankees or so-called Old Americans whose families had already been in the New World for two or more generations, but by the mid-1800s various factors in Europe resulted in intensified migrations to the United States, a condition which began to reflect itself in Dakota Territory shortly after passage of the Homestead Act. This admixture of Old Country cultures, mingled with that of the Dakota Indians, instilled an unusual variety of traditions, customs and values within the territorial population.

While it is difficult to analyze all motivations for immigration and the various trends in movement of ethnic groups to the South Dakota portion of the Territory, there are certain key examples which illustrate the practice of settling in cultural communities as well as in a diffused "melting pot" fashion. [More attention will be devoted to this important subject when the Great Boom from 1878 to 1887 is considered, but to keep the story flowing, some knowledge of the earlier settlement characteristics is necessary.]

Among the '59ers who crossed the Missouri from Nebraska shortly after ratification of the Yankton treaty were Norwegians who established claims on the fertile bottomlands between the Vermillion and James Rivers. In the spring of 1860 another group of the same national origin arrived and settled in the area known as "the lakes" near the site of modern Gayville. They were the forerunners of thousands of their countrymen who came either directly from Norway or after earlier stopovers in various states to the east.

The Norwegians migrated to America — and subsequently to Dakota — primarily because of a lack of tillable farmland and economic opportunities at home. To some degree the principle of *primogeniture* by which the eldest son was favored in inheritance proceedings was a factor which motivated younger heirs to seek their fortunes elsewhere, especially when further divisions would have reduced traditional farmsteads to plots too small to support a family. Other European countries experienced similar problems of succession and the whittling away of property, with out-migration following as a direct result. Unlike some of the other nationalities, however, the Norwegian emigrants were not escaping oppression, starvation or forced military service. In the 1840s when the exodus to America began to increase substantially, their country was faring quite well; and in most cases, those who left were not destitute, just limited in what the future offered.

Emigrants from Ireland, on the other hand, were forced out of their homeland by famine beginning in 1846 when vital potato crops were successively destroyed by blight. Most of those who fled the natural disaster settled first in large eastern cities and then began to move westward primarily as railroad workers. Military service brought others to the frontier, but an attempt to form at least one Irish colony north of Yankton in the 1860s was unsuccessful, and Dakota Territory's first sons and daughters of Erin located as individual families rather than in clannish communities. A minor exception occurred at the settlement of Jefferson (then known as Adelescat) between Elk Point and Sioux City. The attraction there was undoubtedly the Catholic church established by the prevailing French population, a carry-over from the earlier fur-trading days.

In 1869 the first of many Bohemians passed through Yankton to file claims in Bon Homme County near Lakeport, Ziskov and Tabor.

Religion and education were of great concern to Dakota pioneers, many settlements developing around churches favored by particular nationalities. Vermillion boasted a log cabin schoolhouse as early as 1860 (said to be the building at the right in the below photo), and by 1872 had a classically designed Baptist church overlooking the new railroad tracks. (W. H. Over Museum)

[Later the terms Bohemian and Czech were used interchangeably, although the nation of Czechoslovakia which grew out of World War I included Bohemians, Moravians and Slovaks under the Czech designation.] Political unrest, coupled with a potato crop failure not quite as disastrous as those of Ireland, spurred a wave of out-migration in the 1840s which continued despite official restrictions against departures from the central European homeland.

German immigrants to Dakota were less easily characterized in general terms. There were Low Germans who left the coastline of The Netherlands because of poor farming conditions and military conscription. Others found their way out of various provinces of the Fatherland for similar reasons. But of greatest impact on the Missouri River country in mid-America were the Germans-from-Russia (or German-Russians as they were more commonly known), who began to arrive in the Territory in 1873. Two years earlier Czar Alexander II of Russia revoked an agreement which had permitted German colonists to live in his country for more than a century while retaining their own culture, customs and language. The Germans objected strenuously to the new policy of "Russianization" — especially to service in the czar's army — and a mass exodus got underway.

The arrival in the United States of the first immigrants from Crimea, Volhynia and the Ukraine coincided with the availability of homestead lands in Dakota, and for the next two decades thousands

In apparel relatively unchanged for generations, Hutterite children represented the broad admixture of nationalities and cultures in South Dakota. The first Hutterian Brethren arrived during territorial days in 1874. Tenets of their religious faith — notably pacifism and communal living — subjected them to various forms of prejudice through the years. During World War I over-zealous patriots were particularly harsh in dealing with the German-speaking Anabaptists. (Clyde Goin collection)

of the ambitious and tenacious people made their way to a new life of freedom on the prairies. Because they had retained their personal religious preferences through their long sojourn in Russia, their numbers included Lutherans, Swiss-German Mennonites, communal-living Hutterites, Evangelical Christians and Roman Catholics, a fact which some of the other pioneer Dakotans couldn't always keep straight as they referred to all of them simply as "Rooshians."

The Hutterian Brethren (named for Jacob Hutter, the Anabaptist leader who was burned at the stake at Innsbruck, Austria, in 1536) were of particular interest because of their adherence to the communal form of life. The first group of Hutterites came to Dakota Territory in the summer of 1874 after stopping first at Lincoln, Nebraska, where three dozen of their children died in an epidemic of dysentery. The distraught families, hoping to find religious freedom in the United States, waited at Yankton while their leaders completed the purchase of 2,500 acres from Doctor Walter Burleigh, the former Indian agent. They did not want to take up homestead land even though it was much cheaper because they felt it would obligate them to the government and compromise their stand against military service and war. This first settlement along the Missouri River in the vicinity of Springfield became known as the Bon Homme Colony. The members were called *Schmiedeleut* (the "blacksmith's people") because of the trade of their senior elder, Michael Waldner.

A second party — the Wolf Creek Colony — bought land near the James River in Hutchinson County, where after a severe winter in sod huts, they built permanent chalkstone facilities. Their leader was Darius Walther, so they were called *Dariusleut.* A final unit headed by Jacob Wipf, a teacher (and thus called *Lehrerleut),* arrived in 1877 and established the Old Elm Springs Colony farther north on the James. These three bands — numbering less than 400 in all — constituted the original contingent of God-fearing, often misunderstood Hutterites who were to increase and prosper in Dakota through the years. Others of their basic faith who came to the Territory at the same general time chose not to follow the communal tradition and took individual homesteads, later affiliating with the Swiss-German Mennonites in and around the town of Freeman.

Danes came to Dakota Territory during its first decade, too, settling in Swan Lake Township in Turner County astride the Sioux Falls-Yankton stage trail. Many of the young Danes left from the region of Schleswig-Holstein, fleeing a long period of conscription in the German army after the area was ceded to Germany following the Danish-Prussian War of 1864.

Swedes, Finns, Netherlanders, Poles, Swiss and other nationalities were also to be included among immigrants to the Territory — but the point to be made at this juncture of the South Dakota story (in 1873) is that the influx was well underway, and that the early pioneers brought to the challenging land adjacent to the muddy Missouri a rich amalgam of cultures.

Two Generals: An Immediate Tragedy and One Delayed

The significance of the railroad extension to Yankton should not be underestimated as far as the history of South Dakota is concerned. Unimportant as the 65-mile-long Dakota Southern may have been in relation to the giant transcontinental Union Pacific, it was, in effect, an extremely important door-opener to the somewhat isolated Territory. Its impact on the capital and the communities along the route to Sioux City was felt immediately after the gala welcome for the first locomotive to reach Yankton on January 25, 1873, and the beginning of regular passenger service less than a week later.

As exciting as the inaugural trip was, however, it didn't compare at all with an event which occurred later in the spring when — on April 9 — the first contingent of ten companies of the United States Seventh Cavalry Regiment arrived in Yankton on the D.S.R.R. The historic unit had been ordered to frontier duty following two years' service in the South and was under the command of Lieutenant Colonel George Armstrong Custer (a brevet or "temporary" major general during the Civil War). About 800 officers and enlisted men were involved, together with the wives of some of the officers — including Elizabeth Custer — and approximately 40 laundresses. Seven hundred horses and 200 mules were also unloaded, and two alert Yanktonians took advantage of the opportunity to sell the quartermaster 300 tons of hay.

While the wives of the regimental officers were sent to the downtown hotels, Mrs. Custer and her servants moved into a small stoveless cabin near the regiment encamped on the east edge of the capital. For almost a week, living conditions were pleasant and comfortable; then suddenly the mid-April weather took a most unusual twist. A spitting rain turned to a powdery, windblown snow, and abruptly a well organized military cantonment became a frenzied arena of confusion. Before the blinding blizzard completely engulfed the area, the troopers — ill-prepared for the problem because of their extended duty in milder southern temperatures — were ordered to take individual initiative, to try to lead their horses to shelter in Yankton's warehouses, stables and livery barns.

Tents were blown down, and in the Custer cabin the Seventh Cavalry's commander lay feverishly ill under the care of his wife. Snow blew through the chinks in the roof and around the door and ill-fitting windows of the unheated house; it was a terrifying experience for Elizabeth Custer, and in her book, *Boots and Saddles,* she wrote:

> During the night . . . I found the servants prying open the frozen and snow-packed door, to admit a half dozen soldiers who, becoming bewildered by the snow, had been saved by the faint light we have placed in the window. After that several came, and two were badly frozen. We were in despair of finding any

way of warming them, as there was no bedding, and, of course, no fire, until I remembered the carpets . . . which we were not to use until the garrison was reached. Spreading them out, we had enough to roll up each wanderer as he came.

The more weather-wise Yanktonians organized rescue parties to find the women and children along "Suds Row," as the laundresses' area was called. Fortunately, all were saved, including a new-born baby. The storm, which lasted into the second day, piled snow into

Lieutenant Colonel George A. Custer arrived in Dakota Territory in the spring of 1873 in command of the Seventh Cavalry Regiment. After graduating last in his class at West Point, he had a brilliant Civil War combat career during which he rose to the rank of brevet major general, designated by the two stars on his uniform in the photo below. (Yankton Daily Press & Dakotan)

The pictures of Stanley J. Morrow have preserved a graphic account of people, places and events of the territorial period. An assistant to the famed Civil War photographer, Mathew B. Brady, Morrow came to Dakota in a covered wagon in 1868 with a young bride and his camera. He established his studio on Yankton's main street (above) but wandered throughout the region in search of saleable subject matter. (Yankton Daily Press & Dakotan)

enormous drifts, but because of the cooperation of the local citizenry, a major disaster was averted. When the weather had improved and order was restored, Lieutenant Colonel Custer (who also had recovered from his illness) issued a resolution which commended and thanked the Yankton people for preserving "the lives of a great number belonging to this command, besides saving to the Government the value of the public animals mounting to many thousands of dollars."

After a brief period of rejuvenation, the unit made preparations to depart on an overland hike to Fort Rice northward across southern Dakota. Custer staged a formal review for Governor Burbank and the townspeople, and then the Seventh Cavalry's first experience in Dakota Territory came to an end as the ill-fated mounted regiment marched over the bluffs out of Yankton as Strike-the-Ree's followers had done 14 years earlier. The dramatic blizzard episode at the territorial capital was of minor significance to history, of course, but Custer and the unit (during and after his abruptly terminated period of command) were yet to play far-reaching roles in the South Dakota epic.

The Seventh Cavalry came to Yankton because the rail terminus was there, and when the troopers left, the attention of the local businessmen and politicians was again concentrated on the future of the Dakota Southern and the mounting problem of how to pay off the county-backed bonds. The fiscal dilemma especially was the subject of a raging controversy, and a most unfortunate and tragic incident emphasized the intensity to which feelings had been raised.

When it appeared that the feud might result in detrimental publicity to the town and the Territory regardless of who won, a public meeting was called on September 11, 1873, in the Yankton courtroom to try to calm the impending storm. A move towards harmony had been made that same week when the capital had entertained a delegation from the St. Paul Chamber of Commerce — and two of the committee members working on the reception were banker Peter Wintermute and General Edwin Stanton McCook, then the territorial secretary who had a national reputation growing out of the Civil War record of his Ohio family known as the "Fighting Mc-Cooks."

The financier and the secretary were on opposite sides of the railroad issue and had already exchanged angry words over the matter. The general — a large man by 1873 standards, weighing at least 200 pounds and standing six feet tall — was an outspoken supporter of Governor Burbank (one of the railroad's directors), and, as a result, had developed a few local enemies of his own. The editor of the *Dakota Herald,* for instance, on March 25, 1873, had called him an "ignorant, vainglorious, drunken lout, who is an eyesore to our people and a depression upon the good morals of this community."

During the evening of September 11, Wintermute (a slight 135-pound man) and McCook were in the combination saloon and billiard parlor in the basement of the St. Charles Hotel next to the courtroom building when their personal animosities reached a breaking point. Historical reports — including ensuing court transcripts of what actually happened — are extremely conflicting, but a compilation of the testimony, matched with documented facts, spells out a dramatic and tragic story.

Banker Wintermute had apparently gone to the public meeting without a supply of cigars, nor had he brought any money with him. Supposedly he had asked McCook for a smoke or a coin to purchase one, and the latter refused in a manner which incensed Wintermute to a point of retaliation. Whether this was the case or not, a physical tussle occurred between the two, during which the banker had been thrown to the floor and soundly pummeled by his much bigger opponent. It has even been said that McCook rubbed Wintermute's face in the contents of a barroom spittoon. Following the beating, the territorial secretary went back upstairs to the railroad meeting, and the banker went to wash up.

A hundred men or so had gathered in the courtroom to hear arguments from both sides (according to prevailing custom, women seldom appeared at such functions). Ex-Governor Edmunds had been chosen to chair the meeting, and his political adversary in a previous controversy, Doctor Burleigh, had been one of the first speakers, delivering an emotionally-charged oration in behalf of the railroad's plan to sell first and second mortgage bonds to eastern speculators. Solomon Spink (who was to become the third territorial delegate) was in the midst of a rebuttal speech when shots rang out on one side of the room, and General McCook — a blood-red patch erupting on his coat front — came charging through the door from the hallway at Peter Wintermute, who was inside with a smoking pistol in his hand. Though mortally wounded, the territorial secretary grappled with his assailant; there were more shots and Wintermute was thrown to the sawdust-covered floor, at which time John Hanson stepped on his arm and wrested the pistol from him. McCook was still raging, and he attempted to throw the banker through a window which had been broken in the confused and bloody scuffle. And then suddenly it was over.

Wintermute was arrested by the local justice of the peace, and Doctor Burleigh and others helped McCook to his room in the adjoining St. Charles and undressed him for treatment. McCook remained conscious for a time and asked the physician about his chances. Burleigh indicated that there was little hope, and the general sent for his wife and young son. During the night he bled profusely, and early in the morning of the 12th, he died.

The killing rocked the town severely, and the railroad conflict was generally accepted as a contributing factor to the tragedy. To some degree, the shooting caused the citizenry to review the sad state of affairs and to attempt to restore broken relationships. The capital buzzed for weeks about the unhappy event, and then news arrived that another railroad financing plan of a greater magnitude had failed in the East, and the resultant collapse of the banking house of Jay Cooke and Company plunged the nation into the Panic of 1873.

Meanwhile, in a drawn-out epilogue, Peter Wintermute was first convicted of manslaughter and later — at a retrial in Vermillion almost two years after the shooting — a second jury declared him not guilty. The verdict resulted in a storm of protests from within and outside the Territory, but Wintermute, his money and his health gone, didn't necessarily win. Seventeen months later he died of consumption (as tuberculosis was then called) in New York State; it was said that he fell victim to the disease as he languished in his Dakota Territory cell.

The happenings in Yankton which involved the two former generals — one of whom met violent death in 1873 and the other who would be killed at the Battle of the Little Big Horn three years later — were not merely isolated events with no relevance to the South Dakota story. In each instance, the activities were part of the developing narrative and are of greater interest when viewed in the context of the overall tale.

To some degree the year 1873 was the end of the Territory's infancy and the transitional step to a youthful period of blossoming with all its attendant growing pains. The railroad, the steamboats and the telegraph had opened up the region not only to the United States but to the world. The Homestead Act was a lure to increased settlement. The first few towns and villages were beginning to offer services and accommodations which softened the discomfort of frontier living. With the appearance on the scene of more and more women and children, a new emphasis was placed on schools, churches and cultural refinement.

For all the subtle and not-so-subtle changes and improvements, however, there was a missing element, the catalyst to spark a boom. The Panic of 1873 had taken the edge off of railroad expansion for the moment at least, and the seasonal river-shipping business quickly lost its aura of excitement though it was still in its ascendancy. Something new was needed, and it was to come in the form of a magic word: Gold!

BOOK FOUR

THE CHALLENGE OF GOLD

*"As the Christian looks forward with hope and
faith to that land of pure delight, so the
miner looks forward to the Black Hills, a
region of fabulous wealth, where the rills
repose on beds of gold and the rocks are
studded with precious metal."*

— *Clement A. Lounsberry*
Bismarck Tribune
June, 1874

Until 1874 much of the historically significant activity in South
Dakota's past was concentrated in the southeastern sector of the
region, with special emphasis on Yankton because of its status as
territorial capital and terminus of the railroad. At that time the economic future of the Territory was again threatened. The national
depression affected the area drastically, and the much feared
grasshoppers returned again to add to the unfavorable conditions.

The eastern towns were continuing to grow, however, and included were those on the Big Sioux River: Flandreau, Medary, Sioux
Falls (already designated seat of Minnehaha County) and Canton,
then called Commerce City. Still, spirits were generally low, and
some sort of dramatic event seemingly was necessary to overcome the
financial and sociological doldrums. Clement A. Lounsberry, editor
of the *Bismarck Tribune,* summarized the national plight and offered
his ideas for solution in his edition of June 17, 1874:

> The American people need the country the In-
> dians now occupy; many of our people are out of
> employment; the masses need some new excitement.
> The war is over, and the era of railroad building has
> been brought to a termination by the greed of
> capitalists and the folly of the grangers; and depres-
> sion prevails on every hand. An Indian war would do
> no harm, for it must come, sooner or later. A gold ex-
> citement, founded as the Black Hills excitement will
> be, on the report of scientists and officers sent out by
> the Government, will give the restless spirits of our
> land something to do, and all something to think of.
> Then, give us the construction of the Northern
> Pacific and possibly the Southern Pacific, not to
> speak of the many roads which will seek connection
> with them . . . and a new era of prosperity will dawn
> upon our country.

(Public Relations Department, Homestake Mining Company)

Lounsberry's comments were generated by the announcement of an exploratory expedition to be made by Lieutenant Colonel Custer and the Seventh Cavalry into the Black Hills beginning two weeks later. The editor was excited, of course, because the possibility of a gold rush would give Bismarck an economic transfusion, since that city — like Yankton — had also been reached by the railroad a year previously and would therefore be in a good position to serve as a supply point for an overland route to the Hills.

Custer and the War Department, however, continued to stress (before and after the thousand-mile march) that the mission of the expedition was to gain broad knowledge of the region, not merely to ascertain the presence or absence of gold. The fact that two experienced and well-equipped miners were to accompany the unit was evidence that mineral deposits were not going to be overlooked entirely.

The 34-year-old lieutenant colonel also emphasized repeatedly that his purposes were peaceful and that he had no intention of confronting the Indians. His large command of ten companies of cavalry and two of infantry — armed with new Springfield rifles, three ten-barreled Gatling machine guns and one six-pound cannon — was, in effect, a precaution against attack by hostile forces which might or might not materialize. Custer also was well aware of the treaty restrictions which prohibited white encroachment on all lands west of the Missouri in southern Dakota; but he and higher government authorities were equally convinced that previous pacts did not preclude the army from exploration so long as permanent settlement did not result.

Before the Black Hills expedition of 1874 can be discussed and properly assessed, careful attention must be given to a most important document whose provisions were to have great effect on the region not only at that time but would have dramatic legal repercussions a century later.

The Laramie Treaty of 1868: A Dakota Dilemma

Many events directly related to South Dakota did not occur within the boundaries of the future state. Notable among these were the activities of various Teton subtribes and small scattered bands which lived and hunted in various portions of Nebraska, Wyoming and along the Powder River into Montana. These Indians — and especially the Oglala followers of Red Cloud — watched with mounting hatred the effects of the railroad expansion through their once productive buffalo lands and the extension of forts into the Big Horn Mountain country, ostensibly to protect the mining traffic to and from Montana.

Several violent clashes occurred, and it began to appear that a full-scale war might result if a concerted peace effort were not pursued. Accordingly, a treaty commission, headed by General William T. Sherman of Civil War fame, was organized and early in April of

The pre-statehood history of South Dakota was greatly affected by the Fort Laramie Treaty of 1868. The pact, which was ratified by the United States Senate on February 16, 1869, established a permanent reservation to include all of the future state of South Dakota west of the Missouri. Commissioners and chiefs, shown in a council tent at the Wyoming post, agreed to 17 separate articles, obligating both the United States government and the Sioux Indians to specific commitments. (South Dakota State Historical Society)

1868 began to hold preliminary councils with tribal leaders at Fort Laramie. The chieftains entered their complaints about the forts on their hunting grounds and the failure of government officials to fulfill the provisions of earlier agreements. Commission members told of Indian abuses, too, and how the army's presence was not always to be construed as the enemy but as a protector against bad whites who disregarded the law. During one of the meetings, General William S. Harney, a commissioner, explained:

> We know very well that you have been treated very badly for years past. You have been cheated by everybody, and everybody has told lies to you, but now we want to commence anew . . . It is not the fault of your Great Father at Washington. He sends people out here that he thinks are honest, but they are people who cheat you and treat you badly. We will take care that you shall not be treated so any more.

On April 29 the first of the chiefs signed the treaty with its 17 articles. Others made their marks later at Fort Laramie or at Fort Rice where the commissioners held another council. Red Cloud held out, however, until the military posts along the Powder River road — Fort Smith, Fort Phil Kearney and Fort Reno — were abandoned and destroyed. Then he, too, came to Fort Laramie and signed the treaty on November 26. The historic document was ratified by the Senate on February 16, 1869, and proclaimed effective eight days later by President Johnson.

The treaty covered many subjects, but especially pertinent were Article 2, which established a permanent reservation to include all of South Dakota west of the Missouri River; and Article 16, which provided that "the country north of the North Platte River and east of the summit of the Big Horn Mountains shall be held and considered to be unceded Indian territory, and also stipulates and agrees that no white person or persons shall be permitted to settle upon or occupy any portion of the same; or without the consent of the Indians first had and obtained to pass through the same."

The chieftains, for their part, agreed to a series of commitments in Article XI which included withdrawal of opposition to current or future railroad construction not passing over their reservation; a promise not to attack or molest people of the United States at home or on the road, specifically never to "capture, or carry off from the settlements, white women or children" or to "kill or scalp white men, nor attempt to do them harm," and finally an agreement not to object in the future to the construction of railroads, wagon-roads, mail stations or other works of utility or necessity which might be ordered or permitted by the laws of the United States on or off the reservation, although just compensation was to be paid if such activities were carried on within reservation bounds.

It was this Laramie Treaty of 1868 — duly signed and ratified — which affected the planned Black Hills expedition headed by George Custer six years later. Article 2 made an exception, permitting "officers, agents and employees of the Government as may be authorized to enter upon Indian reservations in discharge of duties enjoined by law," and on that basis the army planned its exploration. What happened after the Seventh Cavalry returned to Fort Abraham Lincoln two months later was an entirely different matter.

Gold Fever! A Cry of Mixed Blessings

When the Custer-led retinue departed from the Missouri River post opposite the town of Bismarck on July 2, most of the United States was already alerted to its projected journey by newspapers throughout the nation. In addition, there were five correspondents and one professional photographer included in the party to assure thorough coverage of the excursion. The dispatches of the writers were to have a significant bearing on the future of the region.

Actually, the possibility of finding gold in paying quantities in the Black Hills was broadly discussed even before the expedition was formed. On various occasions rumors of Indians bringing nuggets from the "sacred hills" were circulated. Father Jean De Smet, the Jesuit missionary, supposedly had warned his Indian friends not to broadcast the news that the precious metal existed in the region because he foresaw the stampede which would follow, treaties or no treaties.

There is evidence, however, that individuals or small groups of unknown prospectors had invaded the Hills long before Custer's exploratory venture. When the gold rush did occur (in 1876) rusted shovels and picks with rotted handles were found at various sites. In 1887 two brothers — Louis and Ivan Thoen — found a small slab of sandstone at the base of Lookout Mountain near Spearfish upon which was scratched a crude message. On one side it said:

> Came to these hills in 1833, seven of us, DeLacompt, Ezra Kind, G. W. Wood, T. Brown, R. Kent, Wm. King, Indian Crow. All ded but me, Ezra Kind, Killed by Ind beyond the high hill. Got our gold June 1834.

On the reverse side of the Thoen Stone — as the historic object rather inappropriately came to be known — Kind continued:

> Got all the gold we could carry. Our ponys all got by the Indians. I have lost my gun and nothing to eat, and Indians hunting me.

The authenticity of the Thoen discovery has been challenged by some, but the weight of the total evidence strongly supports the thesis that the prospects of gold had lured numerous eager argonauts into the region in advance of general public awareness. Ferdinand V. Hayden, a geologist, explored the fringes of the Hills in 1856 and reported later that goldbearing deposits were present. All of this, however, was preliminary to the Custer expedition in 1874 which marked an obvious turning point in South Dakota history.

The force of more than 1,000 men (including 50 Indian scouts), 1,900 horses and mules, 300 beef cattle and 110 wagons entered the

The size of the Custer expedition into the Black Hills in 1874 was dramatized by the photograph of the support wagons necessary to serve the ten companies of the Seventh Cavalry and other military units involved. Article 2 of the Treaty of 1868 permitted entry of governmental officers and agents onto Indian reservation land "in discharge of duties enjoined by law," but the Sioux were understandably embittered by the scale of the expedition. (South Dakota State Historical Society)

Black Hills from the Wyoming side, following Castle Creek to the south of Harney Peak to a camp location near the present city of Custer. It was in that vicinity — on French Creek — that the expedition's miners, Horatio Nelson Ross and William T. McKay, first found gold colors in their prospecting pans.

For all the many fact-finding reasons given for the expedition, the discovery or confirmation of the presence of gold in the Hills was to overshadow all other considerations in the months and years ahead. Custer himself was unusually cautious in his references to the precious metal in his official report:

> . . . while the miner may not in one panful of earth find nuggets of large size or deposits of astonishing richness . . . he may reasonably expect in certain localities to realize . . . a handsome return for his labor. While I am satisfied that gold in satisfactory quantities can be obtained in the Black Hills, yet the hasty examination we were forced to make, did not enable us to determine in any satisfactory degree the richness or extent of the gold deposits in that region.

Despite Custer's guarded remarks, the expedition's prime result was to intensify interest in the Black Hills and the potential metallic wealth buried there. Without knowing it, the Seventh's commander

During the 1874 expedition into the Black Hills, General George A. Custer (center) killed a grizzly bear, then existent in southern Dakota. The graphic proof recorded by the camera of William H. Illingworth gave credence to another legend of an earlier date when frontiersman Hugh Glass survived a mauling by one of the huge ursine creatures near the present town of Lemmon. (South Dakota State Historical Society)

had indirectly planted the seeds of his own demise, while directly affecting the immediate and long-term future of the bountiful area.

Paha Sapa: The Great Plains' Alter Ego

The Black Hills were so named because of the ebon hue which thick growths of various coniferous trees give to the isolated mountain range rising in stark contrast above the prairies to the east. According to geologists, the Hills are the end product of upwarping of the earth's crust followed by centuries of erosion to create the present topographic features.

The resultant compact mass is relatively small, with the north-south axis of the elliptical shape measuring less than 90 miles long. In width the Hills span a 60-mile sector, only a small portion of which extends into eastern Wyoming. The ridges average about 3,000 feet above the surrounding flatlands, but Harney Peak (the highest point in the United States east of the Rockies) rises to an altitude of 7,242 feet, giving it a formidable appearance in its pine-wreathed setting. Still another geographic landmark is Bear Butte, a unique 1,200-foot protuberance on the earth's surface which stands isolated on the northeastern edge of the main mass. White frontiersmen and explorers utilized the prominent formation as a point of reference for their travels, while the Indians ascribed religious significance to it.

Oddly enough, neither the Dakota tribes nor those who preceded them in the vicinity actually inhabited the Hills to any great extent. The reasons were both spiritual and practical. The Tetons, for instance, in addition to their recognition of *Paha Sapa* as a sanctuary

Fort Meade was established in 1878 on the fringe of the Black Hills south of Bear Butte, the prominent landmark which provided geographic reference for early explorers and had religious significance for the Plains Indians. Named for General George C. Meade of Civil War fame, the permanent post replaced nearby Camp Sturgis which had been garrisoned in 1876 to protect miners and ranchers following the controversial opening of the area to settlement. In 1892 — at his wife's suggestion — the Fort Meade commandant, Colonel Caleb Carlton, ordered the post band to play the relatively unknown "Star Spangled Banner" at all parades and ceremonies. It was the first known official use of the future national anthem which was finally adopted by Congress in 1931. (South Dakota State Historical Society)

of *Wakantanka* (God) had — with the acquisition of horses — evolved from woodland dwellers into nomadic hunters and warriors to whom the open plains were most ideally suited. Lieutenant Colonel Richard Irving Dodge, who was in the Hills a year after the Custer expedition, wrote of the tribespeople's avoidance of the region:

> Several small parties of Indians, overcome by curiosity, and reassured by the presence of the soldiers, came into the Hills this summer . . . The most intelligent of these, an Indian named Robe Raiser, was quite communicative and informed the interpreter that, though 50 years old and though he has been around the Hills almost every year of his life, he had never before ventured inside . . . His reasons for the Indians not coming in were: First, that the Hills are bad medicine and the abode of spirits; second, that there is nothing to come for except lodge poles, the game being scarce and more difficult to kill than that on the plains; third, that the thickets are so dense that their ponies are soon lost if turned loose and the flies are so bad that they are tormented and worried out if kept tied up: fourth, that it rains very frequently and the Indian does not like rain; fifth, that it thunders and lightnings with terrible force, tearing trees to pieces and setting fire to the woods.

Whether they lived in the Black Hills or not, the Dakota Tetons who then dominated the area had the Treaty of 1868 to substantiate their claim to the coveted land. The time for confrontation — or another round of negotiations — had come.

Jumping the Gun: The Collins-Russell Expedition

Throughout the history of mankind, there are few magnetic forces so attractive to the so-called civilized human being as the lure of gold. Nations, families, kings and commoners have been destroyed in the quest for it, and so it was that the confirmed knowledge of the yellow metal's presence in western Dakota aroused age-old passions and desires which mere laws have never been able completely to quell or thwart. While treaty provisions excluding white trespassers were generally well known, it was difficult if not impossible for most highly obsessed gold-seekers to understand why such agreements which (in their minds) frustrated progress should ever have been entered into by the government.

Plans for private, extralegal expeditions into the Hills were secretly developed, with a leading agitator being General McCook, the territorial secretary who later was murdered in Yankton in 1873. It has been conjectured that had he lived, McCook may have led the expedition to the Black Hills instead of Custer, with the result being a much greater emphasis on gold and the opening of the region to settlement. Meanwhile, in Sioux City, Iowa, another inveterate promoter, Charles Collins, was preparing to challenge both the Indians and the United States troops guarding the closed territory by organizing a party of squatters to get an early start on what he was confident would develop into another full-scale gold rush, treaties notwithstanding.

The proposed venture was typical of Collins, a confirmed Irish nationalist, newspaperman, erratic visionary and prolific propagandist whose place in South Dakota history was secured not so much by what he accomplished but by what he tried. Beginning in 1869, Collins had attempted to establish an Irish colony opposite the mouth of the White River on the Missouri at a site to be called Limerick. His ultimate plan was to form an Irish-American army and at some propitious time to invade Canada and drive the British (whom he hated) out of the continent. The grandiose scheme, though momentarily popular among Fenians, never got much beyond the daydream stage.

By 1872 Collins had turned his attention to the Black Hills and the purported gold deposits there. As editor of the *Sioux City Times,* he wrote glowingly (and imaginatively) of the wealth available there to all who would venture after it. His enthusiasm attracted to the cause Thomas H. Russell, a veteran of the Colorado gold rush, who began immediately to recruit members for a formidable caravan, using as a sales tool appealing pamphlets produced by Collins. When

Annie D. Tallent carved a niche for herself in South Dakota history when she became the first known white woman to enter the Black Hills, arriving in 1874 with the Gordon party. Later, when the Hills were officially opened, she returned to the region to assume a prominent role in educational circles, becoming superintendent of schools for Pennington County. (South Dakota State Historical Society)

the project came to the attention of army authorities, however, an order for the arrest and imprisonment of the leaders of any proposed Black Hills expedition was issued, causing Collins and Russell to abandon their efforts, at least temporarily.

Two years later, following the return of the Custer party to Fort Abraham Lincoln, the two promoters in Sioux City successfully organized a group of 28 persons which ferried across the Missouri on October 6, 1874, ostensibly enroute to the frontier settlement of O'Neill, Nebraska, an obvious ploy to throw government officials off the track. One of the members, John Gordon, was chosen to be the train leader, and because of that, the expedition has generally been referred to as the Gordon party. Collins, the original planner, stayed behind at Sioux City (though he was later to show up in the Hills as editor of several mining camp newspapers, including the *Black Hills Champion* at Deadwood), while Russell accompanied the eager but illegal band. Also among the 28 who started from the Iowa town were 47-year-old Annie D. Tallent, her lawyer husband David and their nine-year-old son, Robert. When the expedition — reduced to 26 by one who died and one who turned back — finally encamped at French Creek two days before Christmas, Mrs. Tallent became the first white woman known to enter the Black Hills. She was later to gain prominence as an educator and authoress of a book titled *The Black Hills; Or, Last Hunting Ground of the Dakotahs.* Interestingly enough, Mrs. Tallent was not the first non-Indian woman to enter the area because a black cook — known as "Aunt Sally" Campbell — had accompanied the Custer expedition and was also mentioned in Mrs. Tallent's book as one of the earliest residents of Crook City.

To protect themselves from attack, the gold "sooners" built a pine log stockade enclosing seven cabins in which they spent the long, confining winter. They were not molested by Indians — as they feared — and when spring came, a detachment of cavalrymen arrived with orders for their immediate removal. Abandoning their small

Contrary to treaty provisions, the Gordon party (also known as the Collins-Russell expedition) from Sioux City, Iowa, entered the southern Black Hills just prior to Christmas in 1874. The gold "sooners" built a pine log stockade on French Creek to protect themselves against Indian attack. They survived the winter but were escorted out of the Hills by United States troops the following spring. (W. H. Over Musuem)

fort and other possessions, the illegal squatters were escorted by the troopers to Cheyenne.

This episode, which in itself was of minor importance, became — like the Custer expedition — a gold-fever catalyst. Collins and other editors added fuel to the ever-increasing fire, and soon it became literally impossible for the army to hold back the anxious prospectors. The government had little choice (other than a war of extermination) but to attempt negotiations for another Indian cession, in this case almost after-the-fact of encroachment. In defense of those federal officials who were fair-minded in the matter, it must be stated that though they were unsuccessful in stemming the tide, had they completely turned their backs without trying, the gold rush might well have occurred two years earlier, with the Indians being quickly outnumbered and frustrated in their attempts to protect their treaty rights without military assistance.

As it turned out, the United States Army forces — which were to be villified by Indians and whites alike — made a vain attempt to enforce the Treaty of 1868 with limited personnel and in the end managed only to enflame the Dakotas further and to goad them ultimately into the unfortunate conflict which was to follow. Though the government in general and the army in particular were not without fault, they were soon to receive almost total blame for what overeager private citizens had perpetrated. This is not said to justify or defend all official action but to stress that in the complexities and confusion of the time there was no single villain nor simplistic solution.

Another Treaty Attempted: The Gold Rush Begins

In an effort to legalize what was already taking place in the Hills, Congress authorized still another treaty commission to meet with the Sioux tribes. As a preliminary gesture, a delegation of chieftains was taken to Washington, D.C., in May of 1875 to confer with President Grant in the company (among others) of John L. Pennington, then the territorial governor. The Indian leaders, who included Red Cloud and Spotted Tail, were no longer so easily swayed by a trip to the nation's capital and they could not be convinced to sign any documents — especially after President Grant didn't permit them to air their grievances in his presence. Consequently, plans were made for a grand council to be held later that fall near the Red Cloud Agency in northwestern Nebraska.

In the meantime, the government approved one more scientific expedition into the Hills, this one led by geologist and mineralogist Walter P. Jenney and accompanied by the previously mentioned Lieutenant Colonel Richard Dodge with a military escort of approximately 400 men. A major responsibility of the party was to obtain as much factual data as possible about the region's wealth in gold so that a realistic price might be arrived at during cession parleys.

The next several months — from June to November — were filled with confusing efforts to achieve some kind of workable settlement. Jenney's miners swarmed over the streams and gulches attempting to appraise the amount of gold available; Dodge's troopers joined in the quest alongside the prospectors, not so much to collect information as to get their hands on some of the valuable yellow stuff.

The geologist's report did not overplay the potential richness of the lodes, and some have said that he purposely underestimated the gold prospects to deter a stampede and to assist government negotiations with the tribes. This charge was never substantiated, however, and Jenney's somewhat modest evaluation might well have been due to his failure to explore the Deadwood diggings. The scientist's findings did include a rather foresighted view: "No matter how valuable the mines may be, the future great wealth of the Black Hills will be its grasslands, farms and timber." Jenney, of course, could not have imagined the area's ultimate importance as a tourist attraction.

Son of an Oglala mother and a Brule father, Red Cloud became a forceful and respected Sioux leader. Warriors under his command were largely responsible for the abandonment of the government forts in the Powder River country prior to the signing of the Laramie Treaty of 1868. Later Red Cloud refused to sign the pact of 1889 which ceded the Great Sioux Reserve west of the Missouri. He traveled to Washington, D.C., on numerous occasions on behalf of his people, participated in many councils and made hundreds of speeches. He died in 1909. (South Dakota State Historical Society)

While the Interior Department's expedition was toiling in the Hills, General George Crook also appeared with a cavalry force and orders to remove all unauthorized personnel as a "good faith" gesture prior to the council meeting. He was only moderately successful. A subcommittee of the treaty commission, accompanied by Chief Spotted Tail and other Indian leaders, also visited the region as part of the preliminary fact-finding process.

When the grand council was convened on September 20, one of the largest gatherings of plainsland Indians ever assembled met the government delegation on the banks of the White River. Estimates of as many as 15,000 individuals — including women, children and elders — were recorded, about one-third of whom were classified as "defiant." Unlike the meetings in Washington, D.C., where the chieftains were virtually alone in strange surroundings, this time the commissioners — headed by Senator William B. Allison of Iowa — were the isolated participants. A badly out-numbered force of some 500 federal troops was on hand to give them protection, but it was quite obvious that had the belligerent Indians risen up at that particular time, the commission's odds for survival would have been slim indeed.

Whether the conditions gave the chiefs a stronger hand or not is moot, but in the end they refused to sell either the Black Hills *en toto* for a proffered $6,000,000 or the mining rights alone for $400,000. The negotiations broke down, and the government response, in effect, was an uncharacteristic "throwing up of hands." Troops were withdrawn from the Hills, and the prospectors — still illegal — were left without protection, to enter or remain in the territory at their own risk.

The result of such a head-in-the-sand decision could only lead to greater problems in the future. With their way no longer barred by United States troops, all gold-seekers brave enough to run the unorganized Indian gantlet rushed into the region. It was as Father DeSmet had predicted, a stampede with little regard for right or wrong.

In the spring of 1876 while the rest of the nation was preparing to celebrate the 100th birthday of the United States at the Centennial Exposition in Philadelphia, the gullies and gulches of the Black Hills echoed with the activities of more than ten thousand argonauts (an expression from Greek mythology used earlier to describe the '49ers of California). There was no turning back the tide as the Gold Rush of '76 spread northward from Custer City, to Palmer Gulch near Harney Peak, to Hill City and finally to the richest strikes of all — in Deadwood Gulch where John B. Pearson was credited with finding the first sparkling placer diggings. At about the same time, additional strikes were made in the adjacent steep valleys of Whitewood and Gold Run Creeks.

Mining camps sprang up like mushrooms after a warm spring rain, at Deadwood, Gayville, Central City, Crook City, Lead, Chinatown, Cleveland, Fountain City, Elizabethtown, Montana City and

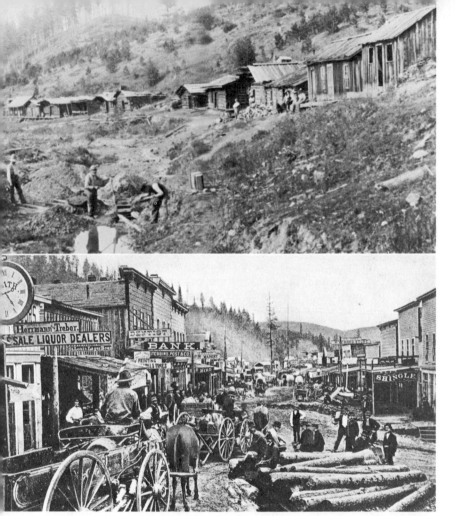

Deadwood in 1876, lower, was a bustling supply and service center for thousands of gold-seekers. Shops and saloons sprang up along its cluttered main street of mud, dust and manure. Prospectors, meanwhile, lived primitively in shacks and tents erected haphazardly in mining camps like Bear Gulch, upper. (South Dakota State Historical Society)

elsewhere. Hundreds of tents and crude shanties housed saloons, eating places and various emporiums as there were as many opportunists and entrepreneurs hoping to get rich off the miners as there were miners themselves.

It is simply not possible in a few short paragraphs or pages to capture the excitement, drama and mining-claim details of the fantastic period during which thousands of men and a few women of varying moral and personal traits were crammed together in the confines of the gold-bearing ravines. Among the masses of unremembered, unsung prospectors, merchants, muleskinners and bawdyhouse girls were a few characters and less flamboyant notables whose names and deeds lived on.

There was, for instance, the colorful and controversial "Calamity Jane" (Martha Jane Canary Burke), who was in her mid-twenties when she came to Deadwood during the gold strike to prove her legendary riding, shooting, drinking and cussing capabilities. In the famous gulch at the same time was James Butler "Wild Bill" Hickok, — scout, lawman, actor and gambler — who was shot in the back of the head on August 2, 1876, by Jack "Broken Nose" McCall, who himself was hanged for the crime at Yankton the following March. Eighteen days after Hickok's murder, Harry Weston "Preacher" Smith — a Methodist and only minister in the Hills at the time — was killed (reportedly by Indians) enroute from Crook City to Deadwood where he was to hold services that Sunday afternoon. One of the men who took it upon himself to inform "Preacher Smith's" friends back East of the itinerant parson's death was 27-year-old Seth Bullock, who the following year was to become chief lawman in the Deadwood area where he built a legendary reputation for toughness and tenacity.

There were others, too — men and women who arrived in 1876 or shortly thereafter — like cigar-smoking "Poker Alice" (Ivers) Tubbs, a British-born gambler who was later to devote her final years in Sturgis to the raising of flowers, chickens and Angora cats; J. B. "Texas Jack" Omohundro and "Potato Creek Johnny" Perrett; "Aunt Sally" Campbell, the Custer expedition's black cook; Charlie Collins, the irrepressible Irish newspaperman; poetry-writing Captain Jack Crawford; Sam Bass, a notorious stagecoach robber; and three rather inauspicious prospectors — brothers Moses and Fred Manuel, who with their partner, Hank Harney, located the claims

Typical of the Black Hills mining towns were Galena City (left) and Gayville (right), both photographed in 1877 by the itinerant Stanley J. Morrow, whose camera recorded much pre-statehood history. While miners and prospectors toiled on their claims, merchants, tradesmen, gamblers and numerous other opportunists established themselves in hastily built structures in the gulches, ready to profit indirectly from the pay dirt. (W. H. Over Museum)

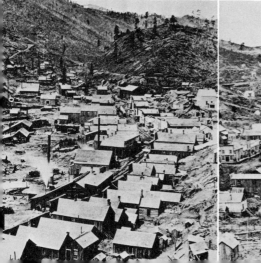

Frontier justice was harsh and often final, and the gallows were used in both territorial and early statehood periods. The above execution of convicted murderer Charles Brown took place in Deadwood in 1897 with the morbidly curious present in great numbers. The most notorious hanging, however, was that of Jack McCall, the slayer of James "Wild Bill" Hickok, who paid for his crime at Yankton in March of 1877. (South Dakota State Historical Society)

which resulted in one of South Dakota's most important long-term industries, the Homestake Mine.

Among several claimants to the title of "Deadwood Dick," the fictional character created by Edward Wheeler in his popular dime novels, was Nat Love, an ex-slave from Tennessee. Love, who came to Dakota as a cowhand, insisted that he had won the "Deadwood Dick" name for his prowess in a riding, roping and shooting competition during a Fourth of July celebration in the unrestrained mining town.

As the months of 1876 slipped away, the activities in the Black Hills grew to crescendo pitch. By the end of the year more than 20,000 gold questers were estimated to be in the northern diggings alone. The permanent communities were established at Deadwood, Lead (named for a gold-bearing ledge or "lead"), Custer, Hill City, Spearfish and Rapid City, which was first called "Hay Town" because of its role as a supply point for the needs of the mining districts.

Miners dug, sluiced and panned (sometimes with cooking utensils) as they produced more than a million dollars in gold in June and July of 1876 at a quoted price of $20 an ounce. Many of the prospectors worked hard and played hard, bringing their buckskin drawstring bags of dust and nuggets to the saloons and gambling shacks which sprang up in all the camps, but especially in Deadwood. Some of the less hardy '76ers — who hadn't counted on such hard work and physical discomfiture — left the diggings quickly; but the trails from Bismarck, Fort Pierre, Cheyenne and Sidney, Nebraska, (then the closest railhead) brought as many or more replacements. The Indians, justifiably angered by the disregard of standing treaty provisions, made sporadic and uncoordinated raids on travelers to and from the Hills with little effect on the traffic volume. However, the anger of the tribes was being felt more pointedly elsewhere.

The Sioux War of 1876: Custer's Undoing

The Indian policy of the United States (before and after 1876) was marked by vacillations and inconsistencies. Some officials honestly tried to develop programs for the mutual good of the tribes and the nation. Others — indefensible under any circumstances — advocated complete elimination of the native Americans or at least the continuation of governmental subsidies and contracts which offered ideal setups for graft and corruption. It must be remembered, too, that the problems relating to plainsland Indians and white settlers in Dakota Territory occurred during a period when other critical events elsewhere — notably the Civil War and its aftermath — were considered to be of much greater importance by a majority of American citizens.

Among the colorful characters of the Black Hills was cigar-smoking "Poker Alice" Tubbs, born Alice Ivers in Sudbury, England. After her first husband was killed in a mine explosion, she married W. G. Tubbs, a gambler whose profession she also followed. In 1928 when she was 75, Governor Bulow sent her a pardon (below) following her conviction on a bootlegging charge because, as he reputedly said, he "couldn't send a white-haired old lady to prison." She died two years later. (South Dakota State Historical Society)

In truth — once the Confederacy had been defeated — Congress and presidential administrations were much more concerned about Reconstruction and the economic well-being of the nation as a whole than with the problems of a meagerly populated frontier. When the West *was* considered in legislative halls and executive conference rooms, the emphasis was usually on such "boomer" topics as Manifest Destiny, the future of the railroads, the opening of new lands to settlement and, of course, gold. Unhappy Indians, miners who disregarded treaties and vociferous settlers who demanded government recognition were all too often regarded as aggravations rather than important issues deserving of solution.

It wasn't right, of course, but the evidence supports such a conclusion. In the East the Sioux Indians were an object of curiosity and endless erroneous news stories. When chieftains were brought to Washington, D.C., their inability to read or write was construed by some shallow-minded bureaucrats as ignorance rather than a cultural difference. Needless to say, the serious conditions developing in and around the Black Hills grew worse because of the low priority of interest nationally and the lack of a clear-cut, realistic policy.

There were so many factors involved: the questionable reputations of many of the soldiers with frontier units, the obsession of gold-seekers, the greed of sutlers and certain agents, the inexperience

Among the noteworthy characters of the early Black Hills settlement period were (left to right): James B. "Wild Bill" Hickok, J. B. "Texas Jack" Omohundro and William F. "Buffalo Bill" Cody. They were the subjects of popular fiction writers of their day, and at one time the three of them performed in a play entitled "Scouts of the Prairies." (South Dakota State Historical Society)

and occasional stupidity of numerous political appointees, the competition among various religious sects in missionary work, and the thievery and malicious acts of some Indians whose attacks frightened white settlers to a point of angry retribution. All of these conditions — and more — added to the complexities of the overall problem; and as one treaty and peace commission followed another, each new stage of negotiations brought more contradictions, more solemn promises which were difficult to keep and an ever-widening chasm between peoples.

So it was that when the Great Council of 1875 failed to offer a quick solution to the Black Hills dilemma, prospects of violent confrontation were increased immeasurably. In the gold camps, miners formed vigilante-type organizations or otherwise kept weapons handy to protect themselves from Indians as well as from white freebooters and claim-jumpers. Young, militant Dakotas (with some Cheyennes and Arapahoes) turned their backs on the reservations and prepared to strike out at the whites — any whites! — in retaliation for the invasion of the Black Hills and other festering injustices.

In the meantime, the restless military — bored and frustrated by mere police work attendant with the unsuccessful attempts to keep prospectors out of a region far too big to oversee — was ready for direct involvement against an enemy in force. Many of the officers and enlisted men were philosophically on the side of the miners anyhow, so turning back wagon trains was a duty performed with little enthusiasm. After all, a battle against an identifiable foe such as a Sioux war party offered greater adventure and might well lead to quicker promotions and decorations than border patrols.

The opportunity for military action came in the spring of 1876 after some 3,000 Dakotas and Cheyennes failed to return to their respective agencies on order from the Indian Bureau and were declared hostiles. In response, three columns of troops numbering about 2,500 men in all were sent out to converge upon the enemy forces which were seriously underestimated both in numbers and strategic ability. One group under General George Crook marched northward from Fort Fetterman on the North Platte; the second led by General Alfred H. Terry (and including Lieutenant Colonel George Custer's Seventh Cavalry) started westward from Fort Abraham Lincoln near Bismarck; the third commanded by Colonel John Gibbon moved eastward from Fort Ellis in Montana. The ensuing battles and lesser skirmishes in which the various units participated were to have a decided effect on South Dakota history, but *all* of the major engagements took place beyond the state's borders, primarily in the Big Horn and Powder River areas of Montana and Wyoming.

The most notable event, of course, was the complete annihilation of Custer and 265 members of the Seventh Cavalry entrapped with him on the Little Big Horn on June 25. The flamboyant officer had divided his regiment into three units in an over-eager attempt to encompass a large Indian encampment. As it turned out, the detach-

Before organized government was established in the gold country, miners depended upon individual effort and vigilante action to protect their interests and possessions against thieves, claim-jumpers, crooked gamblers and gunmen. Deadwood's first jail (right) was an early attempt to curb lawlessness without resorting to more drastic measures like lynching. (W. H. Over Museum)

ment led by Custer himself was cut off instead and totally wiped out before help could arrive. For the Sioux and their allies under Chief Gall and spiritual leader Sitting Bull (both Hunkpapas), it was a momentous victory which was to become as important a milestone in tribal history as Yorktown, Gettysburg and Antietam were to white American heritage.

The steamboat *Far West* — piloted by Captain Grant Marsh, who was said to be capable of navigating a river paddlewheeler over a "sea of dew" — brought out the wounded survivors of the battalion commanded by Major Marcus A. Reno, which was also assaulted by the Indians and prevented from joining Custer's force as planned. In an unprecedented 710-mile race downriver in just 54 hours, they were taken to Fort Abraham Lincoln where their ill-fated march had begun, and then the telegraph clicked out the news of the dramatic and disastrous calamity for the United States Army.

In the Black Hills there was considerable concern about future Indian strategy when it was evident that an overconfident (or ill-advised) War Department did not have the situation completely under control. At the territorial capital the news was greeted with a combination of sorrow laced with pride and anger. Marsh and the *Far West* (the latter being a Coulson Packet Line vessel) were considered Yankton's own; and the Seventh Cavalry, of course, had left an indelible mark on the townspeople three years earlier. A meeting was called at the courthouse on July 7 during which citizens bitterly assailed the Sioux and called for a volunteer militia to destroy the

Indians without further delay. For once, though, cooler heads in the regular service prevailed and a less emotional course was pursued.

The victorious Indians did not choose to follow up on their advantage and withdrew from the battle area before reinforcements from General Terry's main force could become involved.

Few other episodes in the military annals of the United States have been discussed, analyzed and written about more than the clash between the Sioux and the Seventh Cavalry in the Montana hills. It brought an end to the brief but brilliant career of the 38-year-old Custer, who, though brash and showy, reputedly neither drank, smoked nor publicly used the irreverent language so common among his counterparts in uniform. The chain of events which led to his death in the battle which has been labeled popularly as "Custer's Last Stand" actually started with the expedition into the Black Hills in 1874. Though he was not held in the greatest favor among the higher echelons of the War Department because of his willingness to expose army and Indian agency deficiencies to the newspapers, Custer was destined to live on in memory in South Dakota where a city, county and state park were named for him.

To most Americans the far-off Indian war cast only a fleeting shadow over the nation's Centennial celebration, and in the Hills the miners kept on digging with little interruption. In the meantime, the

The Coulson Packet Line steamboat, the *Far West,* had the dubious honor of transporting the wounded survivors of the Seventh Cavalry out of the Little Big Horn country in late June of 1876. Captain Grant Marsh, one of the most noted of the Missouri River pilots, guided his vessel downstream at record speed to Fort Abraham Lincoln near Bismarck where the news of Custer's demise was telegraphed to a shocked American newspaper audience. (W. H. Over Museum)

so-called hostile Indians separated themselves into smaller bands to evade the pursuing army units and to search for food. The lack of buffalo and other game soon left the various leaders with the fateful choice of returning to the agencies (which a majority of the less militant tribespeople had never left) or subjecting their followers to starvation in the winter months ahead. To make the decision more difficult, word had been circulated that some of the first rebels to turn themselves in had had their guns and ponies taken away.

Then another development occurred.

The United States Congress — already disturbed by the failure of the Indians to "sell" the Black Hills which seemed to many members a fair and reasonable thing to do in the name of progress — was in an angry mood when news of the Seventh Cavalry's humiliation began to sink in. On August 15 an Indian appropriation bill was passed which included (among other items), a provision that the Tetons would be cut off from further allotments if they didn't agree to terms for giving up the Hills and all unceded lands outside of the clearly defined reservations. With an explicit law to guide them, a new commission, headed by George W. Manypenny of Ohio, was named to complete the congressional directive.

In effect, it was as if George Custer — in defeat and death — had won a posthumous victory. Congress held the trump hand, and with the food situation growing desperate for the holdout Indians, it became apparent to the leaders of at least some of the small bands that a return to agency existence — however distasteful — was the wisest choice.

The "Battle" of Slim Buttes: "The Horsemeat March"

In the aftermath of their triumph at the Little Big Horn, the various Indian bands scattered to move independently of one another. Two groups under Sitting Bull and Gall ultimately escaped into Canada to remain there until 1881, while another under Crazy Horse, the indomitable Oglala chieftain, roamed the Wyoming wilderness throughout much of the winter of 1876-77, always a jump or two ahead of the federal troops. Before he led his hard-core followers back into the Powder River country, however, Crazy Horse turned up in the Slim Buttes region of South Dakota (in present-day Harding County) where several of the dispersed bands had reunited.

Presumably, many of the Indians were then preparing to go back to the reservations, but whether that was their true intention or not, they were disrupted when an advance party of General George Crook's weary command surprised a small encampment of Brules on the morning of September 8. According to the report of the patrol's leader, Captain Anson Mills, the Sioux were literally laced into their tepees, the leather drawn tight as a drum by an all-night rain. As a result, they had to cut their way out before they could fight back. Chief American Horse (The Elder) and several other Indians died as a result of the skirmish, while one soldier was slain. Most important

Photographer Stanley Morrow recorded the aftermath of the abbreviated skirmish at Slim Buttes. He joined General Crook's forces several days after the event so his pictures were not taken at the scene of the conflict, and some — like the transporting of wounded by travois (right) and soldiers fighting over horse meat — were staged, according to some researchers. The Indians in the (left) photo were identified as prisoners of the campaign. (W. H. Over Museum)

to the troopers, however, was the capture of a supply of dried meat because of the serious need for rations by the military force which by that time was subsisting primarily on a diet of horseflesh from their own wornout mounts. This development caused the Crook campaign to be called "Horsemeat March," and in his autobiography, John F. Finerty, a *Chicago Times* correspondent with the command, described the unusual circumstances:

> While trudging through the mire . . . Lieutenant Lawson and I observed a small group of soldiers by the side of the trail busily engaged in skinning a dead horse, and appropriating steaks from its hinder parts. This was the beginning of our horse rations. The men were too hungry to be longer controlled, and the general wisely ordered that as many horses as would be necessary to feed the men be selected by the officers and slaughtered day by day. Indian ponies captured at Slim Buttes were later substituted for the less palatable cavalry animals.

In the meantime, following Captain Mills' assault on the village, the Indians struck back, apparently with the help of Crazy Horse and his warriors who were encamped several miles away. The captain's report said that after his first attack he and his men were soon surrounded, but fortunately for the detachment, General Crook's main column arrived in time to prevent a repeat of the Custer debacle. Neither the army nor the Indians were in shape for a major showdown battle, so the Sioux disappeared again, some to return to agency control and some not, while General Crook and his hungry, trail-worn soldiers proceeded to the Black Hills where supplies were waiting for them.

It took a final burst of energy for some of the men and horses to get across the rain-swollen Belle Fourche River after an 11-day downpour, but there were no further incidents of note and so the so-called Sioux War of 1876 came to a soggy, undramatic and relatively unproductive close.

When the Manypenny Treaty Commission arrived at the Teton agencies in the latter half of September, the members (including former territorial governor Newton Edmunds, an experienced negotiator) had an agreement for relinquishment of the Black Hills already prepared. The document specifically extended the provisions of the Treaty of 1868 (as modified by the agreement), except that Article 16 — which defined and recognized unceded Indian territory in Montana and Wyoming — was explicitly abrogated.

This time, instead of offering a cash payment of any kind, the government simply directed that compensation would be in the form of rations, educational programs, individual land allotments and houses, support of Indian peace officers on the reservations and other activities to assist the Indians to "become self-supporting and acquire the arts of civilized life." The tribal leaders, faced with what amounted to a sign-or-starve choice, affixed their marks to the treaty-amending document at the various agencies, beginning on September 26 and completing the task a month later. (Congress ratified the agreement on February 28, 1877).

An additional element of the pact offered the Tetons an opportunity to move to the Indian Territory (Oklahoma), and Chief Spotted Tail of the Brules and several Oglala leaders visited the area to consider the proposition. Despite a warm welcome by Cherokee and Creek officials and an invitation from them to bring their tribes southward, the Dakota representatives — with a love of the great open plains too thoroughly ingrained in their nature — rejected the proposal and returned to their people and the reservations established for them under the terms of the Treaty of 1868 and the subsequent agreement.

Spotted Tail, who like Strike-the-Ree of the Yanktons has been chastised by some later-day Indians for his seemingly quick acceptance of governmental authority, was anything but docile when he spoke in councils; and in his commentary at the signing of the agreement in 1876, he expressed his concerns quite pointedly: ". . . when my people are to receive anything from an agreement of this kind, and we sign a paper as we are asked to now, it always turns out we don't get the things that are promised . . . It has been said to us that there is no deceit in touching the pen to sign a treaty, but I have always found it full of deceit."

Spotted Tail wasn't alone in his censure. When the commission submitted the signed papers to Congress, the members took advantage of the opportunity to submit also a comprehensive report which did not hesitate to criticize severely past governmental efforts regarding the Indians and to advocate still greater emphasis of the "peace policy" instigated by President Grant. The commission called for the transfer of all Indian activities from the War Department (where it had long resided) to civil and religious authorities, and decried the loss of capable agents "simply because they would not steal, and could not live on $1,500 a year.'' (This intimated, of course, that those who remained in the Indian service *did* steal.) The report also said in part:

> We hardly know how to frame in words the feeling of shame and sorrow which fills our hearts as we recall the long record of the broken faith of our Government. It is made more sad in that the rejoicings of our Centennial year are mingled with the wail of sorrow of widows and orphans made by a needless Indian war, and that our Government expended more money in this war than all the religious bodies of our country have spent in Indian missions since our existence as a nation . . . We are aware that many of our people think that the only solution of the Indian problem is in their extermination. We would remind such that there is only One who can exterminate. There are too many graves within our borders over which the grass has hardly grown, for us to forget God is just. The Indian is . . . one of the few savage men who clearly recognize the existence of a Great Spirit. He believes in the immortality of soul. He has a passionate love for his children. He loves his country. He will gladly die for his tribe . . . If the men of past generations had reasoned as this generation reasons, none of us would rejoice in the blessings of Christian civilization. A great crisis has arisen in Indian affairs. The wrongs of the Indians are admitted by all. Thousands of the best men in the land feel keenly the nation's shame. They look to Congress for redress. Unless immediate and appropriate legislation is made for the protection and government of the Indians, they must perish. Our country must forever bear the disgrace and suffer the retribution of its wrong-doing. Our children's children will tell the sad story in hushed tones, and wonder how their fathers dared so to trample on justice and trifle with God.

There was a prophetic note in the conclusion of the committee's report as the question of providing justice for the Indian was to persist and grow in the ensuing century. As it developed, the challenge of gold in the Black Hills — so bright and glittering in its spurring of a promising new settlement area in South Dakota — had its tarnished side, too.

BOOK FIVE

THE CHALLENGE OF BOOM AND BUST

We have no wheat, we have no oats,
We have no corn to feed our shoats;
We do not live, we only stay;
We are too poor to get away.
— Mortimer Crane Brown

Before and during the Black Hills gold rush, the homesteaders east of the Missouri River faced a series of morale-shattering challenges, mostly from the vagaries of nature.

While an economic depression persisted on the national scene, Dakotans suffered from drouth and resultant poor crops. Simultaneously, the sun-seared prairies brought disastous grass fires — an anathema to settlers, Indians and buffalo herds. At the same time, grasshoppers (which seemed to survive best when other conditions were worst) returned in force, beginning in 1874. Writer Doris Alsgaard, in her article in *Dakota Panorama* titled "Start With One Cabin," aptly described the extent of the infestation:

> When they [the 'hoppers] struck the ground they
> became part of a dirty brown mass. Chickens ate un-
> til they couldn't walk; cattle and horses were tor-
> mented by the insects which crawled all over their
> bodies, even getting into their eyes, ears and nostrils.
> Cotton mosquito netting, the pioneer's window-
> screening, was eaten first, and when that was gone
> the grasshoppers ate the wooden sash. They ate
> away the soft wood of the handles of pitchforks,
> rakes and hoes. They ate the leaves of vegetables,
> and bored into the cabbage heads like maggots. They
> piled in great windrows around each building. If a
> man walked on the hard ground, he slipped on the
> crushed grasshoppers. If he walked in the grass, they
> flew up in such swarms he almost choked. They
> even got inside his clothing.

Fighting the grasshoppers was almost an effort in futility, and in Union County, near the town of Jefferson, Father Pierre Boucher (said to be South Dakota's first resident Catholic priest) appealed to Higher Authority to help save the crops of his parishioners. On a warm Sunday morning in May of 1876, the white-haired pastor led his congregation (plus members of other denominations) on an all-day procession from field to field where large wooden crosses were erected. The people sang and prayed, imploring Divine assistance to rid them of the insect plague which threatened their very existence.

(W. H. Over Museum)

The resultant legend of the "Grasshopper Crosses" recalled that Father Boucher's pilgrimage succeeded: and after the priest's death, Jefferson Catholics carried on the tradition of his heavenly appeal.

More immediately tangible, however, were the relief supplies delivered by the army and other organizations to the hard-hit farmers. Despite the calamities, though, many of the settlers clung to their land, hoping for a brighter day. By 1877 conditions began to change for the better, and the dominant factor of the dawning era was the steel ribbon of the railroad which began to creep out across the prairie from several earlier terminal points.

What gold did for the establishment of new settlements in the Black Hills, the railway companies accomplished east of the Missouri River. In actuality, though, the valuable discoveries in French Creek, Deadwood Gulch and elsewhere in the *Paha Sapa* — followed by the cession agreement with the Indians — had a lot to do with the extension of trackage across eastern Dakota to the Missouri and ultimately beyond. The founding of towns along the right-of-way in the ceded region was an important inducement to railroad expansion, but with the gold rush in full swing, the shipping of supplies to the mining camps in the Black Hills was where the real money was.

Three Overland Routes: Where Buffalo Once Roamed

A major provision of the agreement of 1876 was "that wagon and other roads, not exceeding three in number, may be constructed and maintained, from convenient and accessible points on the Missouri River, through said reservation, to the country lying immediately west thereof, upon such routes as may be designated by the President of the United States."

Governor Pennington of Dakota Territory promptly appointed commissioners to survey roadways from Bismarck (then the Northern Pacific Railroad terminus) and Fort Pierre, both of which led to Deadwood. A third route, which started at Yankton and followed along the south side of the Missouri and Niobrara Rivers to Custer, received little attention and little use. As might be expected, an intense competition developed quickly between the promoters of the two principal supply lines. Bismarck, with a rail line already completed to the Missouri, had the advantage of one less unloading and reloading process. Fort Pierre, on the other hand, was tied to Yankton and other down-river supply points by steamboat, with goods being transferred from rail cars to the boats at the territorial capital and again from the paddlewheelers to giant ox or mule drawn wagons at the road head. Moreover, the abbreviated steamer season was an even greater disadvantage when ice made it necessary to bring supplies to Fort Pierre by overland vehicles during much of the year. Needless to say, the clamor for a rail line to the Missouri through southern Dakota was loud and forceful.

Until the railroad arrived, the stagecoach was a prime means of passenger transportation in pioneer Dakota. Hot and dusty in summer, cold and unpredictable in winter, the six-horse vehicles were particularly active in the Black Hills during and after the first influx of argonauts, prospectors. Armored coaches were devised to protect outbound shipments of gold. (South Dakota State Historical Society)

Supplying the free-spending miners in the Black Hills — whether from the Missouri River bases or from towns along the Union Pacific in Nebraska and Wyoming — was a lucrative proposition, not only for the freightline operators but for farmers, manufacturers and wholesalers of a broad spectrum of commodities, not the least of which were alcoholic beverages. Unfortunately, all the activity generated by the transportation business — so eagerly desired by the white entrepreneurs — was greeted with an exactly opposite reaction by the Indian tribes. All the fears and dire predictions of the chiefs, both those who conformed and those who held out, were realized.

Stagecoach traffic, as well as freight wagon activity, increased rapidly on the Black Hills routes. As indication of the size of the operations, the Sioux City and Black Hills Transportation Company,

The Black Hills mining country was supplied by ox-drawn freight wagons from Bismarck, Fort Pierre and other railroad and steamboat terminals. This particular caravan was unique because it featured what the Sturgis *Record* called a "bullwhackeress," a lady driver, Mrs. Canuteson, Rapid City. (South Dakota State Historical Society)

for instance, was said to have owned 3,000 oxen and 2,000 mules, while employing 1,500 men. To carry gold out of the mining country, the various firms used steel-lined "battleships on wheels," like the Black Hills Stage and Express Line's "Monitor" which had steel plating five-sixteenths of an inch thick with portholes through which guards could fire. Wells, Fargo and Company hired Wyatt Earp, the renowned gunfighter, to "ride shotgun" on its heavily armored stagecoaches.

A telegraph line connected Deadwood to Cheyenne in 1877, the project bringing not only a force of construction workers but a small army of guards to protect the wires against the depredations of angry Indians. The movement of more and more people back and forth across reservation land, though ostensibly on approved trails, resulted in greater dispersal and destruction of game which drastically affected the livelihood of the Dakotas and drove them more rapidly to dependence upon government rations. Of major consequence, of course, was the fact that the Great Buffalo Era was growing to a lamentable close.

There was no questioning the reality that the white man's rifle and his vast markets for robes and choice morsels of buffalo flesh were responsible to a major degree for the virtual annihilation of the giant herds. Unlimited sport-killing of the animals, especially along the Union Pacific right-of-way, was another factor. Professional hunters like William "Buffalo Bill" Cody were hired to provide a meat supply and to "protect" railroad trains, construction crews and telegraph poles from the buffaloes; and the effects of their sharpshooting were appalling.

The Indians were not totally without fault either. Some of them departed from traditional hunting practices and killed "for market," trading robes and tongues for ammunition, metal implements, cloth, whiskey, coffee and other products of the white man's world. Meanwhile, wolves, coyotes, eagles and various carrion-eaters feasted sumptuously on the decaying remains of thousands of the once majestic creatures. Before all the carcasses were reduced to whitened bones, the stench of dead buffaloes fouled the prairie air during the hot months in a manner which modern-day environmentalists could hardly imagine.

Buffalo herds were further depleted by the reduction of grassland acres. Prairie fires — once started almost exclusively by lightning — were set by ill-tended campfires of white settlers or by Indians as retaliatory measures against homesteaders and other encroachers. There are those who believe, too, that the vast numbers of buffalo in the Upper Missouri country began to decline rapidly following a pathetic episode in the spring of 1868 when tens of thousands of the huge animals were drowned near the border of Montana and northern Dakota. George Kingsbury in his *History of Dakota Territory* described the disastrous natural catastrophe:

Breaking a buffalo to harness was a novel accomplishment of patience, determination and courage. Somehow, though, the sight of the majestic beasts in a subservient role was symbolic of the end of the frontier era. (South Dakota State Historical Society)

A vast herd attempted to cross to the south side of the river on the soft ice . . . when the ice broke, and there was the most fearful and thrilling scrambling and bellowing, leaping and plunging that ever awoke the echoes of the Upper Missouri. The plains north and east of the Missouri had been covered with the animals during the winter, and when the herd started to cross in the spring . . . the column kept moving as buffalo invariably do when on the march, crowding those in front into the death-trap of broken ice until nearly the whole herd was destroyed; and the river for a long distance below was literally covered with their dead bodies. For weeks along the shores, for the distance of a hundred miles, the bodies of the drowned were washed up and piled in heaps where they decayed.

Whatever the reason, however, buffalo herds of any appreciable size were becoming increasingly scarce by the mid-1870s; and accordingly, the Sioux Indians' ability to sustain themselves in their customary nomadic life style was seriously inpaired if not already destroyed.

Political Rivalries: The Territory of Lincoln Rejected

Even before the railroad began to roll back the plainsland frontier at a more accelerated rate, the restless demand for organized government and political involvement was as evident in the Black Hills as it had been a few short years earlier in the southeastern corner of the Territory. Politics on the fringes of civilization not only served the vital function of establishing an ordered society, but the accompanying rallies, speeches and factional rivalries provided diversion from the labors, discomforts and general boredom of mining camp existence.

From a practical point of view, of course, the gold prospectors wanted legal protection for their claims, and a government of some sort was necessary for that. In addition, the capturing and punishing of horse thieves, murderers and other law-breakers were also functions which an unorganized community could not effectively accomplish. Consequently, even before the agreement of 1876 had been ratified by Congress to give after-the-fact approval to the Black Hills encroachment, unofficial delegates from the mining region urged the territorial legislature to push for the organization of counties. The two representatives — Doctor Carl W. Meyer and General A. R. Z. Dawson — threatened to petition Congress for separate status if the Dakota officials did not act in their behalf. They even had a suggested name for their new governmental entity: the "Territory of Eldorado."

Even though the legislature at Yankton had defined the boundaries of Custer, Pennington and Lawrence counties and prepared for their official organization to follow congressional acceptance of the Indian cession, Black Hills political activists continued to pursue the idea of separation. A bill to create the "Territory of Lincoln" actually came before the United States Senate for consideration early in 1877, but it was promptly rejected, a fact which had an obvious effect on the ultimate shape of the South Dakota map.

Meanwhile, as the proposal to split the Territory at its western extremity was being considered, the concept of a north-south division was given more and more attention. A strong rivalry between Yankton and Bismarck — both Missouri River railroad terminals — had developed over Black Hills shipping business. Because of the northern Dakota city's location on a potential transcontinental line, Yankton interests began to fear its ascendancy and therefore did everything to block additional advantages which might go to their up-river competitor. At the same time, Governor Pennington, in collaboration with other politicians and businessmen in the territorial capital, worked hard to establish connections if not control in the Black Hills. When the chief executive appointed men from the so-called "Yankton ring" instead of local citizens to fill many of the offices in the mining counties, animosity between the "Mother City" and the Hills' communities also erupted. With the seat of government as a dominant factor in its favor, Yankton was still the hub of political power in the Territory — but already in 1877 there were signs that new forces were beginning to emerge.

Westward to the River: The Great Railroad Race

The story of railroad expansion and the concurrent development of settlements along rights-of-way through southern Dakota includes a fascinating combination of enterprise, determination, lost opportunities, serious obstacles to overcome and an occasional humorous interlude. Earlier dreams of a transcontinental line passing through Yankton or Sioux Falls had generally diminished by the mid-1870s largely because the Indian reserve and the Black Hills blocked a direct route westward.

Despite bad weather, grasshopper infestations, poor crops and virtually no transportation facilities other than wagons and stagecoaches on rutted trails, a surprising number of homesteaders accepted the Dakota challenge, established claims, founded towns and withstood the worst the Territory had to offer. These hardy young men and young women looked with eager anticipation to the day when the railroads would arrive to solve their supply and marketing problems, to deliver some of the luxuries of life back East and generally to bring a new dimension of excitement into their otherwise drab existence.

Railroad officials needed a more potential market than the sparse population southern Dakota could offer, but when the Black Hills gold rush entered the picture, coupled with an economic upturn nationally, there was reason enough to move rapidly into a westward expansion program. The sale of land-grant property, the lure of immigrants, the platting of townsites and other real estate benefits would provide lucrative bonuses to make the effort doubly worthwhile.

As it developed, two companies had the same idea at approximately the same time. The first was the Chicago and North Western Railway System, whose general manager then was Marvin Hughitt, an energetic young man who had personally visited Dakota to look over a prospective western route. The second was the Chicago, Milwaukee and St. Paul (later known simply as the Milwaukee Road) which was headed at the time by Alexander Mitchell, a successful financier and empire builder.

The C. & N.W. began its move into Dakota from Canby, Minnesota, in the summer of 1878, and by the fall of the following year had a roadway completed through Aurora, Elkton and Brookings (first called Ada) to Volga. During the winter of 1879-80, construction continued on the westward extension to a site on the James River (reputedly selected and named by Hughitt himself). The newly established town of Huron then became the jumpoff point for a tracklaying race across the open prairie between the James and the Missouri. To speed up the process, ties were laid directly on the virgin sod with very little additional preparation. The theory, of course, was that there would be plenty of time afterwards to go back and do a better building job.

Speculators were vitally interested in where the road would terminate on the Missouri, and the best guess was at a site near the mouth of Medicine Creek. While others conjectured, however, Hughitt's land agents — disguised as cattle ranch developers — busily bought up claims north of the small stream and platted a town

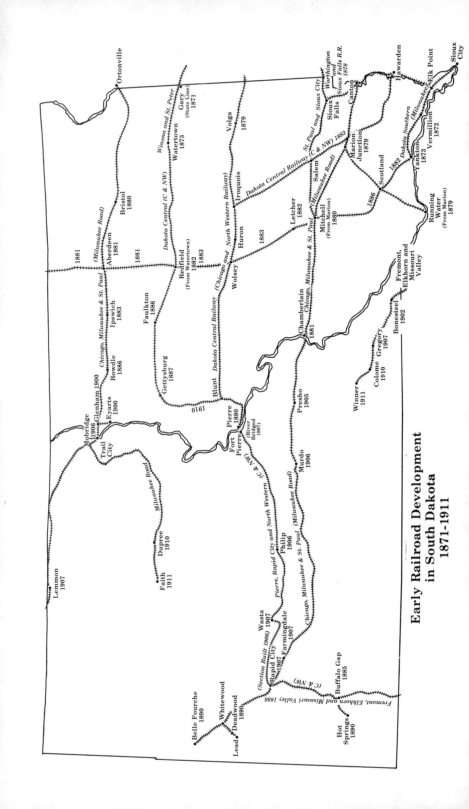

Early Railroad Development in South Dakota 1871-1911

River ferries like the *Josie L. K.* operated regularly on the Missouri River before permanent bridges were built. Smaller boats on rope tows facilitated the crossing of lesser streams where shallow fords were not available. (Yankton County Historical Society)

called East Pierre, later shortened to Pierre. When the construction crews finished their work and the first train arrived on November 4, 1880, the new terminal town was, in effect, company property.

While the C. & N.W. was hurrying westward, the rival Chicago, Milwaukee and St. Paul was not sleeping at the switch. Its entrance into Dakota was via Canton, and by the fall of 1879 it had reached Marion Junction in Turner County. The C., M. & St. P. then unveiled a second strategic move. A branch line was projected southwestward to the Missouri River near Springfield at a landing known as Running Water. This, of course, was a direct blow to Yankton which, up till that time, had enjoyed the benefits of a half-dozen years of near-monopoly over rail-and-river traffic.

The railroad company, at the same time, also pushed its main line westward, crossing the James River, not at Firesteel as expected, but at the new town of Mitchell, ceremoniously named after the

Primary lines and some of the key connections in South Dakota's early railroad development are shown in the map at the left. As tracks were laid, they spawned small towns along the rights-of-way, many of them from seven to ten miles apart to permit settlers to reach a market center and return home in a single day by horse and wagon. Railroad service to small communities reached its zenith shortly before World War I, after which motor cars and trucks began to reduce the interest in and need for restricted, track-bound transportation.

transportation firm's president. From there the track crews proceeded through Plankinton and Kimball enroute to Chamberlain, all infant villages similarly named for railroad officials. Just as there had been speculation over the final location of the Chicago and North Western's river terminal farther north, the C., M. & St. P. also kept the land-manipulators guessing as the line approached the Missouri. Brule City, opposite the mouth of the White River and site of Charlie Collin's unfulfilled Irish dream, was considered the likely choice, but once again the railroad schemers had other ideas and diverted the track toward Chamberlain.

In the exciting era of railroad expansion in southern Dakota, it will be noted that on numerous occasions tracks were laid several miles away from certain established towns and hamlets. This was not necessarily because one route was superior to another for engineering reasons, but usually because the railroad companies directed the new construction across land in which they had vested interest.

The Chicago and North Western won the race to the Missouri River when its rival's track-layers were halted some 20 miles east of Chamberlain by a heavy, early-season snowfall. Completed or not, however, the parallel lines set the stage for a surge of development which in less than one decade would result in the admission of the new state of South Dakota.

While the population had been building up gradually with homesteaders arriving by covered wagon and occasionally by horseback or afoot, the seemingly endless stretches of undulating prairie were still relatively unclaimed. Unlike earlier settlement precedents to the east where railroads came *after* the creation of towns and the availability of markets, in Dakota's case the trains generally led the way into the unsettled regions. It was a calculated business risk (somewhat lessened by the surety of Black Hills trade), and the ultimate result was the Great Dakota Boom.

So certain were Alexander Mitchell and the C., M. & St. P. planners of the profit potential of rails in the vanguard that the company began to install two other lines in the Territory early in 1880. The first one crossed over from Minnesota at the southern end of Big Stone Lake and proceeded to Milbank (for Jeremiah Milbank, a director of the company). From there the rails were extended westward through Webster to Aberdeen, which was platted by the railroad firm and named for Alexander Mitchell's birthplace in Scotland. (British-born C. H. Prior, land agent on the project, apparently was responsible for the fact that English towns like Andover, Bristol and Bath were memorialized in the new villages along the Dakota right-of-way.) Simultaneously, the Chicago, Milwaukee and St. Paul acquired the Southern Minnesota Railway which was projected to Flandreau early in 1880 and from there to Madison, via Egan, Colman and Wentworth during the following year.

Oddly enough, as the railroad expansion spread across the region, two of the leading towns in southern Dakota were not particularly involved. Sioux Falls, whose time had not quite yet come, had been missed by all four of the extension lines, while Yankton, the territorial seat of government, was bypassed and virtually blocked out of the new east-west trade channels. In a little more than a year, the pattern of development in the Territory had experienced a notable change, and the "brighter tomorrow" had seemingly arrived.

Unfortunately, the rosy future was to be dimmed by still more natural calamities.

A Double Blow: The "Hard Winter" and the Flood of '81

Nothing tested the mettle of early Dakotans — red and white — more than the challenge of nature. Survival for the Dakota Indians, of course, depended upon their abilities to cope with the climate and to harvest their food needs from the land and the streams with little control over the source of supply beyond their appeals to *Wakantanka*. The homesteaders, though they tilled the soil and practiced animal husbandry, also had to rely upon the elements for crop-saving rains, and, conversely, for freedom from tornadoes, hail, lightning-ignited prairie fires, insect plagues, drouth, floods and blizzards.

As romantic as the "good old days" may seem in retrospect, there was nothing especially glamorous about life in a tepee or a sod hut during a protracted period of sub-zero temperatures and wind-whipped snows. But the Dakotans of the past not only persisted against the onslaughts of nature, they also seemed to develop a sense of stoic pride in their tenacity. Indian braves passing tribal tests of manhood and white settlers toiling behind ox-drawn plows had more in common than they knew. So too did their wives — Indian women and their white counterparts, struggling endlessly in their respective ways to provide food and clothing for their families while raising new generations under the most burdensome of conditions.

In the late fall of 1880 the future of the region showed great promise. At least for immediate considerations the Black Hills situation had been settled, and the flow of immigrants into the Territory exceeded any previous period. Then, on October 15, a 24-hour snowstorm — unseasonably severe — blanketed eastern Dakota, interrupting railroad construction and delaying service on lines that were already completed. Weather-wise Indians and settlers who had been around for a few years were surprised by the depth of the snow but were not especially concerned because they were sure that mild temperatures would dissipate the cover before later storms arrived. Sadly enough, they were wrong.

Not only did the first snow fail to disappear, but successive layers were added to it in the ensuing weeks and months until Dakotans were literally buried under the white blanket which spread from one border to the other. Hundreds of new settlers were caught ill-prepared for the severe weather, having arrived in the Territory too late to build properly or to lay in provisions. Adding immensely

Not only did the flood of '81 wreak havoc with the steamboat fleet, but the Dakota Southern Railway was also disrupted by high waters and slabs of ice washed upon the tracks. During the previous winter trains had been stalled by massive snowdrifts, and locomotives burned ear-corn when the coal supply ran out. (Yankton Daily Press & Dakotan)

to the difficulties was the fact that the railroads had not yet delivered the regular supply of coal; trainloads of fuel were stranded and lay buried on sidings throughout the winter. Farmers burned twisted hay, straw and ear-corn, while town dwellers cut up small buildings, fences, bridges and precious new lumber from the local yards. Some families moved together to save fuel.

Oil for lamps was also in short supply (as were candles, tallow and lard), so most homes were without light of any kind, a problem made doubly difficult by the fact that many log cabins and sod houses were almost completely covered by snow. Thousands of range cattle perished, and animals which survived and were gathered in crude barns often had to be fed and watered through holes in the rooftops while forage was still available. The homesteaders themselves were drastically short of rations, especially flour. Food supplies in the towns were meted out by relief committees which sought equitable distribution regardless of ability to pay. Farmers who had wheat ground it as best they could in their small coffee mills.

Snow plows and shoveling crews tried to free the trains along the new lines, but they couldn't keep ahead of drifting and additional downfall. Telegraph wires were buried, and in some places the snow piled up two and three times higher than the railroad cars. The track from Yankton to Elk Point was laid on a roadbed several feet above the flat bottomlands, so it was occasionally usable, but even the Dakota Southern was short of coal, and late in December a locomotive made the run from the capital to Elk Point using 50 bushels of ear-corn for fuel. Another train, similarly powered, tried to go from Sioux Falls to Sioux City but was stopped by a gigantic drift 400 feet long just four miles out of town.

And still the Hard Winter of 1880-81 (as the period came to be known) continued mercilessly. Early in February — when it seemed that Dakotans could stand no more — another blizzard, the worst and longest of the season, lashed the Territory as a final memento of nature's winter wrath. Only the hope of an early spring kept the confined homesteaders and townsfolk from cracking under the prolonged strain.

Finally, in the first week of March, the break came — but not in the normal fashion. The massive accumulation of snow in the upper country began to melt and run off before the southern portion of the Territory was similarly affected. Water poured downstream over the ice in the Missouri, James and Big Sioux Rivers; and another catastrophe was in the making. So widespread was the flooding which followed that no chronicle of South Dakota's past would be complete without some detailed report of the destruction and demoralization. George Kingsbury described the nightmarish conditions at one site:

> The ice broke up in the [Big] Sioux River at Sioux Falls on the 20th of March . . . the water began rising, and in twenty-four hours gained a height of about sixteen feet above low water mark, the highest ever known. A torrent over five hundred yards wide ran through the town . . . Three of the bridges . . . went out within fifteen minutes. The upper wagon bridge, a new iron structure, was the first and went whirling down the flood and struck the lower wagon bridge, throwing it in the air, and then the combined wrecks dashed into the Pembina Railroad bridge, tumbling it from its foundation, and the three bridges floated away in company. The big bottom prairie just west of the town was at one time under ten feet of water . . . The farmers lost everything but their land and their lives. Many of them who possessed a small fortune in grain and livestock, buildings and improvements found themselves reduced almost to a beggarly condition. From the highland, buildings could be seen floating in the water, and others were submerged to the apex of their roofs . . . And there was no relief in sight, for there was no way of getting out of the country nor any method by which relief could be sent in.

Downstream the havoc continued all the way to the Missouri. Gristmills and bridges were wiped out, and at Canton the Big Sioux was two and a half miles wide for a time.

Meanwhile, settlements and individual homesteads on the James suffered a similar fate. At Huron there was a reported 20-foot rise in the river as it roared over its banks and down the valley. At Forestburg, then official seat of Miner County, the courthouse was swept away, and the editor of *The Progress* there had to find refuge on the roof of his inundated shop. Scores of sod huts, many of them the first homes of recently arrived German-Russians, were destroyed. Flour mills at Mitchell, Milltown, Rockport and Wolf Creek were smashed completely or put out of commission, all of which added to the aggravated food shortage growing out of the extended winter.

As bad as the debacle seemed to be on the smaller rivers and creeks, the Missouri rampage matched and multiplied the debacle. The lowlands at the new town of Pierre were flooded, and numerous oxen used on the freight route to Deadwood were swept downstream. At White Swan opposite Fort Randall the raging water drove settlers to the high ground from which they watched their worldly possessions float away. Residents of the territorial capital, in the meantime, anxiously awaited the onslaught which on their river front would be complicated by the presence of a wintering fleet of steamers. An eyewitness, Doctor Nelson Armstrong, described what he saw in his autobiographical book, *Nuggets of Experience:*

> On Sunday, March 27th, the ice gave way in the river at Yankton. Hundreds of people were on the banks to witness its going out, and the sight was grand; but as I stood there in silence, gazing upon those acres of ice moving down in a gigantic body, sweeping all before it, a tremulous sensation seemed to creep over me, as if I were dreading an approaching calamity. The steamer *Western,* the only boat not placed on the repair ways, was caught with the earliest moving ice and held so close to the bank as to make her unable to rise with the tide. Men labored with her as in case of saving human life, but she sprang a leak, sank partly under water and was pulverized on the spot. The ice moved out, leaving the river below clear as far as could be seen from the city. The people rejoiced that no more damage had been done; they evidentally thought all danger had passed, but it was discovered later that the ice had first broken at the upper end of the river and gorged near Springfield . . . which very plainly explained the cause of the river being clear at Yankton.

Since the ice had not given way farther down the stream, the water backed up and started to overflow across the lowlands. By the next day the entire James River bottom was inundated, and curious spectators on the high ground east of the capital were able to view the awful scene of farm houses half submerged, cattle and horses struggling in the water, ice floes adrift with chickens and small animals aboard, and — here and there — rowboats and skiffs with heroic rescuing parties at work moving from homestead to homestead.

Up till that time the city itself had escaped relatively unscathed, and the townspeople were sightseers rather than victims. Then, suddenly on Tuesday evening, March 29, a mountainous gorge formed a few miles below Yankton and a massive glacier of jagged cakes of ice built up behind it all the way westward to Springfield. It was a fearful development for which there was no remedy — except to seek high ground, pray and wait.

Just before noon on Wednesday, an immense shudder ran through the entire hulking gorge, and as a reporter for the *Dakota Herald* described it: "The waters gave a mighty roar . . . and with a sudden jerk the whole tremendous mass began to rear, and crash, and tumble, as if it knew of its awful power for destruction." On the city's river front the crushing bergs smashed against the sides of the steamboats on the ways. The previously damaged *Western* was virtually reduced to kindling; the *Butte* was broken in two; the *Helena* was twisted and badly gouged; the *Black Hills* was similarly battered. As the icy water rose, the giant hawsers of the *Peninah*, the *Nellie Peck* and the ferryboat *Livingston* were snapped like store-

In the aftermath of the flood of 1881, the steamboats of the Missouri River fleet which had wintered at Yankton lay smashed and battered amid the ice and debris. The pilot's tower of the *Western* was almost all that remained identifiable of that particular vessel, while others were so badly damaged that they could not be restored to service. With tonnage already seriously reduced by railroad competition, the river transportation industry never recovered from the natural disaster. (Yankton County Historical Society)

The town of Vermillion was virtually destroyed by the flood waters. The twisted printing office of *The Standard* was unsalvageable as were most other frame buildings caught in the ice-laden tide. Undaunted citizens saved what they could and later rebuilt on the high ground overlooking the valley of the Missouri (W. H. Over Museum)

string, and all three vessels were lifted out of the riverbed and deposited grotesquely and brokenly on the shore. On April 2 the *Dakota Herald* reviewed the tragedy:

> People ran hither and thither in wild excitement. Household goods were hastily thrown into wagons and removed to places of safety. Shouting, swearing men, weeping women and children, pawing, frightened horses all combined with the roaring, rushing waves to form a picture to delight the heart of the monarch of Pandemonium. As the waters rose higher and higher, skiffs, yawls and other small craft began to shoot through the streets in lieu of the vehicles. Furniture, clothing and babies were handed out the windows and ferried to high ground. Outhouses and movable truck danced around the surface. Hogs and chickens squealed and squawked and swam and flew to places of safety . . . All through the lower part of the city . . . roared an angry, surging torrent of yellow water, from one to six feet in depth, literally covered with the debris incident to a great flood, all banging, smashing and rolling about in one common medley . . . Down the channel of the river swept haystacks, water-tanks, live animals and the fragments of fences, houses, etc., which had been swept from God knows where up the river.

The incidents of heroism, of tenacity and of terrible loss (at least ten human lives included) which occurred during the fear-filled period were seemingly endless. Yankton had been almost miraculously saved from worse catastrophe by a house-high levee of ice which built up along the river front and diverted the main stream from engulfing the city. Beyond the capital, however, the town of Vermillion — then located on the flatlands below the bluffs — was demolished, the second time in six years it had suffered a major disaster, a fire having destroyed all but three of its almost three dozen business buildings on January 13, 1875. At Gayville and Meckling settlers were marooned on rooftops and haystacks; in barns, attics and corncribs. Seventy-five people were stranded at the Meckling elevator, and 23 were trapped for several days on the upper floor of a granary, living on corn cracked in a small hand-grinder.

In a little more than a week the worst was over, and as the waters of the three eastern Dakota rivers began to subside, a vast panorama of havoc stretched along their destructive paths. Thousands of animals and fowl lay dead in the muck, and in the ensuing warm days, the stench of their decay added a distasteful aspect to the seemingly unachievable task of cleaning up. It had been a terrible ordeal, and from the Yankton Indian agency, old Strike-the-Ree sent a dictated letter to an editor in the territorial capital on April 5, 1881, in which he reminisced:

> It is now some eighty winters that I have seen the snows fall and melt away along this Missouri River, but I never saw a winter of such snows and floods as these . . . Long ago — forty years or more — there was a flood that overtook and killed a large number of Teton Sioux, but even then the flood was not as high as this. Here on the Yankton reservation the water seemed to burst up from beneath and covered the whole plain from bluff to bluff. Though the people fled to the hills and saved their lives, many lost all their property. Forty-three houses were taken away by the flood, with their stoves and other household goods; also stables, haystacks, cattle, horses, cut logs, steamboat wood, mowers, plows and other farming implements.

> As I looked upon the women and children, struck by this great calamity, my heart was moved, and I prayed thus: "God have mercy and look upon me. Look with mercy on these women and children. Give us a way — good, broad and straight — by which they may live.

An Amazing Recovery: Revival of the Boom

As demoralizing as the "Hard Winter" and the ensuing floods were, they did not crush the Dakota spirit nor curtail the influx of new homesteaders. On the contrary, the catastrophe seemed to spur a vibrant sense of revival, and — better yet — the snow-soaked earth was ready to produce crops of cornucopian volume. Instead of taking their losses and pulling out, the railroads likewise rebuilt their lines with renewed vigor, and then added more.

There was one notable casualty, however. For the steamboat industry, as exciting and profitable as it once was, the flood proved to be the fatal blow from which it never recovered. The train service to Chamberlain, Pierre and Bismarck took most of the freight and passenger business, and the expense of restoring the battered fleet at Yankton was too prohibitive to make the effort worthwhile. The Coulson Packet Line operated several boats on the upper Missouri after the disastrous spring, but by 1885 the firm was down to a single vessel which it subsequently sold.

The railroads, of course, provided the driving force for the regenerated boom, and thousands of land-seekers heeded the call to the promising Dakota prairies. Small towns sprang up along the rights-of-way, located by the railway companies every seven to ten miles, an appropriate distance to permit as many farmers as possible to have a marketplace which they could reach by horse and wagon and still get back home the same day. Homesteads were staked first along the tracks, around the villages and along streams, but the demand was so great that marginal land was claimed almost as quickly as the good.

The railroad agents and town developers conducted extensive promotion campaigns, sending bundles of pamphlets and posters which extolled Dakota Territory in glowing terms to Norway, Sweden, Bohemia, the Crimea and other potential sources of immigrants. Representatives traveled to Europe to spread the message of cheap, bountiful acreages to land-poor farmers. Others met ships at New York harbor and offered various inducements to lure newcomers to the flatlands half a continent away. Salesmanship within the United States was also vigorously pursued, and Governor Nehemiah G. Ordway, the Territory's seventh chief executive, participated by fitting out a railroad baggage car with a display of Dakota agricultural products with which he toured New England and other eastern areas. Newspaper articles, letters from relatives and word-of-mouth persuasion attracted hundreds of settlers (American-born and alien) from Minnesota, Iowa, Wisconsin and Illinois, all hoping to improve their holdings farther west.

Boomerism affected town development, too. Seemingly, there were promoters for every little whistle stop on every rail line, each intent upon telling the world that his embryonic hamlet would be the "next Chicago." Truth was not always the principal ingredient in the flowery propaganda printed in frontier newspapers in behalf of their communities. Not all the early-day editors were paragons of virtue; too often they were itinerant opportunists who took advantage of a basic requirement of the Homestead Law. The "proving up" of claims had to be officially advertised, so journals of scant merit appeared in almost every village to print the necessary legal notices at five or six dollars apiece, often more than a hundred per issue. Some rather unscrupulous publishers followed the immigrant trail, profiting heavily from claim advertising when settlement in a particular area was at its height, then moving on when the business tapered off. Such operators were not above embellishing the merits of whatever town they were located in at the time, and the real estate promoters took their flattering handbills and editorials eastward in search of investors and new Dakotans.

A spirit of optimism and eagerness filled the prairie air as trainloads of immigrants poured into the region. For a time there was a literal traffic jam of people in Huron, all needing food, accommodations and a means of transportation with which to begin the search for a farm site. The bustling scene was repeated at Mitchell, Aberdeen and other smaller (but hopeful) towns like Kimball, Plankinton, Ipswich and Woonsocket. Horses, buggies and wagons of all kinds were at a premium as newcomers sought ways to get to where the unclaimed land was. With so much activity — tent cities, lineups at the land offices and trains in parade — it was not difficult for even the most dour citizen to be caught up in the enthusiasm of the times. The weather following the Hard Winter was beautiful, crops were bountiful, and no one seemed to feel that conditions would ever be any different.

Even the earth seemed to respond to the infectious attitude. A new phenomenon — the artesian well (the name being derived from the site of a historic water source at Artois, France) — sent sparkling gushers into the air, symbolic of the buoyant era. More realistically, of course, the discovery of the subterranean supply of water under pressure heralded what seemed to be the answer to one of Dakota's biggest problems: clear water for human and animal needs, water for firefighting, water for irrigation and, hopefully, water for industrial uses.

The first discovery was made at Yankton where a Chicago contractor had agreed to drill to 1,500 feet (at four dollars a foot), with no money to be paid until water was found or the contracted depth reached. On August 29, 1881, with the bit 460 feet into the earth, the first artesian gusher in Dakota Territory was struck. It was a day of great excitement for residents of the territorial capital, anxious to forget the unpleasant water experience of the previous spring; and they turned out in large numbers to see the cascading fountain spilling down the hillside and into the street gutters.

News of the well at Yankton spread rapidly through the Territory, and delegations from many of the water-scarce towns came to see the aquatic bonanza. Within a few months artesian geysers were appearing all over the region, and the energetic boomers began spread-

Artesian wells seemingly promised an unending water supply for South Dakota cities and farms. In time, however, unrestricted drilling proved that the underground sources could be depleted. Gushers, like the one in early-day Yankton above, were not uncommon. (Yankton County Historical Society)

ing the word that Dakota would soon have a bubbling fountain in every quarter section to guarantee an unlimited water supply. Little thought was given, of course, to the possibility that excess drilling would ultimately overtax a natural resource which (like buffalo and topsoil) should have been more judiciously preserved right from the beginning.

In a time of great exuberance, however, the idea of restricting artesian well drilling was quite inconceivable, and millions of gallons of wasted water flowed into creek beds and gullies enroute to the Missouri or one of its tributaries.

A Political Coup: Yankton Loses the Capital

For more than two decades as the territorial capital, Yankton had dominated the political and economic scene, a situation which developed largely because of its position of accessibility on the Missouri River. As other towns to the north and west began to grow and prosper, the "Mother City of the Dakotas" found her once beneficial location becoming an obvious drawback. Legislators from northern Dakota and the Black Hills had to travel disparate distances to attend sessions, and when the steamboat faded as the primary means of transportation through the region, the river port on the Nebraska border lost its extended commercial advantage.

Realistically, the honor of being the seat of the territorial government did not particularly benefit Yankton in a tangible way. On the contrary, when the legislators met to distribute the largesse of government, the Mother City was overlooked because it would appear "too political" to award special favors to the capital. And so the territorial penitentiary went to Sioux Falls in 1881 (after first having been assigned to the village of Bon Homme which failed to survive); the territorial university was granted to Vermillion in 1862, although it didn't start classes until 20 years later when 35 students reported to the first director, Doctor Ephraim Epstein, a former Jewish rabbi; the 1881 legislative session passed an enabling act for an "agricultural college" in Brookings but failed to provide funds to get it underway until $25,000 was appropriated in 1883 for the first building. Similarly, important governmental appointments seldom went to Yanktonians for the same political reasoning; and when the so-called "Yankton ring" did try to achieve a measure of control over outlying counties, the enmity of citizens in the Black Hills, northern Dakota, Sioux Falls and elsewhere was quickly aroused.

The main reason the Dakota Hospital for the Insane (as it was originally known) was located near the capital was because Governor William A. Howard took the matter into his own hands when the

The University of Dakota began operation in 1882 with 35 students in the Clay County courthouse at Vermillion. Local citizens had raised funds for its first permanent building before the 1883 legislature authorized a bond issue of $50,000 for capital improvements. A year later Superintendent Beadle was able to boast that the school had "a good reference library of 500 volumes" for its 116 enrollees. (W. H. Over Museum)

states of Minnesota and Nebraska in 1878 refused to care for mental patients from Dakota as they had been doing under contract. Consequently, the governor, lending some of his own personal funds to the project, had two old lodging houses (which once accommodated incoming German-Russian immigrants) torn down and the materials used to erect the first hospital structure on the school section two miles north of the town. Other than that, about all Yankton had to show for 20 years of political embroilment were mixed emotions about the periodic visits of legislators and federal officeholders (who didn't spend much money) and a deteriorating frame capitol building of the crudest design.

The citizens of Yankton received veiled warning that their capital status was in jeopardy when Governor Ordway (named by President Rutherford B. Hayes to succeed Governor Howard who died in office) indicated in his first message to the legislature in 1881 that a new site would be considered. It was two years later before the threatened action took place.

The fifteenth session of the legislature had convened on January 9, 1883, and after an inauspicious beginning, Councilman George H. Walsh of Grand Forks introduced a bill to move the capital to Huron, a surprising maneuver. Various historians have called Walsh's action a smokescreen strategy which was meant primarily to bring the matter up for debate. It was the concensus that Huron simply could not swing enough votes to win the capital, but with the subject out in the open, a group of conspirators — including Governor Ordway — would be free to manipulate the legislation according to plan.

What resulted, of course, was a political war of intense proportions. In the middle of it with the governor was Alexander McKenzie, forceful lobbyist for the Northern Pacific Railroad, armed with all the power that prestigious company had at its disposal. Aligned against them were the Yankton interests (angered less by the removal than by the deviousness of the scheme to accomplish it) and Richard F. Pettigrew of Sioux Falls, then the territorial delegate to Congress. Pettigrew was not necessarily a supporter of the Mother City, but he had developed a violent distaste for Ordway when the latter had attempted to interfere with the disposition of political patronage. Pettigrew had filed charges against the governor and demanded his removal. In the process the delegate revealed details of a congressional investigation into Ordway's conduct when he was sergeant-at-arms of the United States House of Representatives; and from the chairman of the committee which studied the case, Pettigrew received and published a defamatory letter in which the governor was called "one of the most corrupt and unprincipled men that has ever disgraced and degraded the public service of this country."

When the Huron bid failed to gain support, the legislature created a nine-man capital commission to visit prospective sites, review the bids offered by the competing towns and then vote for the final

A political power struggle revolving around the relocation of the territorial capital was reflected in much legislative action in 1883 relative to schools, colleges and other pet projects. A normal school for the preparation of teachers at Madison (above) was one of those institutions receiving support in the exchange of votes. The need for educators in the Territory's 1,136 schoolhouses as of that year was great, but political expediency was more involved than long-range planning. (W. H. Over Musuem)

choice. Before the commission bill was passed and signed, inordinate pressures were applied and political promises made. Just how much connivance took place between Governor Ordway and Alex McKenzie (who was named to the selection panel) may never be known completely; so many conflicting interpretations of the dramatic and emotional episode have been presented that the matter has been more clouded than clarified.

Before it was over, however, several "political bargains" were quite apparent. The governor succeeded in having his son confirmed as territorial auditor, a potentially lucrative position; he vetoed bills introduced by anti-removalists and signed those sponsored by cooperating members; many of the legislators had new counties named after themselves; and jobs in state institutions were parcelled out. Also figuring in the power struggle was support for the territorial university at Vermillion; normal schools at Madison, Springfield and Spearfish; the agricultural colleges at Brookings and Fargo; the

Deaf Mute School (as it was then called) in Sioux Falls; and a reformatory at Plankinton. Undoubtedly there were other payoffs in speculative property and assorted favors when the final decision was made.

Immediately after adjournment of the legislature, broad opposition to the removal scheme was expressed by a long list of territorial newspapers. The *Parker New Era* editorialized: "Among all our numerous Dakota exchanges we fail to find one newspaper that upholds N. G. Ordway and the corrupt syndicate who have their paws on the throat of the capital." On April 5, 1883, an indignation meeting was held in Sioux Falls and a protest resolution passed:

> Resolved, That we . . . hereby express our condemnation of the gigantic fraud referred to, which was made possible by Governor N. G. Ordway's venality and the prostitution of the powers of his position, and . . . that we denounce the conspirators and perpetrators of this iniquity as unworthy of the positions which they have disgraced, and that it is our earnest prayer that Dakota may be relieved of the official who has been a discredit to the territory and a continual cause of strifes and discords.

A similar meeting was held at Yankton, but meanwhile the capital commission (each member drawing six dollars per diem) had gone into action. One of the provisions of the law required that the group meet and organize at the capital city, and this presented a problem. Fearful of being served with a legal injunction — and of possible physical retaliation by irate citizens — the members gathered secretly in Sioux City where they boarded a special train (reputedly provided through McKenzie's railroad connections) and

Oxen played a significant role in the early days of Dakota Territory, providing transportation, animal power to till the virgin prairie sod and — when dire emergencies came — meat for the homesteaders' tables. The slow-moving beasts of burden ultimately were replaced by horses. (Below: State Historical Society of North Dakota; Right: South Dakota State University)

proceeded through the dark of night to Yankton. Shortly after six o'clock on the morning of April 4, the locomotive and single car crossed the city limits and came to a brief stop. There behind curtained windows the commissioners affected a legal but surreptitious organization as the law required. Immediately thereafter the train hurried out of town.

The next step was to visit each of the bidding locations, each of which had to offer a minimum of $100,000 and 160 acres to be considered; these candidates included Aberdeen, Canton, Frankfort, Huron, Steele, Bismarck, Mitchell, Odessa (Devil's Lake) and Ordway. The latter village — which gained some notoriety as the temporary Dakota residence of writer Hamlin Garland — was the obvious choice of the governor who had extensive real estate holdings there. As brazen as he was, however, the chief executive was unable to push the Brown County town into serious contention because of his patently undisguised connections with it.

Meanwhile, after considerable wining, dining and deliberations, the commission finally got down to voting on June 2 in Fargo. On the thirteenth ballot Bismarck obtained a five-vote majority, with Alexander Hughes of Elk Point providing the margin of victory. Hughes, incidentally, had been appointed to the nine-man panel by the governor himself, and, in addition, Ordway also had had a bill rushed through the legislature on the final day before adjournment approving the Elk Point man as territorial attorney general. In the final tally, Redfield received two votes and Huron and Mitchell one each.

As expected, the news brought a quick real estate boom to Bismarck, and the *Jamestown Alert* commented: "It is said Aleck McKenzie sold $250,000 worth of land yesterday, and that a half million dollars' worth has changed hands within the last couple days." Governor Ordway — who had been present for the voting — was obviously pleased, and on June 5 at Mandan he rubbed salt into the wounds of angry Yanktonians by announcing that "Bismarck is a first-class place for the capital. Yankton is too far away and the people are lacking in public spirit."

The reaction was quick and understandable, and various newspapers castigated the governor in vitriolic terms. Though the legalities of the commission's decision were subject to scrutiny and debate until statehood — and one official (Territorial Secretary James H. Teller) refused to transfer his office to Bismarck — the capital removal fight was, in effect, all over but the shouting and name-calling.

In a delayed aftermath Governor Ordway was indicted for alleged corrupt practices relating to county organization, but his term expired in 1884 and he was never brought to trial. He later became involved in banking and other ventures in northern Dakota, and reputedly served as a special lobbyist for the Northern Pacific in Washington, D.C., thus adding credence to the charge that he had been deviously allied with McKenzie and the railroad company in the Bismarck coup of 1883.

Giants in the Earth: The Pioneer Life

Ole Edvart Rolvaag, in his stirring novel "Giants in the Earth," wrote of the drudgery and loneliness experienced by settlers from his native Norway in the Big Sioux Valley. Hamlin Garland, who took a claim in McPherson County in 1883 when he was in his early twenties, couldn't wait to get out of the Territory, and in the ensuing years he penned disparaging recollections of his brief stay in the country which he labeled the Middle Border. Even Laura Ingalls Wilder — who recalled frontier life in Dakota with nostalgic charm in her books written a half century later — finally moved to Missouri with her husband, Almanzo, when the rigorous demands for survival in Kingsbury County proved more oppressive than they chose to bear.

At the same time thousands of anonymous Dakotans whose stories were never preserved on paper accepted the challenge of the open land, so magnificently described in the promotion advertisements but, in reality, so stubbornly difficult to conquer with plow and seeder. Finding and claiming a homestead was one thing; breaking the sod, erecting a crude shelter and coaxing a paying crop from the earth was another.

This was not to say that the Dakota pioneers were doomed to a hopeless struggle against misery and hardship; but to imply that life on the prairie was a romantic adventure full of hay rides, square dances, quilting bees and festive barnraisings is equally misleading. There is a common human tendency to look to the past through rose-colored glasses — to disregard the bad and accentuate the pleasant times. This very normal trait distorts history, of course, so reminiscences of the "good old days" must be balanced with the stark realities which drove Hamlin Garland to Chicago and New York and broke the spirits (and sometimes the minds) of many disillusioned young homesteaders.

Symbolic of the rugged life on a Dakota claim was the primitive sod house. In a land where wood was scarce and commercial lumber

Sod houses were built in almost every imaginable shape and combination. Most families considered them just a temporary abode before a frame or brick house could be afforded and raised. A storm or root cellar (at left) was a priority item, not only for the preservation of food, but for protection against high winds and occasional tornadoes. (South Dakota State Historical Society)

expensive, a "soddie" was often the first home for bachelors or young marrieds as they began the process of "proving up" the 160 acres they had first recorded at the nearest land office. There was nothing standard about a sod house. They were built in all shapes, sizes and combinations with hillside dugouts and clapboard huts. Most of them, though, were crude one-room affairs seldom bigger than 16 by 20 feet.

In a typical construction process, the homesteader started by scratching out the foundation lines on the ground, the more fastidious builders doing that at night to "square up" with the North Star. The next step was to find a spot where the prairie turf was thickest, followed by the arduous task of cutting the sod "bricks." A walking plow, drawn most likely by an oxen, was used to turn a furrow a foot or more wide. After that, slabs up to three feet long were sliced off with a spade and hauled to the building site on a stone boat.

[A stoneboat, incidentally, was a wooden sled used for gathering rocks from new fields or for collecting buffalo bones which was an early source of revenue for settlers. The bone business was good for the railroads, too, as trainloads of bison remains were shipped east to be used in button, comb, sugar-refining and other industries.]

Erection of a sod house consisted simply of arranging the earthen slabs (four to six inches thick) side by side along the foundation line, except at the door location. On each succeeding course, joints were staggered for greater stability, with every third or fourth course laid crosswise to bind the layers together. Joints were filled with dirt or clay, and the door and window frames (either home-made or store-bought) were set in at the appropriate levels. The pioneer then continued to stack the slabs until the walls were high enough to suit him.

The roof, of course, was the critical phase of construction. Forked trees were cut to hold a ridgepole from which log or rough beam rafters were strung. This often necessitated a long trip to a river or wherever trees might be available. If the homesteader had enough money, he bought boards — often of wiry, warping cottonwood — to cover the rafters. If not, he and his family gathered brush, sticks and even bones to make a first layer, followed by a thickness of prairie hay. The more fortunate families had a tarpaper reinforcement between them and the Dakota skies. Additional sod blocks — not as thick as those in the wall and usually laid grass side down — completed the project, although a flimsy chimney pipe generally protruded through the roof or a wall.

The result was no castle, but it was usually better than sleeping in a covered wagon or a makeshift tent; and since most settlers looked to their soddies merely as a step toward greater things, they moved into them with a feeling of accomplishment and optimism. This spirit usually lasted until the first heavy rains came!

Sod houses had a way of leaking no matter what pains the builder took. The pelting drops would wash away the clay filling between the sod blocks on the roof, and sooner or later, little rivulets of muddy water would begin to trickle down the walls or drip-drip from numerous spots in the crude ceiling. If the house didn't have a raised board floor so the water could run down through the cracks, mud puddles would form in the low spots in the floor. The family learned to congregate where it was driest; or if the storm was particularly bad — especially during the spring and fall tornado seasons — everyone evacuated the house and huddled in a root cellar or cave used interchangeably for food storage and protection.

Rain-soaked roofs of soddies were heavy and dangerous. Occasionally they collapsed, injuring and even killing family members. Wet snow was similarly worrisome when it collected too deeply overhead. Compared to dugouts and flimsy shacks, though, sod houses

Boredom was a major problem of frontier living so diversions of any kind were welcome. Music was a universal relaxer whether it was provided by a lone fiddler at a barn dance or an organized group like the Clear Lake, Dakota Territory, band below. (State Historical Society of North Dakota)

were generally warmer in winter and cooler in summer — but for a neat housekeeper, they were a constant aggravation. Bits of dirt and straw kept falling from the walls and ceiling. It was especially bad when the dwelling was built against an embankment so that animals — domestic and wild — could walk on the roof and jar down more trash, sometimes right in the supper dishes. It was not totally uncommon for a settler's wife to look up and see a cow's leg dangling down into her one-room hovel which she so desperately tried to make into a home.

A few soddies were plastered and whitewashed inside. Others had walls and ceilings covered with cheesecloth or unbleached muslin to catch or deflect the falling particles. Newspapers — filled with claim notices and patent medicine advertising — were sometimes used to hide the earthen walls. Outside, the more esthetic homesteaders trimmed the walls neatly, and a few even tried various types of plaster or stucco finishes. In the spring and summer roof tops might be colorfully adorned with sunflowers and other prairie blossoms growing from the slabs.

Household furnishings were meager and often handmade. A cookstove was vitally important, of course; and gathering fuel to last the winter was a major chore for every family. When wood wasn't available, buffalo chips and twisted prairie grass were used. Special stoves for burning hay were invented, and the Dakota town of Hayti in Hamlin County was presumably named for the process of preparing winter fuel. Crude beds had mattresses filled with straw or cornhusks; and tiny cribs — made of packing cases or steamer trunk boards — were in steady use in most soddies where young wives bore their babies (often with little outside assistance) and, unfortunately, lost many of them to respiratory diseases and other maladies attributable to their dark, dank, poorly ventilated dwellings.

So many facets of frontier living strained the imaginations, physical stamina and mental stability of the prairie newcomers, that it is a wonder that so many of them persisted. Collecting water in rain barrels or hauling it long distances from streams or springs by stoneboat were challenges faced by many families. The preparation and preservation of food supplies were continual problems. Battling mosquitoes, flies, grasshoppers and other pests was a frustrating experience. Finding ways to overcome boredom, to cure illnesses without doctors, to maintain religious faiths without ministers and to keep clean and reasonably presentable with minimal sanitary facilities and caustic, homemade soap were nagging tests of mettle. It was not altogether uncommon for mothers to prepare their own children for burial and for fathers to build the crude wood caskets and dig the graves for tiny sons and daughters.

What kept the homesteaders going, of course, was hope — hope for a better tomorrow, a nicer home, a successful crop and possibly a small luxury like a pipe organ, a new rifle, a doll or coaster wagon for a youngster and maybe a store-bought dress for a wife. When there was so little, of course, each new improvement or trinket — however

Artist-illustrator Harvey Thomas Dunn, who himself was born in a Dakota sod shanty in 1884, depicted homestead life on the prairies in a series of canvases, several of which emphasized the hard life of pioneer women. Before his death, Dunn willed many of his paintings "to the people of South Dakota," and a memorial art center was built in Brookings to house them. (South Dakota State University)

small — assumed greater importance. This spirit of fulfillment is described in the following excerpt from *The Prairie Is My Garden*, a biography of the famed South Dakota artist-illustrator Harvey Dunn:

> . . . by mid-summer [1882] the newlyweds were as settled as they could be in a seven-by-nine-foot hut made of crude lumber and sod spaded from their own land. The shanty was erected not just for their own protection but to fulfill the requirements of the law. In this claustrophobic setting, the indomitable couple spent almost two years. Meanwhile, Tom Dunn broke a few acres of the deep rooted prairie sod with the help of his ox team. To the north of his igloo-like house, he spaded in saplings of cottonwood and box elder, the two species of trees which — like the men who planted them — proved that they could survive the great extremes of Dakota weather. And that's what it was for Tom and Bersha: a survival existence. Somehow the warmth and the beauties and the bird-music of spring helped them withstand

the scorchingly hot winds of summer, just as the blazing colors and weather respite of early autumn fortified them for the rigors of winter.

Almost by frugality alone, they saved enough money to buy a few pieces of lumber, several window panes and some square-edged nails. Alongside the original hut, Tom erected a 12-by-16-foot house with a small attic. To the young pioneers it was a grand mansion when compared with their earlier dwelling. As the winter of 1884 waned, Bersha was content and gigantically pregnant in her new home . . . Before dawn on the morning of March 7, Tom yoked his oxen, secure in the belief that there was plenty of time to drive to DeSmet for supplies before his wife would need him. At the county seat town, he loaded his wagon with provisions and carefully covered them with a buffalo robe, hair side in to protect a special purchase he had made.

Snow began to fall, driven blizzard-like by a brisk March wind. On the morning of the eighth, the storm grew worse, and at the Dunn homestead the sod stable was barely visible from the house as the oxen plodded stoically into the yard. Tom's timing was almost too close. At about ten a.m., still chilled from the wind-whipped ride, he was nervously present for the birth of his first male heir — a robust, squalling little Dakotan who was given the name Harvey Thomas Dunn . . . When he had recovered sufficiently from the drama of his son's arrival, Tom went outside to the wagon and unloaded his special acquisition. Carefully and proudly he carried it into the house and presented it to his 22-year-old wife.

No pioneer woman could have been happier! On the very same day, she had been blessed with a fine man-child — and a brand new sewing machine.

"Home sweet home" for Dakota pioneers was often a clapboard shack, a cottonwood log cabin or merely a hole in the side of a hill. While real estate agents and railroad land promoters circulated glowing accounts of prairie life among prospective settlers in Europe and the eastern United States, those already on the scene faced the reality of a rugged, challenging existence. (South Dakota State Historical Society)

Dakota Indians, who had long traveled afoot, on horseback and with travois, adopted wheeled vehicles as they did other elements of the white culture. With the buffalo gone, nomadic wanderings were reduced to periodic treks to council meetings, ration allotments or religious gatherings. This particular photograph of a Sioux caravan on the trail showed graphically the vast openness of the west-river plains in the late 1800s. (South Dakota State Historical Society)

It has been one of the weaknesses of early recordings of Dakota history that all the emphasis has been placed on the strength and doggedness of the white settlers who withstood the challenges of the prairie weather. It should not be forgotten, however, that other South Dakota pioneers — the Sioux Indians — lived through the same arid summers and harsh winters, protected only by their buffalo-hide tepees and undergoing the same privations, the same physical discomforts and the same familial heartaches. They, too, looked to the future with hope — but their particular hopes were fulfilled less and less as the homesteader prospered more.

Prairie Melting Pot: People, Religions and Cultures

The boom years of 1878 to 1887 brought a continuing admixture of nationalities to Dakota Territory. Those who had arrived earlier and had established themselves successfully wrote back to the Old Country and encouraged friends and relatives to join them. It is interesting to note, of course, that most of the immigrants came from countries in Europe north of the 44th parallel which runs through South Dakota (generally along the route of the modern Interstate 90). In only isolated instances did Spaniards, Italians, Greeks or other Mediterranean area inhabitants migrate to the American interior where variations from their native climate could be considerable.

In general, families coming to southern Dakota tended to homestead in localities where others of the same origin had settled. These groupings were not highly organized (except in such cases as the Hutterites) but developed because of language ties, a desire to preserve Old World customs and, realistically, for the comfort and security of having "something in common" with neighbors in a new land.

Often the different nationalities clustered about places of worship: Poles, Bohemians, Slovenians, Irish and French in Roman Catholic parishes; Scandinavians principally in Lutheran communities; various German-speaking peoples in Mennonite, Evangelical, Congregational, Lutheran or Catholic congregations; and Hollanders around Dutch Reformed and Christian Reformed churches. European traditions were strongly entrenched and continued to persist a century later.

Scandinavians — Norwegians, Swedes, Danes and Finns — constituted the dominant foreign-born element in Dakota. They settled generally in the eastern and southeastern counties of the Territory, though the mining region of the Black Hills attracted some Finnish families. The Scandinavians, though ethnically related, maintained their separate identities, traditions and relationships with particular Lutheran synods. Emigrants from Norway were the most numerous, and in later years South Dakotans of all national origins were to become well acquainted with the popular Norwegian food specialties, *lutefisk* and *lefse* (codfish cured in lye and potato flatbread).

The German-Russians, divided though they were in regard to religion and customs, added to the burgeoning population of German-speaking Dakotans during the 1880s, while emigrants directly from *Deutschland* itself also arrived in greater numbers. The extension of the Chicago, Milwaukee and St. Paul westward from Aberdeen to Eureka coincided with increased German settlement. The expansive grain fields of McPherson, Edmunds and Campbell counties were a strong lure to an agriculturally-minded people, and for a time Eureka was reputed to be one of the largest wheat shipping centers in the world with 20 or more elevators in operation. Bowdle, Ipswich, Leola (rebuilt after being destroyed by a prairie fire in 1889) and other small towns in the area were heavily German in character. The *Die Eureka Post* was one of South Dakota's few foreign language newspapers, and like the *Dakota Freie Presse* at Yankton, was a bond of communication among the Teutonic farmers.

Not to be confused with the Germans were the Dutchmen who also entered Dakota in increasing numbers during the boom years. Small parties of Hollanders homesteaded in various locales along the new railroads, but concentrated settlements were established in

A bill to forbid "persons of color, bond or free" from residing in Dakota Territory passed one house of the first legislature and was narrowly defeated in the other, indicating the Southern sympathies existing in the region at that time. Though the number of blacks in early-day South Dakota was never large, the Ku Klux Klan actually fomented race-hate attitudes in the state for a time. (South Dakota State Historical Society)

Douglas and Charles Mix counties at Platte, New Holland, Harrison (originally New Orange) and Armour. Wooden shoes were made and worn by some of the industrious Dutch farmers who also smoked the traditional long pipes. Close ties were retained with larger colonies of Hollanders in Iowa, especially through the Dutch language newspaper, *De Volksvriend* ("The Peoples' Friend"), published in Orange City.

Bohemians who had located settlements in Yankton and Bon Homme counties almost ten years before the boom, similarly attracted additional countrymen to the swelling Dakota population. Some came westward to escape factory work in eastern cities, while others were beckoned directly from Europe. Tabor, a village established in 1872, was to become the hub of the particular culture in Dakota where the Bohemian *Sokol,* a festival of dancing and gymnastics, was preserved.

In the mid-1880s small Polish communities developed at Grenville in Day County and at Lesterville northwest of Yankton. The Black Hills gold rush was a magnet for numerous Chinese immigrants — possibly as many as a thousand — who congregated in and around Deadwood where they had their traditional "josh house" or temple and a few opium dens. On the streams they meticulously worked the tailings left by less careful miners and usually found as much gold the second time through as the first

Forts Meade, Randall and Wadsworth (Sisseton) were the United States Army's so-called permanent installations within the bounds of South Dakota, although all three ultimately were abandoned or declared inactive by the government. At Fort Randall (below) black troops of the 25th Infantry Regiment were prepared for inspection and parade by white officers, then a standard army procedure. Military service exposed many black soldiers — mostly ex-slaves or their sons — to the plains of South Dakota, but few of them remained or returned following their enlistments. (Yankton Daily Press & Dakotan)

sluicers did. Often victims of prejudice, they ultimately faded out of the region, leaving only slight traces of their short-lived presence. Slovenian miners (plus some Irish and Italians) who came to Lead to work at the Homestake formed a large Roman Catholic congregation which, in turn, resulted in the establishment of South Dakota's second bishopric of that denomination in the Hills city.

The boom years also attracted a few black freedmen to Dakota. In the early 1880s Norval Blair came to Sully County with his six children, all of whom filed claims. Later they were joined by other ex-slaves until there were almost 400 blacks in the vicinity of Onida. Blair became well known as owner of a string of race horses, including "Johnny Bee," reputedly the fastest horse in the state and instigator of many wagers shortly after the turn of the century.

Another small colony from Eufaula, Alabama, settled in the southeastern corner of the Territory, and by 1887 an African Methodist Episcopal church had been erected in Yankton to serve them. Unfortunately, they — like the Indians, Chinese and, to some degree, the Hutterites — were tolerated but not particularly welcomed by the dominant society. In time the pressures of bias, isolation and hard times caused many of them to leave. Commentaries in pioneer newspapers give evidence of degradation which early black Dakotans suffered in the relatively short period after slavery. Ku Klux Klan activities — which continued beyond World War I — added to the very special challenges faced by hopeful settlers of African descent. In South Dakota, as elsewhere, white-sheeted bigots and burning crosses were facts of history — but certainly not commendable ones.

Territorial pioneers from the British Isles included emigrants from England, Wales, Ireland and Scotland who in most cases were not first-generation arrivals. A colony of Welsh homesteaders settled clannishly in Edmunds County after an earlier stop in Wisconsin. In several instances Irish families located near one another in small communities (such as Walshtown in Yankton County), but generally they were laborers rather than farmers so they congregated in the towns along the railroads. On the other hand, the Scotsmen and Englishmen — partly because they did not speak a "foreign" language — did not tend to settle in groups nor did the majority follow agricultural pursuits, becoming interested instead in river shipping, merchandising, banking and other business enterprises. Many of them were affiliated with the Episcopalian (Anglican) church which, in turn, was deeply involved in the Indian mission service.

By 1885 the boom period had passed its peak, although the influx of settlers continued for at least two more years at a gradually diminishing rate. By the end of 1887, however, the best of the public land was gone, and the enthusiasm generated by the early railroad company promotion had worn off.

In 1870 the region which was to become South Dakota had a non-Indian population of less than 12,000. In ten years there were slightly more than 80,000, a figure which was to triple by 1885. As statistical proof of the boom movement's scope, the federal census of 1890 reported the new state's total population to be 348,600, of which 19,848 were Indians.

Boom in the Black Hills: The Phenomenal Homestake

While the homesteading fever raged east of the Missouri River, the Black Hills region was having a growth surge of its own. Despite their isolation beyond the Indian reserve and dependence upon overland transportation to bring supplies in and carry bullion out, the western counties had established themselves solidly and were well past the instabilities of a gold rush district.

An economic development which occurred shortly after the stampede of '76 was the introduction of cattle to the rich grazing lands in the foothills and valleys of the *Paha Sapa*. Herds from Texas and the depleted ranges of Wyoming and Nebraska were brought into the region where the longhorned animals fattened rapidly on the grass which had once supported thousands of buffalo. Not only that, but the free-spending miners provided a profitable market near at hand, thus eliminating the expensive and wasteful shipment to consumers in the East. Mammoth cattle companies — drawing considerable capital from England and Scotland — were involved, but at the same time smaller, individually owned ranches

The Homestake and other mines attracted men of varied national origins, with Slovenian, Welsh, Irish and Italian surnames showing up prominently on work rosters. So-called "Cousin Jacks" from Cornwall, England, also were well represented, and their traditional food delicacy — the Cornish pasty — was as well known in Lead as Norwegian lefse and Bohemian kolaches were in the east-river country. (Public Relations Department, Homestake Mining Company)

The Black Hills region was dependent upon overland freighting until 1885 when the first railroad reached Buffalo Gap from Chadron, Nebraska. Thousands of plodding oxen were used by the transportation companies whose wagons wore rutted trails across the prairies which could still be seen almost a century later. (South Dakota State Historical Society)

began to appear. Off-limits, of course, was the vast expanse of Indian land between the Hills and the Missouri, but with cattle numbers in the area totaling more than three-quarters of a million head, it followed that the Sioux chieftains would be approached again for another land parley.

In the meantime, British investors were becoming deeply involved in another Black Hills enterprise which had national and international implications. Tin — presumably in paying quantities — was discovered in the vicinity of Harney Peak in 1873, and because it was a relatively scarce metal in great demand because of the developing food-canning industry, the potential of the find was seemingly enormous. Huge investments were made in mining and processing facilities (especially at Hill City); great quantities of the ore were assayed at the new Dakota School of Mines in Rapid City and at Cornwall, England, then a major source of the world's tin supply; and international financiers became involved in claim purchases and complex stock manipulations. As promising as it seemed, however, the great "tin dream" faded almost as abruptly as it developed when the economic problems of extracting the ore (which proved less extensive than first believed) were apparently too great to overcome at a profit.

The tin episode was not totally without benefit, however. It rekindled the excitement generated by the earlier gold rush and kept Dakota Territory in general and the Black Hills in particular in the national news. It also was a factor in the acquisition of the first railroad line into the region. In 1885 the Fremont, Elkhorn and Missouri Valley Railroad (which became part of the Chicago and North Western System) extended its track from Valentine, Nebraska, through Chadron to Buffalo Gap, D. T., the terminus being named for the pass in the southern Hills through which herds of bison traveled in their seasonal wanderings. At the celebration marking the railroad's arrival, the ceremonies included the symbolic driving of a tin spike, and within a month a four-and-a-half ton specimen of tin ore was hauled to the Buffalo Gap station where it was loaded on a car for shipment to the East for analysis.

In 1886 the rail line was completed to Rapid City, with an appropriate dedication program taking place on the Fourth of July. From that day on the Black Hills was freed from reliance upon oxen,

Long before steam or gasoline engines reached the Black Hills, horses were used to haul the gold-bearing ore from the depths of the Homestake mines. As the search for gold took the miners deeper and deeper into the earth under the original claims of the Manuel Brothers and others, the Homestake Company found the need to run its own sawmills. These mills cut the support timbers that held the shafts and tunnels which led to the rich ore. (Public Relations Department, Homestake Mining Company)

mules and horses for economic well-being. Unlike eastern Dakota where the railroads had spurred the homesteading boom, in the Hills the first track was laid to take advantage of what had already occurred.

One of the most important developments, of course, was the Homestake Mining Company at Lead where the Manuel brothers had discovered the rich outcropping of ore on April 6, 1876. In the following year the Manuels sold their original claim of less than five acres to George Hearst for $70,000, and on November 5, 1877, the Homestake firm was incorporated in San Francisco. Hearst, who was already a wealthy man following mining successes in California and Nevada, teamed with his principal partners, James B. Haggin and Lloyd Tevis, to acquire adjoining and nearby claims and to begin production on an organized and efficient basis. The legal complications were enormous and the physical problems greater yet. The closest rail connection was then 270 miles away at Sidney, Nebraska, but the massive ore-crushing and refining equipment was hauled in on giant freight wagons, and the Homestake became one of the world's richest gold mine properties of all time.

In 1889, the year South Dakota became a state, the Homestake Mining Company was already an extensive industry which would continue to affect the economy not only by its gold production but through the taxes it paid. In 1891 George Hearst, the principal stockholder, died; and thereafter, his widow — Phoebe Apperson Hearst — assumed a strong role in managing the family fortune and philanthropies. As a result, her influence was widely felt in Lead. (South Dakota State Historical Society)

By the end of its seventy-fifth year, the company had extracted 21,000,000 ounces of gold from more than 76,500,000 tons of ore. Some 6,000 acres of mining claims were added to the first small acquisition from the Manuel brothers, and shafts reaching 5,000 feet into the earth became part of the scientifically engineered operation. In 1949 South Dakota replaced California as the leading gold-producing state. A further item of interest is the "Black Hills gold" jewelry industry which dates back to the original rush. A craftsman by the name of J. B. LeBeau began to manufacture the grapes-and-leaves designs of colored or alloyed gold in Central City in 1876. Others later appropriated the patterns and technique.

A Little Baby

ONE YEAR OLD, THIS IS

South Dakota

Huron says this Baby never will grow any larger; that in twenty years it will be still a little sick baby

"On the Town"

From this she argues that as

HURON IS SICK

The two ought to go together and Huron be the Capital.

Pierre says South Dakota is a Lusty Yearling Baby.

And in twenty years will astonish the world. She has EVERY RESOURCE necessary to make ALL HER PEOPLE RICH. She has the greatest artesian basin in the world, extending from Minnesota to Wyoming and within a short time this country will be covered with artesian wells at the

Expense of the United States Government

FREE TO SETTLERS.

She has the unrivaled agricultural resources east of the Missouri River and

NO POOR SOIL!

The country west of the Missouri River is yet but little understood and has been constantly slandered for a purpose. THERE ARE NO POOR LANDS! IT IS WELL WATERED! It is suitable either for AGRI-CULTURE OR STOCK RAISING! It is covered over its entire area with the richest grass in great variety. Natural hay is abundant and of all crops the hay crop is the most valuable of the United States, and of nearly every state. Running streams, more abundant than any other part of the West, as follows:

Grand River, 200 Miles Long. Moreau River, 300 Miles Long. Cheyenne River, 300 Miles Long. Bad River, 120 Miles Long. White River, 200 Miles Long.

And over 200 creeks, many of them furnishing fine water powers. It will be seen from the above that Western South Dakota is the best watered country in the west. The water is pure and sweet.

Stop and think what this country of 37,000 square miles will be twenty years hence, and sit down on all idiots who tell you that South Dakota has stopped growing. Now add to the above

THE BLACK HILLS COUNTRY

THE MARVEL OF THE UNITED STATES

BOOK SIX

THE CHALLENGE OF STATEHOOD

*The people of Dakota have carved
the new state out of the wilds
of the prairie ... at a touch
of the magical wand of progress.*

— *Arthur C. Mellette
Territorial Governor
1885*

The rapidity with which Dakota Territory went from a sparsely populated prairie wilderness to a well settled, highly productive land of promise was a unique historical achievement. So much occurred in a few short years that "growing pains" were understandable. The vibrant young people who claimed homesteads, searched for gold in the streams or established businesses in railroad towns before the track-layers had finished driving their spikes were in a hurry to build and prosper. As a result, mistakes were made and the seeds of future problems planted, but the contagion of the boom fever was a disease no one feared nor cared to check.

Despite restrictions of travel and transport, controversial Indian treaties, natural calamities, the ineptitudes of some territorial appointees, political confrontations such as the capital removal, the head-over-heels rush for public land and a sizable quantity of greed thrown in for good measure, the Territory developed with a surprisingly solid foundation. Because so much happened concurrently during the first 30 years, it is difficult to relate the main thread of the story without complicating it with side issues and the interesting but endless local and personal events and accomplishments. The quick rise and fall of hopeful towns missed by the railroads; the rousing — and sometimes bitter — fights for county seats; the individual survival tales of thousands of pioneers, so much alike and yet all different; the successes and failures of businesses, churches, schools, clubs, lodges, lawmen and firefighters; the lengthy oratory and complexities of frontier politics — all were intimately part of the larger epic which unfolded so quickly and dramatically on the "ocean of grass."

It is probable that many of those involved in the Great Dakota Boom thought that the bubble would never burst. Nature had cooperated admirably to assure ample crops for several successive years; and the mines, mills, railroads and general construction provided

An intense interest was shown in education at all levels as the frontier receded in territorial Dakota. Among the numerous schools established was the Wessington Springs Academy (later Wessington Springs Junior College), founded by the Free Methodist Church in 1887. Twice — in 1908 and 1918 — the school's administration building burned, but on each occasion the loss was restored by dedicated supporters. In 1964 the institution became a private four-year high school. (South Dakota State Historical Society)

regular or part-time jobs for all who cared to work. In southern Dakota factories of various kinds sprang up during the exuberant 1880s; a meat-packing plant at Oelrichs, an oatmeal mill in Parker, the seven-story Queen Bee flour mill in Sioux Falls, a tow mill at Scotland to process flax straw into usable fiber, a linseed oil plant at Groton, a woolen mill at Yankton and a paint factory at Watertown were all examples of industrial development. Creameries, cigar factories, slaughter houses, soap and cornstarch plants, brick kilns, saw mills, canneries, quarries and breweries added to the excitement of the homestead binge which brought more than a quarter of a million people to the south half of the Territory in just ten years.

A new challenge — a political one affecting the future government of their ebullient land — faced the farmers and townsfolk of Dakota. Should they remain a territory subject to the whims of Congress and each new presidential administration, or should they strive for statehood which would permit greater control of their own destiny?

An Ordway Veto: Southern Dakotans Unite

The issue of admission to the federal union was not a simple, clearcut matter to be resolved by a quick vote or stroke of a pen. The idea of statehood "some day" was as old as the Territory itself, but even when the population grew sufficiently to support a change of status, not everyone favored the concept nor did many of the later immigrants understand the difference.

If statehood were to be pursued, a basic decision first had to be made: Should there be one state or more? As early as 1874 a move had been made to divide Dakota and organize the northern half as

The Big Sioux River provided water for various industries at Sioux Falls such as the Cascade and Queen Bee mills. In the exuberance of pioneer development, many other small factories were started in the various towns, but the limitations of population and rapidly changing demands of consumers caused a high percentage of failures during the state's formative years. (W. H. Over Museum)

General William Henry Harrison Beadle played an important role in South Dakota history, especially in the preservation of school lands. He served as president of Eastern Normal College at Madison which for a time was also known as General Beadle State Teachers College. Beadle County was also named for him. (South Dakota State Historical Society)

the Territory of Pembina. Three years later (after the gold rush) the plan for an east-west split was proposed, with the western sector becoming the Territory of Lincoln. In 1878 Governor Howard suggested the possibility of creating three states on the basis that the north, south and Hills sectors were widely separated, had diverse economies and were tied by the railroads to different outside markets. None of these proposals gained serious support, but they did give indication of a trend in sentiment for division.

On Thanksgiving Day, 1879, a private informal meeting took place in Yankton at the home of Congregational minister Reverend Stewart Sheldon. On hand — among others — were Reverend Joseph Ward (Sheldon's brother-in-law who was to establish Yankton College two years later), Governor Howard, Territorial Attorney General Hugh J. Campbell, Chief Justice Alonzo J. Edgerton and General William Henry Harrison Beadle, territorial superintendent of schools. A lengthy discussion of the statehood question followed and from it emerged a small clique of division proponents who singly and collectively became deeply involved in the events, the arguments and the political contentions which occurred during the next ten years.

Beadle was interested because he had a plan under statehood to preserve the value of school lands (sections 16 and 36 in every township). Reverend Ward was an advocate of prohibition and, at that time, thought it should be included in any new constitution. Campbell, a dynamic orator, wanted to be one of southern Dakota's first United States senators. Governor Howard (who was to die in office enroute to Washington, D.C., the following spring) and Judge Edgerton were, like other Republican leaders, partial to the idea of two states being formed because their party held a strong edge among the voters of the Territory.

While the Yankton meeting cannot be credited with the birthing of the statehood movement entirely, it did stir the participants to action in behalf of the cause, and gradually interest blossomed in various parts of Dakota south of the 46th parallel. It must be borne in mind that the homestead boom was just getting underway which meant that few of the new settlers flocking to the region were remotely aware of the issue. The idea of statehood was fostered primarily by territorial "old-timers" rather than late-comers whose first concerns were providing roofs, planting crops and proving up. A Citizens' League was formed, and in June of 1882 a constitutional meeting was held in Canton to consider the proper course for a campaign which had not yet caught fire.

When the territorial legislature convened in January of 1883, however, the assembly passed a bill authorizing the southern counties to hold a constitutional convention as a prelude to statehood. Governor Ordway pocket-vetoed the measure, and that action — coupled with the capital removal fiasco — provided the necessary spark to enflame the lagging effort.

Within two decades after the territory was created, there was a headlong rush to establish schools and colleges, both denominational and public. In Sioux Falls the Baptists opened the doors of Dakota Collegiate Institute in 1883 (later to be renamed Sioux Falls College). Lutheran Normal, which became Augustana College, was founded in the same city six years later. (W. H. Over Museum)

On June 19, less than three weeks after the capital had been awarded to Bismarck, 188 delegates from southern Dakota gathered in Huron where the governor was loudly villified; and, because he [Ordway] was against dividing the Territory — after the control had moved northward — the convention presented a solid front for separation. Congressional Delegate Pettigrew, violently anti-Ordway, joined the movement, as did Father Robert Haire, a Catholic priest who had built a sod church near Columbia in Brown County and was espousing social reform. With or without official approval, the statehood drive was underway and the next stop would be to draft a constitution and convince a skeptical Congress that South Dakota was ready to join the galaxy of stars in the national flag.

The Sioux Falls Constitution: Cart Before the Horse

Sioux Falls, in the fall of 1883, was beginning its gradual ascendancy to its ultimate position as southern Dakota's foremost city. In its developing years it had suffered several reversals — evacuation because of the Indian scare of 1862, a population exodus as a result of the grasshopper plague in the mid-'70s and finally the destruction caused by the flood of 1881 — but always it had bounced back. In a way, Sioux Falls had grown quietly and without excessive fanfare. Most of the dramatic events and political activities of the Territory had centered primarily at Yankton, Fort Pierre, Bismarck and Deadwood, and all three railroads which were pushed westward to spur the homestead frenzy had bypassed the Minnehaha County seat.

Nonetheless, Sioux Falls — under dynamic leadership of men like Richard Pettigrew and E. A. Sherman — had attracted new citizens and was prospering. Typical of the city's seemingly casual approach to growth was the welcome given the arrival of the first railroad described in the *Pantagraph* of July 31, 1878:

> Without any gush or hurrah, Sioux Falls last evening received a visit from a locomotive, the track having been laid during the day to a point between the two mills. The first warning of the presence of the long-looked for engine was a couple of toots from its whistle — the first sound ever made by a steam whistle in Sioux Falls . . . Almost any other community under the sun would enthuse over such a piece of fortune as has finally reached us; but our people are very matter of fact, and it is glory enough for them to know that the road has got here.

Other rail connections were to follow and with them came the development of a quarrying industry to utilize the native pink quartzite (Sioux Falls granite) underlying much of the original townsite. By 1882 the territorial penitentiary was ready to receive Dakota prisoners who previously had been held in the Detroit, Michigan, detention center. The School for the Deaf, started as a private enterprise, had been accepted by the legislature for support in 1881, and two years later Sioux Falls College (then known as the Dakota Collegiate Institute) was established under the sponsorship of the Baptist Church. The falls of the Big Sioux River (which Doctor F. V. Hayden had described in 1866 as "the most valuable water power I have ever seen in the West") had been harnessed for just that purpose by the Queen Bee flour mill and other enterprises, and the city in general was enjoying a boom quite apart from the homesteading activity elsewhere in the Territory.

On September 4, 1883, 125 delegates — unauthorized because of Ordway's veto — gathered in Germania Hall in Sioux Falls to draft a constitution for the yet unborn state of South Dakota. In some respects it was a repeat of the premature "squatter government" attempt to secure territorial status 25 years earlier at the same location. The average age of the delegates was 35, and many of them had been in the Territory ten years or more. They included 42 lawyers, 31 farmers, 13 newspapermen, 11 land agents and 28 from other professions and occupations. Only 17 were foreign born which indicated an "old guard" composition.

Arthur Calvin Mellette, an attorney who had come to Dakota as a federal land official, was elected temporary chairman until he was succeeded on the second day by Bartlett Tripp of Yankton as president of the convention. This was significant because Tripp was a prominent Democrat, and his election emphasized the singleness of purpose of the conclave which was predominantly Republican. The pugnacious Hugh Campbell played a prominent role during the 15 days of deliberations which followed. He continued to advocate his philosophy that southern Dakota could, in effect, secede from the Territory and proclaim statehood without congressional action. This "we are a state" concept, as it came to be known, was later to be a detriment to the campaign because of its rebellious tone and negative effects on certain members of Congress.

The first Sioux Falls constitutional convention cannot be disregarded because out of it came a lengthy document which, with minor changes, was to become the basic law of South Dakota when statehood was finally granted. Doctor Ward had withdrawn his insistence on a prohibition clause to avoid a major conflict which might result in the defeat of the constitution over that issue alone. (His judgment may well have been correct because the saloonkeepers and brewers were already mounting a strong lobbying force.) General Beadle succeeded in gaining acceptance for a provision which would prohibit sale of school land for less than ten dollars an acre (a relatively high price at that time).

Women's suffrage was discussed by the all-male group which agreed that qualified female electors should be able to vote in elections held solely for school purposes but they could hold any office in the state not specifically denied them by the constitution. (Despite the latter phrase, all state officials mentioned in the document were referred to by masculine pronouns.) Further proof that the rights of women were not yet ready to be taken with complete seriousness were the bursts of laughter which punctuated discussions on that issue, even when delegate Gideon C. Moody of Lawrence County proclaimed:

> I favor woman suffrage . . . Give woman the ballot, let her hold office, and you raise her at once in intelligence. I know of no reason why my wife and daughter are not as able to hold office as I am, though they may not be as willing.

Had there been women present, they undoubtedly would have been outraged by the reaction — but the political arena was still an exclusive male domain.

Statehood Rejected: A Second Convention

The Sioux Falls constitution was submitted to a vote of the people of southern Dakota and approved 12,336 votes to 6,814. The results were gratifying to the statehood proponents, except for one weakness: there were at least 30,000 citizens who failed to cast ballots, and six counties didn't even submit returns. As might be expected, when the Dakota representatives presented their petition to Congress, the apparent lack of enthusiasm on the part of the electorate was used as a negative argument against admission as was the unofficial nature of the constitutional convention itself.

There was opposition from the Territory, too. Governor Ordway used what residual power he had against the move, and so did other northern Dakotans who favored a single state with Bismarck as the seat of government. In Brown County the vote had gone against the constitution ostensibly because there was hope that with one large state, Aberdeen might be able to secure the capital because of its central location. Another factor was a growing enmity against the railroads by farmers who insisted they were being overcharged and coerced in the shipping of agricultural commodities because of the monopoly control and political power of the transportation companies. It was insinuated that the new constitution was pro-railroad because it did not contain specific provisions for limiting them.

Despite the anti-division sentiments in the Territory itself, Senator Benjamin Harrison of Indiana (who had helped get his friend

Pink quartzite, popularly known as Sioux Falls granite, was used widely for building stone and paving blocks in many South Dakota towns and cities. The Rowena quarry, photographed in 1890, was one of several such operations centered largely in Minnehaha County. Stonecutters came from England and Scotland to find employment in the industry which flourished into the first decade of the new century. (W. H. Over Museum)

Arthur Mellette the territorial land office job) introduced a statehood bill which passed favorably in the Senate. Unfortunately, the House failed to act on the measure, and the first effort of the southern Dakotans was frustrated.

The rejection did not dampen the hopes of the separation forces, however. To overcome a major defect of their original move, they went to the territorial legislature early in 1885 and secured passage of another constitutional convention bill and this time the act was signed into law by Governor Gilbert A. Pierce, the Chicago newspaperman who had been named to succeed the much-maligned Ordway.

Again the delegates met in Germania Hall in Sioux Falls, convening on September 8, 1885, and selecting Judge Edgerton as president. This time the body stayed in session for 17 days, mostly satisfying themselves that the constitution of '83 had been thoughtfully drawn and was still valid. The prohibition clause was again kept out of the document, but was to be submitted separately to a vote of the people. Certain constraints were placed on the railroads, but no changes were made relative to women's suffrage despite a fervent letter to the convention from Marietta M. Bones of Webster, an officer of the National Woman Suffrage Association, which included:

> In your wise deliberations let me implore you in behalf of your sister, mother or wife, to place the women of our glorious territory on an equality before the law with yourselves . . . Give us equality, not to make us manly, but more womanly . . . as a pecuniary interest to Dakota, what can your convention do more than to make the grandest state in the Union for women? Then will they emigrate here by thousands, to a land where they are not taxed without a voice . . . [and] giving to our marriageable men wives that are free instead of slaves.

Of considerable importance was the change of the proposed state's northern boundary to the 7th standard parallel which had been used for surveying county lines and was approximately four miles south of the 46th degree of north latitude which had been adopted in the constitution of '83.

The final document was endorsed by unanimous vote which, according to Kingsbury, "was followed by loud and long continued applause." Eighty-nine delegates signed the product of their labors which was to be submitted to a vote of the people of the affected region on November 3. In the interim before the election, the Republican Party held a convention of its own to offer a slate of candidates for the offices specified in the second Sioux Falls constitution. The Democrats declined to participate. Also involved was a campaign for a temporary capital of the state in which Huron, Pierre, Chamberlain, Alexandria, Redfield, Watertown and Sioux Falls were contenders.

Once again a relatively small vote was cast, but the constitution was approved 25,138 to 6,527; prohibition won a slight majority 15,552 to 15,218; Huron was chosen temporary seat of the nonexistent state with 12,695 votes to Pierre's second-place total of 10,574; and Arthur Mellette was elected governor without opposition.

Senator Benjamin Harrison repeated his favor to the southern Dakotas and his friend Mellette by sponsoring a second bill for division and statehood which also was passed by the Senate. Again the Democratically-controlled House of Representatives killed the measure. What followed was a lengthy period of heated debates, alternate proposals and political foot-dragging. President Grover Cleveland, who listened courteously for an hour to the representatives of the "State of Dakota" as they presented their case for admission, thereafter named Louis Kossuth Church to be Dakota Territory's first and only Democrat governor — and Church was opposed to division. Senator Harrison finally spelled out the political realities of the situation in a statement made late in 1887:

> I don't think there is any prospect for the admission of any of the territories before the presidential election of 1888 . . . the democrats in the House are determined to control the Government at any cost, and they will not consent to the admission of any new territory which might by any probability cast its electoral vote for the republican ticket.

The senator's remarks were prophetic, and when he himself was elected 23rd President of the United States — with Republican control in both houses of Congress — the long drawn-out struggle came to a hasty close. Before President Cleveland left office, an Omnibus Bill to admit Washington, Montana, North Dakota and South Dakota to the federal union was hurriedly prepared. One-state backers in Dakota Territory quickly changed their tune and fell in line with the new political development, and earlier congressional opponents of the Sioux Falls constitutional government were suddenly neutralized or switched their position. On February 20, 1889, the Omnibus Bill was finally passed, and President Cleveland signed it two days later with a quill pen made from the feather of an eagle killed in Dakota Territory which after 28 years of turbulent existence was soon to pass into history.

The Blizzard of '88: A Tragic Interruption

While the quest for statehood was reaching final stages in the halls of Congress and the meeting places of the persistent southern Dakotans, the forces of nature — over which no political party had control — were delivering two fateful blows to the people who were trying to wrest a livelihood from the stubborn prairie land.

The first occurred in the winter of 1886-87 when severe storms struck the western region and took a heavy toll of cattle on the open ranges. Many of the animals from warmer southern climates were unable to withstand the subzero temperatures and perished. Losses were so heavy that the huge companies involved in the so-called "bonanza ranching" were forced to reduce operations or quit. The ultimate result of the disaster was a different approach to cattle raising, with emphasis on permanent ranch units, winter feeding and hay production.

The second calamity struck on Thursday, the 12th of January, 1888. The particular day dawned balmy and pleasant despite the midwinter date; children had trudged off to rural schools; farmers had driven to market or were away from home doing seasonal chores. Suddenly the mild southeast breezes brought a shower of rain, and then without warning, the wind switched to the northwest, the temperatures plummeted and the rain turned to sleet and granular snow. For more than a dozen hours the blizzard raged across the Territory. Men were trapped in the fields; livestock wandered aimlessly until they became stranded in drifts to freeze; but saddest of all, many youngsters were released by their teachers when the weather began to change and before they could get home, they were engulfed by the storm. In southern Dakota the gale gusted to more than 60 miles an hour and the mercury dropped to 20 degrees below zero or more.

Just as suddenly as it appeared, though, the "children's blizzard" passed out of the region. On Friday the 13th, survivors emerged from their places of safety to search for those who were not so lucky. When the gruesome figures were tallied, it was revealed that the storm had left at least 112 dead in the southern half of the Territory, with Bon Homme County losing 19, Beadle 18 and Hutchinson 15. There was no way to determine how many others died later as a result of complications from exposure and freezing or how many amputations frontier doctors had to perform. In later years the tales of tragedy and heroism related to the infamous blizzard of '88 were recounted by territorial pioneers as stark examples of the harsh challenges faced on the Dakota prairie.

South Dakota: Under God the People Rule

Passage of the Omnibus Bill did not make South Dakota a state. The act required a third constitutional convention which was held in Sioux Falls beginning appropriately on the Fourth of July. Though they remained in session more than a month, the delegates did not accept any amendments to the constitution of 1885 other than to make it conform to the federal law; no one wanted to rock the boat with the end so near. A commission settled financial matters between the northern and southern sectors of the Territory, requiring the southern counties to pay $42,000 because they had received greater appropriations for institutions. By a vote of 72 to 0 the constitution was approved for submission to the people, and 200,000 copies were ordered printed, to include 20,000 in German, 20,000 in Norwegian and 10,000 in Russian.

After that, both major political parties held conventions to select candidates for all state offices, and on October 1 the people were called to the polls. The constitution was accepted resoundingly, and the special prohibition amendment received a majority of 5,724. After a spirited campaign Pierre was chosen as the temporary capital, and the full slate of Republican candidates elected. Arthur Mellette, whom President Harrison had named territorial governor within a week after his inauguration, was further honored by being selected as first chief executive of the new state. There was still more preliminary work to be done, however.

At that time the federal constitution provided for the election of United States senators by state legislatures, and so the newly elected representatives had to hurry to Pierre to accomplish that important task. The temporary capital city was not ready for the sudden influx of more than a thousand politicans and their friends, but the challenge was met and the state senators convened in the Presbyterian church and the representatives in the county courthouse. In the senate there were 41 Republicans, three Democrats and one Independent Republican; the house was made up of 111 Republicans, nine Democrats and one Independent Republican. There was, of course, little doubt which party would control the selection of the two important national officers.

When the oratory and balloting were completed, South Dakota's first United States senators were lawyers Gideon C. Moody of Deadwood, Civil War hero and member of the New York colony which migrated to Dakota in 1864, and Richard F. Pettigrew, a 41-year-old native of Vermont who came to the Territory with a surveying crew, staked a land claim near Sioux Falls and became an energetic leader of that growing city. With that decision made, the final act to accomplish statehood rested with President Harrison.

On November 2, 1889, the Chief Executive signed the proclamation which created North and South Dakota as the 39th and 40th

Because of its central location, Pierre enjoyed an advantage over other towns seeking the state capital. Competition was keen, however, and the choice had to be defended on several occasions at the ballot box and in the legislature. The Hughes County courthouse dominated the scene in 1890 before any state buildings were erected. (South Dakota State Historical Society)

states of the Union. In doing so, the President shuffled the documents under a covering paper and signed them in such a way that no one would ever know what state preceded the other into the national federation. "They were born together — they are one and I will make them twins," Harrison said. Consequently, it is only by alphabetical order that North Dakota is generally accorded the lower number.

The *Yankton Daily Press & Dakotan* carried a single-sentence telegraphic report of President Harrison's action in its edition of November 2, but a series of one-column headlines proclaimed:

WE ARE A STATE
The Proclamation Issued For
South and North Dakota

Two New Stars Shining from the
Firmament of the Union

Ring the Bells and Shoot the
Cannon — E Pluribus Unum

A Brief Announcement of the
Glorious News, But it
is Enough

South Dakotans greeted the news with less excitement than they did most Fourth of July celebrations, probably because the happening was almost anti-climactic after the earlier passage of the Omnibus Bill. Of the leaders in the statehood movement, Mellette became governor, Pettigrew and Moody senators and Edgerton judge of the circuit court. General Beadle was named president of the State Normal School at Madison. Hugh Campbell, angry and belligerent on most occasions, was removed as territorial attorney general when he was brought to trial for neglecting his duties and other charges growing out of his personal attacks on Governor Ordway. He was acquited finally, but his hopes for a senatorship were never realized. Reverend Joseph Ward, the pioneer churchman from Yankton whose influence was felt in government, education and business circles, did not have the privilege of participating in the development of the state he helped to create. On November 11, nine days after President Harrison had signed the admission proclamation, he died of a carbuncle infection at the age of 51. Among his other contributions, he left a five-word living memorial which expressed his personal beliefs and became South Dakota's official motto: "Under God the People Rule."

State of Frustration: A Troubled Beginning

While South Dakota's political leaders were intensely involved in the birthing of a new commonwealth, the homesteaders — who had come to the region so eagerly with high hopes and low capital reserves — were facing a struggle of their own. The boom years had also been good crop years, and then, in the summer of 1889, the cycle changed abruptly. A searing drouth struck the area and destroyed the harvest, especially in the central and northern counties where so many new settlers were vitally dependent upon their wheat yields.

Hundreds of young families, with no credit and no money, packed their meager possessions and headed back east. Mortgaged homesteads were left to banks and other lending agencies, some of which promptly failed because they needed interest money more than deeds to land nobody wanted. Governor Mellette personally visited destitute families to learn their situation firsthand. After a tour of Miner County — one of the worst hit — he appealed to the state's citizens for food, coal, clothing and shoes for the suffering farmers trying to hold on. Many churches, organizations and private individuals throughout South Dakota contributed to the relief fund, with the Farmers' Alliance being particularly active.

Any excuse for a parade or party was welcomed by pioneer South Dakotans, with Fourth of July being a special gala event in all communities. This gathering in Madison featured a band with a banner reading "Huron for Capital." A street corner sign also invited celebrants to a baseball game, a popular Dakota pastime even before statehood. (W. H. Over Museum)

Later the governor traveled to Chicago and other eastern cities to seek help, and though this effort was gratefully appreciated by those in need, it was strongly criticized by businessmen in the towns and cities not yet hurt by the crop failure who believed the problem could be solved at home. The land boomers in particular wanted to minimize the effect of the disaster, and Governor Mellette was subjected to "shameful abuse" (in the words of historian Doane Robinson) for carrying the negative message out-of-state. The chief executive was undaunted by the selfish detractors, however, and reportedly donated several thousand dollars of his own money to pay administrative costs of the relief fund he raised.

There was absolutely no way to hide the calamity, of course. The fleeing families carried their stories of the parched earth with them, and South Dakota's image as a bountiful land suffered accordingly. It was a morale-shaking, unpreventable reality which got the infant state off to a shaky, troubled start.

The first state capitol building in Pierre was a large frame structure with little charm or architectural imagination. The box-like legislative hall served the purpose, however, especially since other cities were not yet ready to agree that a final choice had been made so that an investment in a more elaborate edifice could be justified. (South Dakota State Historical Society)

A Permanent Capital: Victory for Pierre

During the territorial period, intense rivalries developed between various towns over the location of county seats. In one case, two companies of militia were ordered to Redfield in 1884 after eager citizens of that town had seized the government records from (Old) Ashton and were about to be attacked by an armed and angry mob trying to get them back. This so-called "Spink County War" typified the importance placed on possession of the courthouse.

Similar fights took place between Travare and Wilmot in Roberts County (with Sisseton later winning the prize); between Estelline (originally Spalding) and Castlewood in Hamlin County before Hayti became the final choice; Forest City and Gettysburg in Potter; Onida and Clifton in Sully; and Big Stone City and Milbank in Grant. There were others, too, but though they were temper-raising affairs locally, they did not have the significance of Bismarck's dethroning of Yankton or the Pierre-Huron battle for the permanent state capital.

Twice in pre-admission elections Huron had been named the seat of government; then in the balloting following the Omnibus Bill, Pierre had emerged the winner. In November of 1890 a fourth vote was ordered, presumably to make the decision final. The Missouri River city had the advantage of its selection as temporary capital and had proved its interest by building a large hotel (the Locke) in 90 days — just in time for Governor Mellette's inauguration. Huron, however, had no intention of forfeiting the honor it had long sought, and so a heated campaign got underway.

Both cities indebted themselves heavily to pay for the advertising, political chicanery and vote-buying which followed. (It took Pierre more than 30 years to pay off its obligations which, with principal and interest, amounted to almost half a million dollars.) Watertown had intended to enter the race, but withdrew in favor of Huron, undoubtedly with proper persuasion. Pierre used the boomer approach, promoting its location as gateway to the Great Indian Reserve between the Cheyenne and White Rivers which Congress had opened to settlement the previous February. One of its promotion posters proclaimed:

> Pierre says South Dakota is a Lusty Yearling Baby and in twenty years will astonish the world. She has every resource necessary to make all her people rich. She has the greatest artesian basin in the world, extending from Minnesota to Wyoming, and within a short time this country will be covered with artesian wells at the expense of the United States Government free to settlers. She has unrivaled agricultural resources east of the Missouri River and NO POOR SOIL.

The extravagant advertisement urged readers to "sit down on all idiots who tell you that South Dakota has stopped growing." Overlooked, of course, was the drouth-forced exodus already in progress; but in the end, Pierre's optimistic spirit — and more realistically, the city's location in the geographic center of the state — resulted in a relatively easy victory for the Hughes County rivertown, 41,969 votes to 34,610. In the same election Governor Mellette — who was thinking more of the plight of the homesteaders already

The Deadwood Central Railroad was a narrow-gauge line operating in the Lead-Deadwood mining region. The first steam train ran in 1888, but later electric trolleys were installed to provide interurban passenger service on the same trackage. In 1889 high water in Gold Run Creek created a roller-coaster effect on the roadbed. (South Dakota State Historical Society)

on the scene than of those yet to come — was returned to office, but the overall Republican strength showed considerable erosion due to the growing appeal of the populist movement spurred by the Farmers' Alliance against railroads, financial institutions and big business in general.

One thing was certain: as the baptismal year of statehood drew to a close, South Dakota was already facing its first crisis.

———————————

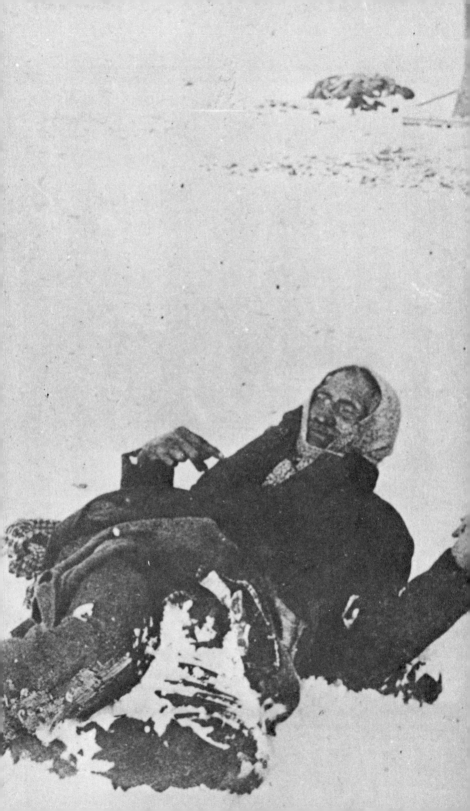

BOOK SEVEN

THE CHALLENGE OF WOUNDED KNEE

*Greed and avarice . . . in other
words, the almighty dollar, is
at the bottom of nine-tenths of
all our Indian troubles.*
— *General George Crook*

In the 14 years following the Custer defeat in Montana and the opening of the Black Hills, the Dakota Indians were subjected to an erratic system of dole and control which was characterized by an enormous ignorance of the native people, their beliefs, their traditions, their nomadic lifestyle and even their capacity to comprehend what the white man called "civilization." Though President Grant's "peace policy" had some merit for its attempt to take Indian affairs out of the hands of politicians and military officers, the emphasis was placed on Christianizing and industrializing the tribespeople with little thought apparently given to the depth or the values of the Indian culture itself.

Under the peace system, the various tribes throughout the nation were assigned to specific religious denominations which were to recommend the agents to be chosen and to play a direct role in educating the Indians to take their places ultimately in the white society. In southern Dakota all Sioux agencies were placed under the jurisdiction of the Episcopal Church, except that of the Sissetons, which became the responsibility of the American Board of Commissioners for Foreign Missions (a joint Congregational and Presbyterian organization), and Standing Rock or Grand River under Roman Catholic authority.

The allocation of tribes to particular sects did not bar other missionaries from ministering to the Dakota bands, but it did create further bewilderment among the Indians who — in addition to their other adjustments — had to cope with the revelation that Christianity came in different forms. Though the church representatives generally were sincere in their efforts to "help" their assigned wards, they exhibited varying degrees of intelligence, ability and zeal — and, in fact, competed for the souls of the Sioux who were referred to by some as "heathens," "pagans" and "savages."

Among the dedicated missionaries were Presbyterians Stephen Return Riggs and Thomas S. Williamson, who translated the Bible into the previously unwritten language of the Dakotas. Williamson had one son and Riggs had two, who — like their fathers — were ordained and worked among the tribes under the auspices of the Presbyterian-Congregational arrangement. Assisting Reverend Thomas

Chief Big Foot as he was found frozen in the snow where he fell during the Wounded Knee Massacre. (South Dakota State Historical Society)

L. Riggs (founder of the historic Oahe Mission) was Mary Clementine Collins, a 29-year-old volunteer who later became a medical doctor and Congregational minister.

Bishop William Hobart Hare, the leading Episcopalian missionary, arrived at Yankton in 1873 a few days after the April storm in which General Custer and his Seventh Cavalry had been trapped. Thereafter the 38-year-old clergyman began a career of service on the frontier which earned for him the title: "Apostle of the West." Hare's Catholic counterpart was Abbot Martin Marty, who came to Dakota three years later and became known among the Sioux as the "Lean Chief." He was consecrated a bishop in 1880 and established the first Catholic diocese with his official residence at Yankton. Later, when South Dakota became a state, he transferred the see to Sioux Falls. These and other priests, ministers and lay people faced the difficult task of trying to accomplish what guns and sabers had failed to do.

Under the "peace policy" of President Grant, the various Indian agencies were assigned to specific religious denominations, though missionaries of different sects were not barred from preaching their particular brand of Christianity on any of the reservations. Presbyterians and Congregationalists operated jointly under the American Board of Commissioners for Foreign Missions, and among their activities was the Congregational Mission at Greenwood serving the Yankton Indians. (W. H. Over Museum)

Return of Sitting Bull: No Boom for the Tribes

While the white Dakotans were caught up in the excitement of the homesteading rush, the red Dakotans were undergoing a difficult period of transition to a new way of life. After the victory at the Little Big Horn, the old patterns of casual wandering were forever gone. There were no buffalo to pursue, and the non-agency bands became fugitive nomads, short of food and constantly seeking to avoid the relentless army patrols.

Chalkstone from deposits along the Missouri River was used for permanent construction before brick kilns began to fill building needs. Soft enough to be sawed, the yellow-white limestone was sufficiently durable to provide substantial structures like the Episcopal Mission at the Greenwood Agency. (Yankton Daily Press & Dakotan)

In 1877 Spotted Tail, the perceptive Brule chieftain, helped persuade Crazy Horse — almost 20 years his junior — to give up the futile roaming and submit to governmental control. The young Oglala leader, then in his mid-thirties, agreed to bring his people in, but when he himself tried to leave the agency, he was arrested and returned to Fort Robinson. While he was being led to a guardhouse at the northwestern Nebraska post, his aversion to detention was so great that he resisted his guards and was promptly bayoneted. He died that same night — September 5 — an uncompromising warrior to the very end.

Spotted Tail, meanwhile, attempted to lead his people along a conforming course which would benefit them while not destroying their dignity. He even sent several of his own children to the new school for Indians at Carlisle, Pennsylvania, though he later became dissatisfied and had them brought home. On August 5, 1881, the Brule chief was shot and killed by a fellow tribesman, Crow Dog, while he was riding away from a council meeting at the Rosebud Agency. The true motive for the murder has continued to be a point of argument. Was it an internal tribal struggle for power? Was it the result of a quarrel over a woman? Or was it a government conspiracy to eliminate a strong figurehead to further disorganize the Indians?

Regardless of why it came about, Spotted Tail's assassination was just one more disturbing episode to add to the general confusion. Crow Dog was convicted of murder in a Deadwood trial and sentenced to be hanged; after a lengthy appeal he was granted his freedom by the United States Supreme Court on jurisdictional grounds and

Chief Spotted Tail, a Brule Teton, was an influential leader who faced difficult decisions trying to find solutions which would permit his people to live in dignity while adapting to conditions imposed by the dominant whites. In his willingness to attempt the melding of cultures, he sent four of his sons to the Carlisle Indian School in Pennsylvania. He withdrew them later, however, when they were baptized and given Christian names without his permission. (South Dakota State Historical Society)

the additional fact that his family had settled with Spotted Tail's people in the time-honored Indian custom for absolving such crimes.

In the month prior to the tragic incident on the trail at Rosebud, Sitting Bull, the unyielding Hunkpapa leader, rode into Fort Buford from Canada with all that remained of his hungry and ill-clad followers. The Canadian government had not been as generous to him as he had hoped; after all, he was an American Indian and not one of theirs. Several years earlier Father Marty had traveled north of the border to urge his surrender for the good of his people. Later a commission headed by General Alfred Terry (the same man who in 1876 had overall command of the army force which included

Dejected but unyielding, Sitting Bull (Tatanka Yotanka) was detained in custody after his return from Canada in 1881. He was taken to Fort Randall with a small party of relatives and faithful followers as a precaution against emotional uprisings which might be incited by his presence. The unidentified white woman pictured with him and members of his family was apparently the wife of a military officer. (South Dakota State Historical Society)

Sitting Bull received nationwide attention when he traveled with Buffalo Bill Cody's Wild West Show following his release by federal authorities. The taciturn Hunkpapa medicine man obviously was exploited, and he accepted gratuities for autographs and camera poses with customary aloofness. Still rejecting conformity to the white man's world, he returned to the Standing Rock Reservation where he was killed at his cabin on the Grand River just prior to the massacre at Wounded Knee. (Smithsonian Institution, Bureau of American Ethnology)

Custer's ill-fated regiment) received permission to visit the Hunkpapa rebel and offer him amnesty if he would return to the Standing Rock agency. Gall, who had fled northward with Sitting Bull, had relented earlier in the spring after his band suffered severely through a harsh Canadian winter. Gradually the roundup of all the recalcitrant Tetons was coming to a close and, at long last, it seemed that the conflict between Indians and whites could be resolved by the peaceful assimilation of the former into the latter's world.

Though his power had apparently waned, Sitting Bull was one of those rare personalities whose mere presence caused an emotional stir. Government officials feared this ability to incite strong feelings, and largely because of that, he was taken to Fort Randall with some of his relatives and faithful followers where he was retained in custody during a lengthy cooling-off period. Later he was permitted to return to Standing Rock and from there he departed on an historic tour with "Buffalo Bill" Cody's Wild West Show which brought him much notoriety.

All this time the various mission schools were being established and the process of de-Indianization begun. English was taught, gardens planted, Christian hymns sung, and the once mobile and masterful Tetons had little choice but to adapt to the system — or lose their rations. As far as the eastern idealists were concerned, the education concept was paying off quickly. Charles Alexander Eastman, a Santee Sioux, had been graduated from Dartmouth College and was attending the Boston University medical school. Luther Standing Bear, a young Oglala student, had led the Carlisle Indian School brass band across the Brooklyn Bridge at its dedication in 1883 and later was a trainee in the famous John Wanamaker's store in Philadelphia. In the opinion of the absentee critics, these were obvious examples that the "peace policy" was on the right track, and that the "Sioux Indian problem" was finally coming to a happy, harmonious close.

End of the Great Sioux Reserve: Old Wounds Reopened

It had long been a pet philosophy of humanitarians and social theorists that the sooner the Indians were put on their own farms and released from the agency and annuity system, the better off the country (and the tribespeople) would be. This concept led to the Dawes Allotment Act of 1887 which made it possible for the head of each Indian household to claim 160 acres of land, with smaller tracts going to women, children and single men. Those who fulfilled the requirements of the law were to be granted immediate citizenship, and as soon as all tribal members had secured an allotment, the government was to offer the surplus land for sale, with the proceeds going into a special trust fund for the Indians.

This meant, of course, that sooner or later the influence of the old tribal structure would be eliminated, and the government could

The process of "de-Indianization" which many white social workers and government officials thought was the only answer to the "Indian problem" was actively pursued in day schools and boarding institutions on and off the reservations. Oglala youngsters (above) demonstrated "before" and "after" appearances on reporting to school and receiving uniform apparel. (South Dakota State Historical Society)

then deal with the Sioux as individuals — and citizens — rather than as an organized group. It also meant that less total land would be required by the Indian farmers, thus making it possible to open to white settlement vast tracts of territory previously unavailable under old treaties.

Almost from the moment the Black Hills cession agreement went into effect in 1876, agitation was started to open the corridor between the White and Cheyenne Rivers. The Hills people wanted a closer tie with the east than provided by the three roads granted under the pact; the giant cattle companies wanted more open range;

and the railroads had extended their lines to Pierre and Chamberlain on the assumption that in time the tracks would go all the way through to Rapid City or some other western terminal. During the boom years government commissions tried to get the Dakotas to relinquish the land without success, and finally in the spring of 1889, another official delegation — this one headed by General George Crook — was dispatched from Washington under congressional directive.

Crook, who was respected by the Indians and respected them in return, had been convinced that the offer he was authorized to present to the Sioux was in their best interests; and beginning at the Rosebud agency, he pursued the task of acquiring the necessary signatures (three-fourths of all adult males) with serious dedication. After nine days of discussions, a majority of the men at Rosebud "touched the pen" in approval of the agreement which doubled the allotment acreage to 320 for heads of families. At Pine Ridge, Red Cloud's objections held the total down, but at Lower Brule, Crow Creek and Cheyenne River, the response was better. The final decision, however, hinged on the success at Standing Rock. Sitting Bull opposed the offer, of course, but John Grass, an orator of considerable ability, effectively convinced enough of his fellow tribesmen to accept the inevitable and try to make the best of it, after which they provided the necessary signatures to legalize the cession.

A concerted effort was made to teach "white men's ways" to young Indians in fulfillment of treaty provisions. Unfortunately, the preservation of tribal values, traditions, religious practices and the Sioux language itself were not melded into the educational process. At the Oglala Boarding School students learned printing, baking, harness-making and home economics, among other skills. (South Dakota State Historical Society)

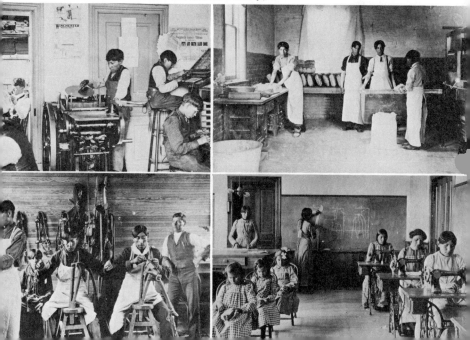

Indian leaders were brought to Washington, D.C., on numerous occasions, hopefully to impress them and sway their opinions during treaty negotiations. This delegation in October of 1888, the year following passage of the Dawes Allotment Act, included Sitting Bull (27) at far left, aloof even under such circumstances. Other individuals of historic note included Governor L. K. Church of Dakota (5), John Grass (39), Gall (40), Standing Rock Agent James A. McLaughlin (42), American Horse (53) and Bull Head (79). (Harold W. Shunk collection)

The commission did not complete its work until September, too late to permit a fall opening. Even so, hundreds of "sooners" began to gather on the east side of the Missouri with the mutual desire of racing to the best land opposite Pierre and Chamberlain the moment the signal was given. Throughout the winter months, troops were required to hold back a premature invasion, and several clashes in the Fort Pierre area occurred as the result of "sooner" anxiousness. Finally, on February 10, 1890, President Harrison signed the proclamation to wipe out the Great Sioux Reserve, and the mad rush across the Missouri ice began. Eye-witnesses estimated as many as 5,000 land-seekers participated in the bedlam at Chamberlain, with as many or more at Pierre where a local newspaper described the frantic scene:

> Men had stood in great crowds on the streets all day anxiously awaiting news and when it was known, a mighty cheer went forth and the scene of excitement beggared description. The crowd made a break for the river bank and participated in a grand rush for the other side. When the news was made known in the state house by the firing of a cannon, the members of the Legislature arose from their seats and gave three long cheers . . . Flags floated from every building and several bands played. Those who did not go across in the rush kept up the general hurrah in the city till nightfall. Teams hitched to wagons had been stationed all along the river

bank on this side all day and countless boomers remained by, ready to make a start for the promised land. When the word was received, each team, with the wagon filled with men, started, and many races were had to see which would gain the other side and be the first to get on the choice quarter sections.

Needless to say, the long negotiations for the cession and the tidal wave of invasion (possibly consisting of more speculators than actual settlers) rekindled the smoldering resentment of the tribes.

Beef issue day was a gala occasion at the Sioux agencies as various bands and family units gathered for their rations delivered "on the hoof." There were occasions when steers were turned loose on the plains so that Indian riders could shoot them on the run in a somewhat unfulfilling reenactment of the old buffalo-hunting days. (South Dakota State Historical Society)

Throughout history there are numerous examples of nations clutching at straws in time of intense crisis, and the Sioux Indians — in their frustration and anger — were understandably receptive to any course which might bring back the old ways. Not only had their traditional nomadic lifestyle been destroyed, but on March 2, 1889 — just eight days after President Cleveland had signed the Omnibus Bill to authorize the creation of South Dakota — six permanent reservations had been officially established in the vicinity of the old agencies even before the Crook commission arrived to begin its work.

In addition, the drouth which was wreaking havoc with the homesteaders had also descended upon the Sioux, burning up their tiny gardens and hayfields. They were even worse off than the white farmers because of their inexperience in agriculture and the poor

The agency on each reservation was the headquarters for administration, annuity distribution, law enforcement, mission activity, grievance councils and social events. Rosebud Agency in present-day Todd County (bottom) was a well-established community in 1889 when the permanent reservations were designated. (Top) White staff members posed with Indian policemen at the Standing Rock Agency in 1880. (South Dakota State Historical Society)

quality of their land for farming purposes. They had, however, learned enough from various advisers and missionaries to produce sufficient food during normal years to supplement the treaty rations; but when the crops failed, the unelastic government neglected to increase the provisions accordingly, and some bands were soon on the verge of starvation.

It was no wonder that the Dakotas listened intently when they heard of a new Indian Messiah who was preaching a message of hope near Pyramid Lake in Nevada. Wovoka, a Paiute dreamer known less glamorously as Jack Wilson, claimed to have had a revelation telling him, in effect, to promote a religion of non-violence and love which also included a ceremonial rite called the Ghost Dance. To learn more about the Messiah and his doctrine, the Sioux tribes sent representatives to the west about the time the Great Reserve stampede began. The delegation — dominated by Short Bull, a strong-willed Oglala — was impressed by what was seen and heard and returned to spread the word.

It is generally believed that the Messiah's tenets — stressing mostly the Christian virtues of hope and love — were misinterpreted or purposely altered by the Dakota representatives to fill the emotional needs of their people at that particular time. They brought back the morale-boosting message that if everyone danced the Ghost Dance, the buffalo would return, the white men would disappear, their relatives would rise from the dead, bullets would not penetrate their flimsy calico "ghost shirts" and all their lost land would be restored.

The opening of the Great Sioux Reserve in 1890 and surplus reservation lands after the turn of the century attracted large crowds of homestead-seekers like the one below near Pierre. In the earlier instance, a first-come-first-served race to the most desirable claims was a dramatic part of the exciting process. Later government-operated lotteries were held to reduce the number of applicants to match the available acres. (South Dakota State Historical Society)

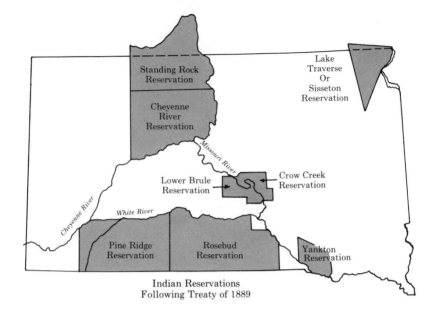

Indian Reservations
Following Treaty of 1889

The Treaty of 1889 defined the boundaries of the Standing Rock, Cheyenne River, Lower Brule, Crow Creek, Pine Ridge and Rosebud Reservations, thus opening up the corridor of land between the White and Cheyenne Rivers for homesteading. The Yankton Reservation and the unique triangular Lake Traverse or Sisseton Reservation were established earlier by separate treaties.

The Ghost Dance and the garbled philosophy reached the Sioux just when they needed it most, and supposedly the transformation was to occur when the grass began to grow in the spring of 1891. Since dancing was a cherished part of Dakota religious expression (a custom whites had difficulty understanding), many Indians welcomed the new cult and its ghostly features. It filled a void, and it had nothing to do with an armed uprising; after all, the message promised that all they had to do was wait, dance and "do right" and their burdens would be lifted with no further action on their part.

Since Wovoka's influence was being felt among various tribes throughout the West, government officials tried to comprehend the meaning of the Ghost Dance religion and to decide whether it was harmful to the "peace policy" or not. Certain missionaries worried that the new beliefs would undo all their teaching. At Pine Ridge Doctor Daniel F. Royer, a totally inexperienced and frightened new agent whom the Sioux nicknamed "Young-Man-Afraid-of-Indians," send out a frantic call for troops when he thought an uprising was imminent.

About the same time James "Scotty" Philip, a pioneer rancher who was to gain fame later for his efforts to prevent extinction of the buffalo, rode into Pierre to tell Governor Mellette of the impending troubles, and the chief executive promptly alerted the militia in Walworth and Campbell counties. He also wired General Nelson A.

Miles in Chicago about the tinderbox state of affairs, and army reinforcements were dispatched to the reservations. On November 20 three troops of black cavalrymen of the Ninth Regiment arrived at Pine Ridge to fortify Royer, the nervous physician-businessman from Alpena.

In 1890 a situation was developing at Pine Ridge (above, on ration-issue day) which the inexperienced agent, Dr. Daniel F. Royer, could neither understand nor handle. The Ghost Dance, while it tended to intensify anti-white attitudes among the participants, was not a preparatory ritual for revolt as suspected; but when troops were called in, the stage was set for the emotional explosion which followed. (South Dakota State Historical Society)

Tragedy at Grand River: Death of Sitting Bull

At Standing Rock the Ghost Dancers also were having an agitating effect. Agent James F. McLaughlin had better control than Royer, but he also had Sitting Bull, who was then living in a log cabin on the Grand River. It was rumored that the Hunkpapa leader was somehow involved in the new religious fervor and would use it to foment a revolt, so to head off such an eventuality, the commandant at Fort Yates was ordered to apprehend him before greater trouble developed.

In the early dawn of December 15, a detachment of 43 Indian policemen headed by Lieutenant Bull Head arrived at Sitting Bull's cabin. They were supported by a detail of cavalry troopers who halted outside the camp to avoid inciting any unnecessary conflict. A scuffle followed Bull Head's confrontation with the aging medicine man, and in the exchange of gunfire which followed, Sitting Bull and Bull Head were mortally wounded, along with six of the Indian police unit and an unknown number of the resisting warriors. The brief fray ended with the arrival of the cavalrymen.

The news of Sitting Bull's death spread rapidly to the southern reservations, and fear of army retaliation against the Ghost Dance caused many of the practitioners to flee into the Badlands to join others already there. The controversial and colorful Hunkpapa —

hated by some and called the greatest of all Sioux leaders by others — had resisted the white encroachment to his final breath, when, ironically, he — like Spotted Tail — was killed by a bullet from a gun in the hands of another Indian.

Troopers at Fort Meade on the northeastern fringe of the Black Hills were kept in a state of readiness primarily to discourage trouble between Indians and whites. The routine of garrison life was broken by maneuvers and drills, which included the training of cavalry horses to lie quietly on a battlefield to serve as shields for their riders when such a drastic strategy became necessary. (South Dakota State Historical Society)

Despite the approaching holiday season, troops began to station themselves at specified positions on the reservations, and one unit — the reconstructed Seventh Cavalry — was ordered to intercept and disarm a small band of Minneconjous under Big Foot which was preceding southward through the Badlands, either to turn themselves in at Pine Ridge (as the Indians later claimed) or to join the Ghost Dancers of Short Bull (as the army believed).

The elderly Big Foot, suffering from pneumonia and riding in the back of a wagon, was hardly the picture of a defiant fighter, and in his cold and weary band of less than 350 individuals, not even a third could be classified as warriors. The Indians were overtaken by the cavalry force of four troops under Major Samuel Whiteside, who informed the ailing chief that his people were to proceed under escort to Wounded Knee Creek, some 17 miles northeast of the Pine Ridge headquarters, where they would be disarmed before being permitted to go any farther.

Massacre at Wounded Knee: An American Tragedy

Major Whiteside had Big Foot transferred to a more comfortable army ambulance for the march to Wounded Knee, and when they arrived, he had a field stove placed in the chief's tepee and ordered a regimental surgeon to treat his illness. During the night the remainder of the Seventh Cavalry rode in, and Colonel James W. Forsyth assumed command of the operation. Two batteries of Hotchkiss guns (successor to the earlier Gatling) were mounted on a rise overlooking the camp which was also surrounded by guards.

At dawn on December 29 a bugle sounded, and a hard-tack ration was issued to the Indians. Afterwards they were told to bring out all their weapons and stack them in the center of the camp. Because the colonel was not satisfied that all rifles had been produced, he ordered a search of the tepees, wagons and the blanket-clad warriors themselves. Though the Indians resented the indignities, they did not resist, and soon kitchen knives, awls, axes, tent stakes and all sharp-pointed implements they possessed were added to the pathetic pile of arms.

And then suddenly there was a shot.

The versions of the incident are many and conflicting, but apparently a young warrior (who some said was deaf and couldn't hear

Following the disaster at Wounded Knee Creek, Drs. Valentine T. McGillicuddy (left) and Charles A. Eastman provided medical care for the living victims of the slaughter, many of them women and children. McGillicuddy, a former Indian agent, had warned that interference with the Ghost Dance would bring serious consequences. For Doctor Eastman the ordeal was particularly difficult because he was a Santee Sioux who had pursued "white man's ways" in eastern schools, only to have his Christian ideals shattered by the apparent act of vengeance during the Christmas season of 1890. (South Dakota State Historical Society)

the orders) pulled his rifle from his blanket. The army reported he fired the shot which precipitated the gory affair; Indian survivors swore he was merely trying to resist losing a new rifle which had cost him dearly. Whatever happened, it set off an immediate murderous barrage from the rapid-fire Hotchkiss batteries and the carbines of the troopers stationed around the encampment.

Chief Big Foot crumbled and fell under the first volley and so did many of the other unarmed Indian men. Some of the warriors engaged in hand-to-hand combat with the dismounted cavalrymen until they were gunned down by other troopers who outnumbered them almost four to one. Women and children who survived the first terrible blast ran screaming for the shelter of a nearby ravine, many of them being shot as they fled.

The carnage was indescribable. No exact figure of Indian dead was ever established, but estimates ranged from a low of 200 to a high of well over 300, including infants. How many of the wounded perished in the snow and cold which followed the terrible onslaught could not be accurately determined. According to the official surgeon's report, the Seventh Cavalry lost one officer and 29 enlisted men killed and a similar number wounded. (Other references say 20

After the Wounded Knee massacre, a small chapel at Pine Ridge was converted into a temporary hospital with straw strewn on the floor as the only beds for the massacre's victims. Despite the imperfections, this historic photograph depicted graphically the crude conditions under which physicians worked in their effort to save lives. Ironically, Christmas decorations were still hanging in the mission church when it was taken over to provide emergency medical care. (Denver Public Library Western Collection)

soldiers were killed during the fray and 16 died afterwards.) Since very few Indians had firearms, it has been assumed that most of the army casualties were caused by the vicious Hotchkiss and carbine crossfire.

In the aftermath, the wounded soldiers and some of the Indians were taken to Pine Ridge for medical care. A small Episcopal mission church not far from the smoking remains of Minneconjou tepees was converted into a field hospital after benches were removed and hay spread on the floor. Doctor Charles Eastman, the Santee Sioux physician at Pine Ridge, hurried to the scene; he was assisted in his ministrations by Doctor Valentine T. McGillicuddy, former agent at Pine Ridge who had come from Rapid City to try to help ease the tension and who earlier had warned that trying to stop the Ghost Dance would undoubtedly lead to serious trouble.

In his memoirs, Bishop William Hare described what he saw when he arrived at the Wounded Knee mission shortly after the calamity:

> On the church floor, instead of the pews on either side of the aisle, two rows of bleeding, groaning, wounded men, women and children; tending them two military surgeons and a native physician assisted by the missionary and his helpers . . . Above, the Christmas green was still hanging . . . a mockery to all my faith and hope.

On New Year's Day, a burial detail of soldiers returned to the site of the massacre to gather up the Indian dead who had been frozen into grotesque shapes when the temperature dropped sharply. A mass grave was dug and the victims of the deplorable slaughter were interred without dignity. Throughout most of South Dakota, homesteaders were almost totally unaware of the developments leading to such a tragic end until they read about it in their newspapers. Like the Sioux, many of them were cold and hungry, too, and looking for better things — when the first grass grew in the spring.

Understandably the Wounded Knee tragedy was to leave a lingering scar on white-Indian relationships. Greeted first as a great army "victory" to avenge the Custer massacre, the historic event gradually took on a new meaning as emotions subsided and the facts became known. Through the years the story has been told and retold, slanted first in favor of one side and then the other. Regardless of presentation, however, it emerges always as a nightmarish episode in which no one can take pride. Wounded Knee — an Alamo for the Sioux — can have positive meaning only if it becomes symbolic of a continuing challenge to resolve the conflict of cultures.

Another Stampede: Opening the Sisseton Triangle

While the Western Sioux were involved in their desperate struggle to adapt to the realities of a changing world, the Santee tribes in the northeastern corner of South Dakota were living under circumstances which lessened the impact of the cultural collision. The Sissetons and Wahpetons were less nomadic than their Teton cousins, and through the years they had had more intimate exposure to white traders, settlers and missionaries, especially the Presbyterian churchmen assigned to their triangular reservation established by treaty in 1867.

Some of the Minnesota Santees had rebelled in 1862, of course, but after that shortlived outbreak, the white-red relationship had been generally peaceful. The principal figure on the reservation was Chief Gabriel Renville, a mixed blood whose uncle (Joseph Renville, a trader) had helped missionaries Riggs and Williamson translate the Bible into the Sioux language. Chief Renville, as a youth, had been sent east to school but ran away and managed to return to his people. He had not participated in the Outbreak of '62, and afterwards he became a member of the Indian scouts appointed to serve with government troops at Fort Wadsworth (founded in 1864 and renamed Fort Sisseton in 1876). Gabriel Renville had been part of the delegation which went to Washington, D.C., in 1867 to negotiate

Young Man Afraid of His Horses was an Oglala chieftain who returned to Pine Ridge from an extended hunt shortly after the Wounded Knee disaster and was instrumental in re-establishing peace on the reservation. Like other perceptive leaders, he did not necessarily agree with imposed government conditions, but he recognized realities and acted accordingly. His name, and that of his father, should more correctly be expressed as "the man of whose horse we are afraid." (South Dakota State Historical Society)

for the Sisseton-Wahpeton Reservation, and though he never learned to speak English, he was named by the government to head the combined tribes.

Geographically, the region inhabitated by Renville's people offered an unusual contrast to the typical flatlands of Dakota where life for other Sioux Indians was more rigidly dependent upon the buffalo. Dominated by the Coteau des Prairie (prairie hills), the lake-dotted area provided bountiful fish and game resources and an ample supply of timber (including oak not common to South Dakota as a whole). Northeast of Fort Wadsworth was an extensive wooded ravine known as Sica or Sieche Hollow ("place of evil" according to Indian tradition) where artesian springs created rust-colored bogs which emitted "swamp gas" or methane to add to the eerie effect of the locale.

Soldiers, settlers, missionaries and Indians mingled without particular problems within and adjacent to the three-sided reservation. Only one historic incident — the dramatic "false alarm" ride of Samuel J. Brown on April 16-17, 1866 — interrupted the otherwise unruffled coexistence of Indians and whites. In that instance, the 21-year-old mixed-blood scout had galloped out of Fort Wadsworth to spread the warning that a Sioux war party was heading toward the populated country. Through the night he rode westward to the Elm River scout station in Brown County; then, when he got there, he learned to his dismay that the information was erroneous. Realizing that a similarly false alert message would go out from Fort Wadsworth the next morning to the commander of Fort Abercrombie, young Brown felt compelled to head off the misleading dispatch and immediately mounted a fresh horse to begin the return trip. During the course of the eastward dash, a freezing rain started to fall, and then a springtime blizzard overtook the courageous horseman. Miraculously, Brown made it back to the fort — after traveling approximately 150 miles in less than 15 hours. When he fell exhausted from his horse, however, his leg and back muscles had undergone such punishment that paralysis set in and he never walked again. He died at age 80 in 1925.

In the ensuing years the Indians of the Sisseton-Wahpeton Reservation adjusted to the pattern of living imposed by the white society. They were almost completely unaffected by the Ghost Dance or the problems peculiar to the Western Sioux. Agriculture became an important factor in their economy, and as they located more and more on individual farms, the need for a large tribal reserve diminished. Renville and other leaders refused to negotiate for the sale of surplus acres in the early 1880s because the government showed no inclination to consider prior claims for which the Indians insisted settlement must be made. However, when statehood was imminent and a more liberal attitude was adopted by Congress regarding compensation, Chief Renville, Governor Mellette and others went to Washington to discuss the possibility of opening the excess land not taken in severalty by Indians. A commission was appointed, and after 160 acres of land were allocated to all tribespeople — regardless of age or sex — the remaining territory, consisting of some six hundred thousand acres, was released for sale to homesteaders, with the opening to take place at high noon on April 15, 1892.

The stampede for cheap land was similar to the mad dash across the Missouri two years earlier at Pierre and Chamberlain. Hundreds of land-seekers awaited the sound of the bugle and then the reverberation of carbine shots as cavalrymen posted along the borders echoed the starting signal. A St. Paul newspaper reporter described the scene:

> ... from every spot bordering on the reserve that could shelter a man, horse or wagon, there sprang hordes of homeseekers ... about one thousand made the rush from Browns Valley. About five hundred started from the little town of Travare, four miles from the lake. At Wheaton, where the approach to the promised land was over a private bridge whose owner attempted to stem the flood of boomers in the interest of a land company, six hundred people crossed the bridge regardless of orders, and the police force of the town was overwhelmed ... At Waubay, South Dakota, close to the line to the southwest, between 500 and 600 people, with picks and spades,

In the days immediately following the Wounded Knee massacre, General Nelson A. Miles (right) arrived to take personal command of the still explosive situation at Pine Ridge. He replaced the inept Doctor Royer as agent and managed to prevent further military confrontation. On January 16, 1891, he was photographed with "Buffalo Bill" Cody (left), one of several men experienced in Indian-white relationships who were brought to the scene to help re-establish peace. (South Dakota State Historical Society)

joined in one grand rush for the choice lands . . . at Wilmot, South Dakota, there was a grand rush for a town site. A train on the Milwaukee road, with 500 people on board, pulled out for the line at 11:30 this morning. At the stroke of 12 the train was rushed a few miles further [sic] to the end of the track, from which place fast mustangs carried the town-site boomers. These mustangs were provied by thrifty Indians at big prices.

On that particular day, the new town of Sisseton was established almost in a matter of minutes. By the end of the summer at least 50 buildings had been erected on the site, and in 1893 the railroad was extended to the flourishing community. In a way, the reservation opening and the mushrooming birth of the Roberts County town gave a much-needed boost to the infant state of South Dakota which had very little to shout about in its first years of existence.

The year 1893 brought another development farther south on the Big Sioux River which had indirect historic ties with the activities in the Sisseton area. On March 7 that year an Indian boarding school began operation at Flandreau on a 160-acre tree claim which United States Senator Pettigrew had sold to the federal government in 1891. The Senator had championed the cause of the school, telling potential voters in the town that it would mean more to them in the long run than acquiring the state capital (of which there was little chance, of course).

The school — which opened with 98 pupils and 12 staff members — was named Riggs Institute in honor of Reverend Stephen R. Riggs, the Presbyterian minister who had served the Sisseton-Wahpeton reservation for so long. The general choice of location came about because of the settlement near Flandreau of a band of Christian Santees who had left the reservation in Nebraska in 1869 to set up homesteads in Moody County. The Board of Missions had established a day school for the independent group in 1876, which later was taken over by the government and ultimately became the nucleus for the larger institution serving tribes in South Dakota and beyond. After several name changes, it was finally designated the Flandreau Indian School, the largest such facility in the nation with the longest continuing history.

BOOK EIGHT

THE CHALLENGE OF A NEW CENTURY

> *"Ye gods, what a spectacle South Dakota must present to the outside world."*
> — *The Brookings Register*
> *1895*

The great spirit of optimism which spurred the statehood movement was desperately needed to maintain the morale of the citizens during South Dakota's first years. The widespread drouth and the Wounded Knee debacle imposed serious setbacks before the government really had a chance to function. The fact that Governor Mellette was able to provide some carryover from the territorial system was a small advantage, but there was no question about it: South Dakota did not start with its best foot forward.

The economic conditions greatly affected politics, of course. Farmers continued to be dissatisfied with rail rates and the prices they received for their limited crops and livestock. The Populist or People's Party — headed by Henry L. Loucks — became a factor to be considered in South Dakota elections. Disenchanted Republicans and Democrats, prohibitionists, women's suffragettes, the Knights of Labor and the promoters of unrestricted silver coinage aligned themselves with the rural element as numerous factors complicated the political picture. The Chautauqua movement — which featured touring lecturers and entertainers — helped expand public awareness of social and economic issues.

While the Women's Christian Temperance Union and other anti-alcohol groups were delighted with the outlawing of intoxicating beverages in the state, the breweries, saloons and liquor distributorships were forced to close, which — understandably — caused the out-of-business operators to organize a retaliatory campaign. This tied in, too, with a loophole in the law which permitted divorce with less restrictions than in most other states, a fact which led to an influx of wealthy clients for attorneys becoming proficient at dissolving marriages. Prohibition was not favorable to such "legal tourists" who wanted to celebrate during the short residency period and after the decree. Churches especially began to pressure for a statute to eliminate the deficiency which earned for Sioux Falls the uncomplimentary title of "divorce capital of the nation."

In addition, the issue of silver money, which Populists believed would improve conditions for the tightly strapped farmers, obviously ran counter to the desires of Homestake Mining Company officials and other Black Hills voters to whom gold represented the dominant

Though it was originally bypassed by the main east-west rail lines, Sioux Falls grew rapidly and by 1890 was established as the state's leading city. A laxity in South Dakota's early laws made dissolution of marriage relatively easy, and Sioux Falls became known for a short time as the "divorce capital of the nation." Many visitors arrived at the train station married and departed single before the legislature plugged the legal loophole. (W. H. Over Museum)

source of wealth. The rich and powerful railroads — with their "free pass" system for politicians — were able to exert a strong influence over bills affecting them, despite the feelings of the majority of citizens.

Even with the growing unrest, however, the Republicans were able to re-elect Mellette in 1890, though the legislature chose a Populist — James Henderson Kyle, a Congregational minister from

The Chautauqua movement, named for the New York town in which the educational and cultural program was developed, found ready acceptance in South Dakota where visiting speakers, musicians, acting companies and other entertainers brought diversion to the somewhat isolated state. The opportunity to obtain a completion certificate, roughly equivalent to a high school diploma, was also available. The Lake Madison Chautauqua Association, established in 1891, held periodic three-week sessions in a comfortable hotel. Other towns had to be satisfied with tent Chautauquas. (W. H. Over Museum)

A natural phenomenon in Fall River County in the southern Black Hills was responsible for the development of Hot Springs as a tourist attraction and health spa. Mammoth Springs, the largest of several flows emanating in the area, delivered 100,000 gallons an hour to the popular indoor Evans Plunge. The Fremont, Elkhorn & Missouri Valley Railroad brought many guests to the five-story Evans Hotel, pictured here as it was in June of 1893. (South Dakota State Historical Society)

Brown County — to replace Senator Moody. Two years later the G.O.P. again managed to retain control of the statehouse when Charles H. Sheldon — a Civil War veteran and former member of the territorial legislature who farmed near Pierpont in Day County — became South Dakota's second governor. He took office just in time to face new economic and social woes.

The site for the territorial university was established at Vermillion by the first legislature in a political bargain which gave Yankton the capital and Bon Homme the penitentiary. The school, which became the University of South Dakota, held its first classes in 1882 and suffered a temporary setback when its principal building — Old Main — was gutted by fire in 1893, a bad economic year for the state and the nation. (W. H. Over Museum)

The quest by women for recognition beyond traditional domestic roles was aided in the late 1800s by increased educational opportunities. Exposure to discussions of social problems — even in such obviously restricted settings as the study room at South Dakota Agricultural College in Brookings — led to more and more involvement in suffrage and temperance movements. (South Dakota State University)

A National Panic: Scandal in South Dakota

The Panic of 1893 — blamed by President Cleveland on excessive cheap paper money — aggravated the already bad situation in South Dakota. Business firms joined farmers in failure as a combination of natural and man-made calamities hit at the same time. Altogether some 600 banks across the nation closed their doors, and 74 railroads (including the Northern Pacific and Union Pacific) fell into receiverships. To make matters worse, the drouth in the summer of 1894 matched or exceeded any of the previous dry spells since the earliest territorial days.

The South Dakota Agricultural College (which was to become South Dakota State University) at Brookings was established by the territorial legislature in 1881, but it was three years later before the first classes were taught. The school survived a "revolt" of students and faculty in 1893 during which Governor Sheldon visited the campus in an attempt to restore harmony. Instruction in progressive agricultural methods, including the use of steam power, received primary emphasis. (South Dakota State University)

Governor Sheldon faced serious financial problems in government as tax collections failed to meet the state's needs. Relief programs were established and special rain-making conventions held.

In acquiring its ranking as the state's major city, Sioux Falls began to take on an air of sophistication in the 1890s with its electric trolley line and the ample accommodations of the Cataract Hotel. The city's growth momentum continued, and it soon out-distanced any possible contenders for the honor of being South Dakota's population center. (W. H. Over Museum)

Amid all the other difficulties, a controversy at the South Dakota Agricultural College in Brookings grew to such proportions that more than half of the students went home. Politics, personalities and basic philosophies were involved, and Governor Sheldon added fuel to the fire by saying that the state didn't need "professors of agriculture"; it needed "teachers of farming".

But, for the chief executive, the worst was still to come.

Governor Andrew E. Lee, native of Norway, was elected in 1896 and began his tenure by insisting that all of the state's funds be brought to Pierre and physically counted. It was a unique and controversial move, but he wanted to be sure the treasury was in order following an embezzlement scandal during the previous administration. The Vermillion Populist posed with his daughter and wife, Annie Chappell Lee, who like many women of the period was an active member of the Women's Christian Temperance Union. (South Dakota State Historical Society)

After he had been re-elected to a second term, Sheldon publicly praised retiring State Treasurer William Walter Taylor for protecting the public funds throughout the unstable fiscal conditions created by the national depression. Then, on January 8, 1895, it was revealed that the former Redfield banker had fled to South America and that the treasury was short $367,000. The monstrous scandal was almost the last straw for a state already reeling under other adversities; and Governor Sheldon — to say the least — was embarrassingly red-faced. After several months Taylor returned to South Dakota, was convicted of embezzlement and sentenced to 20 years in prison, the term being reduced later to two years which the ex-treasurer served. His personal assets, the state funds he foolishly had placed in the hands of his Chicago attorneys (who apparently had advised him to leave the country) and the forfeiture of his bond restored a major portion of the missing sum, but when it was all over, the people of South Dakota still lost almost $100,000.

There was an additional unhappy sequel to the episode, too. Ex-Governor Mellette, who had been badly cripped in a fall from a buggy before his term ended, had returned to Watertown to practice law. He also was a bondsman for Taylor, whose past record gave no indication that he was untrustworthy. The default wiped out Mellette's personal fortune, and he moved to Pittsburg, Kansas, broke and humiliated. He died within a year on May 25, 1896, at the age of 52.

A Populist Governor: Counting the State's Money

The Taylor affair reflected negatively on the entire Republican Party in South Dakota, and in the election of 1896, the Democrats supported the Populist gubernatorial candidate, Andrew E. Lee of Vermillion, who won a convincing victory. Lee, a native of Norway, gave immediate evidence of a tight-fisted administration when he insisted that the state's money be brought to Pierre and be counted before approval of the new state treasurer's bond. In the past, certificates from the banks where the funds were deposited were accepted as proof that the accounts were in order, but the new governor wanted to see the cash personally, all $257,482.71 of it.

Six guards accompanied $190,000 from depositories in Chicago, with a detachment of the South Dakota militia joining the security force at Huron. Some $46,000 was hand-carried in satchels to the state legislative hall from three Pierre banks under military escort. The lengthy counting process (which made a lot of people nervous) was finally completed, and no irregularities were found. The anxiety was extended, however, when the train carrying the money back to Chicago was snowbound near Highmore and a rescue train from Huron was unable to proceed beyond Wolsey. Fortunately, no misfortune befell the funds, which — if stolen — would have bankrupted the state. Lee's stubborn insistence upon the physical inventory was widely criticized for its impracticality, but he got his way, and somehow the unusual episode seemed to signal the coming of a brighter, more prosperous era.

The best remedy — which no governor nor political party could deliver — was ample rain, and after the lengthy dry spell, the weather once again began to cooperate with the hardy farmers who had persisted through the bad times. Morale improved with successful harvests, and South Dakota — at last — began to move forward toward the potential the old-time boomers had prophesied for the region.

Spanish-American War: A Presidential Visit

To the chagrin of the W.C.T.U. and other prohibition forces, South Dakota saloons were reopened in 1897. The state's voters approved an addition to the constitution which provided for *initiative* and *referendum* procedures by which citizens could enact or annul laws by direct petition and ballot (a reform achievement credited to the Populists and for which South Dakota gained favorable national recognition for its leadership in progressive legislation). The electorate did not endear itself to the exponents of women's suffrage, however, when an amendment to secure the vote for female citizens was defeated by a substantial margin.

The emergence of women as a factor to be considered in future political and other leadership activities was a reality which could no longer be denied. Prohibition had given the women a cause beyond the kitchen, church and school, and many W.C.T.U. banner-carriers became active suffragettes. Rigid European and tribal traditions governing the role of the female were difficult to overcome, but gradually individual women began to break away from the pattern and to become active in various business and professional roles.

For instance, Mrs. Alice R. Gossage — a former teacher, typesetter and church organist — had assumed the management of the *Rapid City Journal* in 1890 when her husband became ill. As editor of the pioneer newspaper (founded as the *Black Hills Journal* in 1878) she was a strong advocate of equality at the ballot box. Annie Tallent, the pioneer Black Hills "sooner," had proved her capabilities as superintendent of public instruction in Pennington County and president of the board of education in Rapid City. Phoebe Apperson Hearst, who became actively involved in directing the Hearst enterprises after her husband's death in 1891, made her presence felt in both business and social affairs of the Homestake Mining Company and the city of Lead. In the early 1890s, the ranks of practicing physicians in South Dakota included, among others, Doctors Flora H. Stanford, Deadwood; Sarah M. Wayman, Spencer; Elizabeth S. Boulter, Roscoe, Ruth E. Swift and Harriett B. Conant, Yankton; and Flora May Betts, Sioux Falls. Not to be overlooked were the Catholic nuns who came to the Territory in virtual anonymity to work among the Indians and in various other charitable capacities.

As the twentieth century dawned, small towns continued to develop along railroad extensions. Avon, on the Milwaukee's line to Platte, was a typical case, as an earlier post office was relocated closer to the tracks in 1900, after which a growth spurt followed. Named for the New York home town of an early settler, the Bon Homme County village was the birthplace of Senator George S. McGovern, candidate for the United States presidency in 1972. (South Dakota State Historical Society)

Just when South Dakotans were beginning to enjoy a period of crisis-free progress, a national emergency developed. On February 15, 1898, the United States battleship *Maine* was sunk in the harbor of Havana, Cuba. The American public, aroused by inflammatory newspaper editorials, was convinced that Spain brazenly perpetrated the disaster which took the lives of two officers and 258 seamen. "Remember the *Maine*" became a much-echoed slogan, and Congress voted a declaration of war effective on April 21; just nine days later the South Dakota militia was ordered to duty.

The First South Dakota Volunteer Infantry Regiment, under Colonel Alfred S. Frost, was hurriedly assembled in Sioux Falls. Governor Lee chose not to call the legislature into special session to authorize funds for the unit; instead he appealed to private firms and individual citizens for the $14,000 needed for transportation, rations

Troops of the First South Dakota Volunteer Infantry were rushed into federal service following the declaration of war on Spain in April of 1898. Various companies were assembled in Sioux Falls and ultimately shipped to the Philippine Islands where they fought Filipino insurrectionists and not Spaniards. (Yankton County Historical Society)

Dr. Niels E. Hansen, a Danish immigrant who became a professor of horticulture at the South Dakota Agricultural College in 1895, revolutionized farming practices in mid-America by introducing hardy plants and trees from Siberia and other remote areas of Asia. The seeds of the wild alfalfa he fed the camels in Semipalatinsk, Siberia, in 1913 ultimately helped establish the important forage industry in South Dakota. (South Dakota State University)

and other necessities until the troops could be federalized. The campaign fell about $3,000 short, and the governor himself made up the difference. Later the private donations were refunded by the government.

After a month of disciplinary training and organization, the regiment was sent to San Francisco to prepare for overseas shipment, and in late August the South Dakotans found themselves encamped — not in Cuba — but on Luzon Island in the Philippines. In the

An unusual three-deck railroad arrangement existed in Lead shortly after the turn of the century. The trolley line of the old Deadwood Central was on the lower level; the Homestake's ore trains ran on the high trestle; and the Fremont, Elkhorn and Missouri Valley (acquired by the Chicago and North Western) operated in between. (South Dakota State Historical Society)

meantime, the Spanish fleet had been quickly destroyed and the "official war" was ended by the Treaty of Paris on December 10, 1898. By its terms Spain relinquished sovereignty over Cuba and ceded Guam, Puerto Rico and the Philippine Islands to the United States.

When it became apparent to the Filipinoes that they were not free but had merely traded what they considered to be one foreign overlord for another, an insurrection under Emilio Aguinaldo was launched. The South Dakota regiment almost immediately became actively involved in the swamp-and-jungle warfare which erupted on February 4, 1899. The unit fought with distinction for 126 days on the line until disease, exhaustion and enemy fire seriously reduced the organization's effectiveness. Historian Doane Robinson reported that on June 10 when the unit was relieved from its outpost position, "there was not more than eight men to a company capable of doing duty".

Back home the "war after a war" had lost much of its patriotic flavor, and angry demands were made for the return of the volunteers. Finally on August 5 the First South Dakota was relieved by the 25th United States Infantry regulars and subsequently transported to San Francisco where it was officially mustered out of federal service. Of the 64 men who didn't return, 20 were killed in action, eight died of wounds, one was drowned and 35 succumbed to various diseases.

The regiment was greeted joyously on the Pacific coast by the state's congressional delegation, many of its other elected officials and numerous personally interested South Dakotans. The ensuing rail trip home was made by way of the Northern Pacific to Jamestown, North Dakota, and thence down the James River Valley. So much political furor had been generated by the Philippine acquisi-

Historically, South Dakota has always been an agricultural state, but its farm successes have been due in large measure to continuing improvements in seeds, livestock breeding and operational techniques. Pioneers did not enjoy the advantages and yields of Cossack alfalfa, hybrid corn, soybeans, rust-resistant wheat, brome and crested wheat grasses, sunflowers, sugar beets and other new or improved crops which were developed later to fit the state's climate and soil. (South Dakota State Historical Society)

In 1904 the buffalo no longer existed as a wild species in South Dakota, but efforts to preserve the animal from extinction were already underway. When a number of bison escaped from a herd purchased by Scotty Philip, an old-fashioned buffalo hunt was planned with Governor Charles N. Herreid (right) as honored guest. Since then many dignitaries through the years have shot surplus bison from private and government herds for sport and publicity. (South Dakota State Historical Society)

tion and the involvement of state militiamen in the campaign against Aguinaldo that President William McKinley scheduled a western tour so that he would be in Aberdeen when the South Dakota veterans arrived from California. Not only did he greet them there, but his special train hurried on ahead of the soldiers to Redfield,

J. C. H. Grabill, another of Dakota's pioneer photographers, captured on film the mess camp of a ranch crew in 1887. In later years movies and television shows glamorized the cowboy so much that the modern version no longer reflected the drudgery, the lonely, body-breaking work — in good weather and bad — which was the true lot of the early-day cattleman. (Clyde Goin collection)

Huron, Sioux Falls and Yankton where he repeated his welcome and words of appreciation on behalf of a grateful nation.

Another South Dakota unit — officially known as the Third Regiment of the United States Volunteer Cavalry but popularly called Grigsby's Cowboys after its commander, Colonel Melvin Grigsby of Sioux Falls — was also activated and sent to Chickamauga, Georgia, for training. The majority of the privates in the five troops listed their occupations as cowboys or miners, and there was general disappointment throughout the entire regiment when it was never ordered to combat duty.

End of the First Decade: A Minor Boom

The federal census of 1900 showed South Dakota with 401,570 residents of whom 20,218 were Indians. The total reflected a reversal of the downward trend from 348,600 in 1890 to 330,975 in 1895.

Good weather, new railroad extensions, potential reservation openings and a more scientific approach to agriculture were instrumental in reviving the state's growth pattern as the 19th century faded into history. Eastward from the James River Valley, greater corn plantings brought crop diversification and swine production. In later years pigs came to be known in South Dakota as "mortgage-lifters". Professor Niels Ebbesen Hansen, the state's famed plant scientist, had returned from the first of eight exploration trips to such far-off Asiatic destinations as Turkestan, western China and Siberia. In the five carloads of seeds and plants he had shipped home was a foundation stock of crested wheat grass and hardy Cossack alfalfa, each of which was to become a valuable addition to South Dakota's list of farm crops. In the early 1900s the first experiments to overcome stem rust in wheat were begun at the South Dakota Agricultural College, and west of the Missouri River cattle and sheep operations were flourishing on the former Great Sioux Reserve.

As conditions improved for farmers (including a voluntary reduction of railroad rates in 1901), the Populist Party disintegrated and disappeared from the South Dakota political scene. In 1900 the Republicans elected Governor Charles N. Herreid, a Leola banker, whose two terms of office were unmarred by the economic and social problems faced by his three less fortunate predecessors. Senator Pettigrew, the strong-willed Sioux Falls attorney who had adopted Populist views while in office, was replaced by Republican Robert J. Gamble of Yankton; and Senator James H. Kyle, who was elected as a Populist, died at the age of 47 and Alfred B. Kittredge was named by Governor Herreid to succeed him.

At Yankton the State Insane Asylum (as it was then called) received positive attention from the legislature following a disastrous fire in 1899 during which 17 patients died — just when a legislative committee happened to be on an inspection tour at the institution. On September 14, 1901, a national tragedy occurred when

President McKinley was slain by an assassin, and Theodore Roosevelt, a special friend of the Dakotas, succeeded him. A time of great change was imminent. Spindly motor cars began to make their appearances on the dusty main streets of prairie towns, and the advent of the machine age signalled the gradual ending of the pioneer era.

The Cheyenne Strip: Cowboys and Indians

Like many facets of South Dakota's heritage, the story of the western cattle industry deserves book-length treatment by itself. The "shortgrass country" (somewhat erroneously titled because the vegetation often grew waist high or taller) had been the natural feeding grounds of the buffalo. Decimation of the bison herds, coupled with the meat demands of the Black Hills miners, made the open-range grazing of imported longhorns a highly profitable venture.

Even before the cession of the Great Sioux Reserve in 1889, permanent ranches started to develop, and barbed wire (first patented by Joseph F. Glidden in 1874) began slowly to partition off the once unrestricted plains. Shorthorn and Hereford bulls were brought in to improve the quality of the tough, gangly bovines of the old trail herds. The severe weather of the early 1890s affected the ranchers as much as it did the eastern homesteaders, so further expansion was curtailed, but as the new century arrived, the cattle business re-blossomed with it.

First of all, the homestead lands between the White and Cheyenne Rivers began to attract settlers again; and, since it was the major railhead for the western "empire of grass," Pierre — for a time — enjoyed the unofficial title of the world's largest initial shipping point for beef on the hoof. Belle Fourche previously had claimed that same honor, shipping 4,700 carloads of cattle in 1894.

The second major development occurred in 1902 when the Indian Service decided to lease un-utilized tribal lands to ranchers on behalf of the Indian owners. This was a special bonanza for the huge companies which gradually had been losing valuable grazing acreage

For a brief period after the turn of the century, the railroad terminal town of Evarts on the east bank of the Missouri north of Pierre was a major cattle shipping point and the prospective river crossing for the Milwaukee Road's transcontinental line. When the stream ultimately was spanned at Mobridge, Evarts (shown as it was in 1903) faded into oblivion. (W. H. Over Museum)

Ed Narcelle demonstrated what the well-dressed nineteenth century cowboy wore. The Narcelle name was prominent during the heyday of the huge cattle companies. Paul Narcelle, Edward's father, came to the region as a fur trader in pre-territorial days. Another son, Narcisse, was at one time considered to be the largest individual ranch operator in the nation, with livestock ranging over the entire Cheyenne River Reservation. (South Dakota State Historical Society)

to smaller operators or "nesters" taking claims on the public domain. Where the Standing Rock and Cheyenne River Reservations came together, the Milwaukee Road had negotiated a lease for a sliver of land (on the latter reservation) six miles wide and some 87 miles long. The Strip, as it was called, was a fenced lane over which the ranchers could drive their herds to the Milwaukee's rail terminus at Evarts on the east bank of the Missouri. A pontoon bridge and a ferry facilitated the river crossing. The Indians were paid 25 cents a head for all cattle and horses using the Strip, but sheep were excluded. The railroad company provided dams and water holes at intervals where natural streams or lakes were not available.

Among the companies served by the unique cattle thoroughfare was the giant Matador of Texas with the Drag V brand, its top boss in South Dakota being Murdo MacKenzie after whom the Jones County seat of Murdo was named. The Flying V was the brand of the Sheidley Company whose management ranks included G. E. (Ed) Lemmon, namesake of the Perkins County town on the North Dakota border. A. D. Marriott's H.A.T. outfit (with three brands shaped like square, round and pointed head gear) was another major lessee. The Indians themselves — primarily mixed bloods of French and Sioux derivation — also used the Strip for shipping purposes.

This was the heyday for cowboys in South Dakota, and the extensive leases on Indian land made the traditional roundups, trail drives and tedious fence-riding necessary. As long as the railroad tracks stopped on the east side of the Missouri, the Strip played an important role in delivering beef to Chicago and other eastern markets. However, the ranchers continued to apply pressure to have the river bridged so that the rail cars could be taken to the cattle and not the other way around.

Crossing the Missouri River was a major problem for pioneer Dakotans and their Indian predecessors. Winter travel over the ice was a common but occasionally hazardous practice. Pontoon bridges provided summertime facilities at several locations such as Chamberlain where the floating span was also used for cattle drives. (South Dakota State Historical Society)

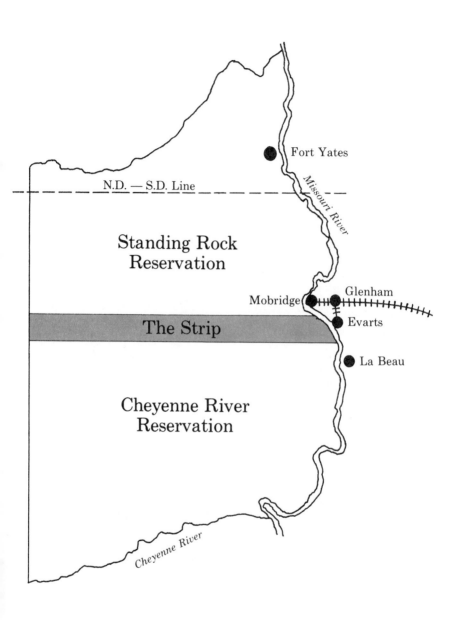

A corridor of land six miles wide and more than 80 miles long between the Standing Rock and Cheyenne River Reservations was fenced off shortly after the turn of the century to facilitate the shipment of cattle from the huge ranches on the old Great Sioux Reserve. Herds using "The Strip," as the lane was called, crossed the Missouri by pontoon bridge to Evarts, then the Milwaukee Road's terminus. When the rail lines were extended westward from Mobridge, Pierre and Chamberlain, The Strip lost its purpose and was discontinued. The cattle towns of Evarts and La Beau faded with it.

Mitchell's Goal: The Capitol and the Corn Palace, Too

While the railroads were committed to the development of the livestock industry, the Milwaukee and the North Western also became deeply involved in still another capital fight. Challenging Pierre for the governmental prize was the ambitious Davison County city of Mitchell which was gaining considerable local and national notoriety because of its unusual Corn Palace.

The Mitchell Corn Palace festival was first staged in 1892. Despite early success, the event was curtailed by drouth and hard times before it finally became an annual affair beginning in 1902. John Philip Sousa brought his nationally famous band to the exposition in 1904 (after much persuasion and hard cash), and he enjoyed it so much he returned in 1907 when the above photo was taken. (South Dakota State Historical Society)

The latter had its birthing in 1892 when Mitchell civic promoters adopted the idea of staging a harvest festival in a grain-decorated building. Prior to that time, Sioux City, Iowa, had been holding a similar event, first begun in 1887. However, when the fifth venture in 1891 was a financial failure, the backers decided to forego any future shows and it was then that the South Dakota town alertly seized the opportunity to capitalize on the Corn Palace theme. Despite hard times and bad weather, the celebrations in 1892 and 1893 attracted large crowds. Economic problems continued, however, and the exposition was not resumed until 1900 when presidential candidate William Jennings Bryan, a powerful orator, became the leading attraction of the third Corn Palace event. After another layoff in 1901, the fourth show was held in the agriculturally festooned hall in 1902, and thereafter performances were scheduled annually.

Then, on the theory that being nearer the center of population was more important than being at the geographic midpoint, Mitchellites helped persuade the state legislature to put the nagging capital question to the vote of the people again in 1904. The referendum was a tough blow for Pierre, still heavily indebted from the previous competition, but the citizens of the Missouri River rail terminus agreed that possession of the statehouse was worth the effort — and so the campaign got underway in earnest.

The Milwaukee Road (serving Mitchell) and the North Western (serving Pierre) provided free transportation for all South Dakotans wishing to visit the competing towns, with an estimated 100,000 passes being issued before the election was over. Hotel and restaurant accommodations were unable to keep up with the trainloads of curious guests, and so local residents were called upon to share their homes and larders with potential voters.

For two months the expensive and wearying sales effort continued. A carnival atmosphere prevailed in both towns as each tried to out-entertain the other. Pierre received considerable help from feather-bedecked Indian dancers and riders, and Mitchell gambled a huge advance fee to lure John Philip Sousa, the nationally famous conductor and composer of military marches, to lead his band in the Corn Palace for six days. During the annual fete, Pierre was denied exhibit space in the gaudy arena, so its boosters erected a display in a local hotel room.

In 1908 Gregory was a registration point for 4,000 new homesteads released for purchase in Tripp County. Named for John Shaw Gregory, a member of the first territorial legislature, the town was itself a product of the earlier Rosebud land opening in 1904. The "corn palace" idea did not catch on in Gregory as it did in Mitchell. (South Dakota State Historical Society)

As it turned out, Sousa was a great success, but the Mitchell capital quest failed. With heavy Black Hills support and the backing of many other South Dakotans who were tired of the repeated resurrection of the removal question, Pierre retained the seat of government by a vote of 58,617 to 41,155. It was a festive but wasteful campaign; the one gratifying note was that the citizenry had demonstrated quite conclusively that it wanted the statehouse located in one place permanently, no matter who could stage the biggest party.

The Rosebud Lottery: More Homesteaders Than Homesteads

Pierre and Mitchell were not the only South Dakota towns drawing crowds in 1904. Based on the agreement of 1889 whereby unallotted reservation land could be purchased by the government and released for homesteading, federal representatives began negotiating with tribal leaders to accomplish the objective. Early in the year a total of 385,817 acres in eastern Gregory County was declared surplus, and the General Land Office made plans to open the territory to settlers.

Because it seemed apparent that there would be more applicants than the 2,412 claims of 160 acres each in the original Rosebud Reservation, it was decided to distribute the land by lot. From July 5 through July 23, registration offices were to be established at Bonesteel, Chamberlain, Fairfax and Yankton, and when the hour arrived for the signup to begin, it was obvious that the authorities had guessed right.

Even an August rain in 1897 could not deter the citizens of Deadwood from turning out with their umbrellas to hear William Jennings Bryan, the silver-tongued orator from Nebraska who was the losing candidate in three presidential elections: 1896, 1900 and 1908. President McKinley, who twice defeated Bryan, also was a South Dakota visitor. (South Dakota State Historical Society)

The opening of reservation lands to settlement attracted huge crowds to registration centers. In 1904 the interest in the Rosebud lottery was so great at Yankton that additional signup accommodations were necessary to reduce the long lines. Though none appeared in the above photos, a few women applied for and won homestead sites. (Yankton County Historical Society)

In Yankton, for instance, Great Northern, North Western and Milwaukee trains shuttled eager land-seekers in and out of the city by the thousands. Hundreds of applicants slept all night in lines leading to the registration booths, and during the day opportunists rented out chairs, sold boxes for seating, peddled food and picked pockets. Some of the more enterprising individuals sold their places near the head of the line to less patient waiters — then started all over again themselves.

Winning the opportunity to buy a homestead on surplus Indian land was one thing; establishing a home and eking out a living from a treeless claim was another. The crudest kind of shacks, dugouts and soddies provided shelter for pioneer families. The ability of frontier women to survive the harsh conditions and to raise their children often without basic necessities is especially noteworthy. (South Dakota State Historical Society)

Altogether 106,296 hopeful homesteaders participated in the lottery for the 2,412 claims, more than half of them signing up in Yankton. Bonesteel, which had the second highest total, experienced the only trouble of consequence. The event attracted an assortment of gamblers and other questionable characters, and when the local authorities — with volunteer help — decided to drive the hoodlums out of town, several volleys of gunfire echoed through the warm July air. When the fray ended, one gambler lay dead and two were severely wounded in the brief altercation which came to be known as the "Battle of Bonesteel."

The first Rosebud opening initiated a series of similar land releases stretched out over a period of eleven years, all of them utilizing some form of lottery system. In 1907 a 55,000-acre tract on the Lower Brule Reservation drew 4,350 applicants for the 343 homesteads available. During the following year 114,769 registrants flocked to Dallas, Chamberlain, Gregory, Presho, O'Neill and Valentine

When surplus Indian land was freed for purchase and settlement, homestead seekers included a small number of women. At one signup point in the first Rosebud opening, a 13-year-old girl asked to register and was refused. When she presented proof that she was a divorcee and mother of a young son, her application was accepted. (South Dakota State Historical Society)

(the latter two in Nebraska) in quest of 4,000 land units in Tripp County. That second Rosebud opening topped the first by 8,000 signers.

In October of 1909 there were 81,456 hopeful enrollees at Aberdeen, Pierre, Le Beau, Mobridge, Lemmon and Bismarck (North Dakota) for approximately 10,000 160-acre plots on the Cheyenne River and Standing Rock Reservations. A million and a half acres in Mellette, Washabaugh and Bennett counties (Rosebud and Pine Ridge) attracted proportionately less applicants in 1911 because of the poor quality and inaccessibility of the land, an extremely dry year and undoubtedly the fact that the novelty of the land lotteries was wearing off.

After a span of four years, a final opening of approximately 100,-000 acres on the Standing Rock Reservation brought to a close the wholesale dispersal of surplus Indian lands bought and then resold by the United States government.

The first decade of the 20th century in South Dakota might well be called a maturing stage of the state's development. For all practical purposes, homesteading of the better quality unallocated Indian lands was completed during the period; and despite the so-called Panic of 1907 nationally, the long-awaited Missouri-to-the-Hills railroads were built. A second track-laying race between the Chicago and North Western from Pierre and the Chicago, Milwaukee and St. Paul from Chamberlain converged on Rapid City and brought into being a string of small towns along the right-of-way. (The North Western reached the goal on July 10, 1907, ten days ahead of its rival's first train.) The Milwaukee Road also crossed the Missouri at Mobridge, and its projected transcontinental line reached Lemmon in October of 1907, thus making additional public domain land along the Grand River accessible to settlers.

Politically, the era featured a split within the dominant Republican Party between the progressives and conservatives (also referred to as the "stalwarts"). In 1904 the conservatives elected Samuel H. Elrod to succeed Governor Herreid. The new state executive, who practiced law during territorial days in a one-room shack in Clark where he also survived a typhoid fever epidemic, managed in two years to clean up the state's obligations and put it on a solid fiscal footing. Though his record was relatively good, he was caught in a tide of the progressive movement in 1906 and defeated for renomination by Coe I. Crawford. Two years later Crawford won the senate seat of Alfred Kittredge, the "stalwart" candidate; and Robert S. Vessey, a Wessington Springs merchant and banker, became the second progressive governor.

During this unusual political period — when the Democrats were virtually a third party — the progressive Republicans fostered legislation to eliminate the free passes which railroads had used to such great lobbying advantage; to assess higher taxes on corporate property, railroads in particular; to establish direct primary elections; to provide free textbooks in public schools; and to require a bona fide one-year residence as a means to overcome the state's "easy divorce" reputation.

Economically, the state made considerable progress, though the Panic of 1907 had a delayed depressing effect on cattle prices and caused some western ranchers to switch to sheep-raising. In 1908 the Robert Hunter Granite Company opened the first large commercial quarry to capitalize on the high-grade, fine-grained stone found in Grant County. The following year John Morrell and Company — originally an English corporation — established a plant in Sioux Falls to supply pork products to customers in the British Isles. (In its first year the South Dakota branch processed 89,000 hogs in leased facilities; the firm moved into its own new building in 1911.)

Iowa-born Coe Isaac Crawford (right) was elected governor of South Dakota in 1906 as a progressive and United States senator two years later. His law partner in Pierre, Charles E. DeLand (left), became a prolific writer on historical subjects, particularly the La Verendrye explorations and the inhabitants of Dakota prior to the Sioux. (South Dakota State Historical Society)

Horsepower — from the animals themselves — played an important role in the development of permanent roadbeds for rail lines. Earlier, ties and tracks were laid directly on the prairie sod in the interests of speedy construction. A Milwaukee Road grading crew was photographed on the job near Chamberlain in 1905. (South Dakota State Historical Society)

Yankton suffered an industrial reversal in 1909 when the Western Portland Cement Company — which also had been started by British interests in 1890 — succumbed to the burden of high production costs and dismantled its huge plant, a move which stripped the former territorial capital of its "Cement City" nickname.

In the Black Hills the Homestake Mining Company survived a serious underground fire in 1907 which required an estimated 80 million cubic feet of water to subdue, but production in other shafts continued high as the demand for gold by the United States Mint maintained the firm's profit status. In late 1901, however, the company closed down the entire mine in reply to an ultimatum by the Western Federation of Miners which declared that its members would refuse to work with non-union employees. Mildred Fielder in her book *The Treasure of Homestake Gold* reported the effects of the tense situation:

As the track-laying race across western South Dakota progressed, small villages developed along the rights-of-way as they had earlier in the eastern part of the state. Among them was Belvidere on the Milwaukee Road — named for Belvidere, Illinois — reached by the first passenger train on April 4, 1907. (South Dakota State Historical Society)

First Passenger Train at Belvidere

The lockout began on schedule on the morning of November 25, and continued through the rest of that year. It was a time of fear and hate in the town. The company began recruiting men from other parts of the United States to build an adequate working force, and the union men in town knew this. Attempts at destruction of the company property were made, but the company hired over one hundred guards and Pinkerton detectives and placed them at strategic points on its property and the homes of its officials. They installed hugh search lights to play over the town at night and discourage night sabotage . . . Families were split in their loyalties. Many miners left town, but those who were left were adamant in their demands.

In 1909 in Sioux Falls John Morrell and Company established a packing plant which was to become one of the state's major employers. The complex was photographed as it appeared in the 1930s. Other early industrial ventures were not as successful as agriculture continued to provide the economic base for the region, while manufacturing, mining, food processing and other businesses were supplemental factors. (Clyde Goin collection)

Fortunately, the threat of violence passed with little more than a few bloodied noses and angry verbal interchanges. Before long the economic pinch became so great in the community that some of the union miners joined the non-members in requesting a return to work. The company relented and by mid-January, 1910, the Homestake was humming again.

A Welcome Immigrant: The Chinese Ringneck Pheasant

While all these varied activities were occurring across the state, a rather inauspicious development — which would produce unexpected long-range benefits for South Dakota — was taking place with little notice. Citizens were growing more and more concerned about the condition of the area's wildlife resources. Belatedly the realization of past sins of greed — the wanton slaughter of buffalo herds and indiscriminate market-shooting of prairie chickens and waterfowl — began to haunt a new generation starting to recognize that nature, too, had limitations.

Harry J. Teer, who worked 49 years for the Homestake Mining Company before his death in 1927, guarded bars of crude bullion containing both gold and silver prior to their shipment to the United States Mint. By standards of the 1970s — seven decades after this picture was taken — the eight bricks were worth a half million dollars or more. (Public Relations Department, Homestake Mining Company)

Governor Robert Scadder Vessey (center), who took office in 1909, was the first chief executive to serve in the new capitol dedicated the following year. A progressive Republican, the Wessington Springs banker and merchant appointed the first state game warden and fostered development of a game and fish department authorized by the legislature in the year he was inaugurated. (South Dakota State Historical Society)

In 1909 the legislature authorized a Department of Game and Fish to be managed by a commission consisting of the governor, the attorney general and the state game warden. Appointed by Governor Vessey to the $1,500-a-year job, W. F. Bankroft, the first warden, was authorized to spend just $200 annually to propagate game and fish without further commission approval. Under Bankroft the first serious law enforcement efforts were made to conserve South Dakota's wildlife, and numbered among the species to be protected was an Asiatic import called the Chinese ringneck pheasant.

In 1880 the United States consul in Shanghai — O. N. Denny — shipped 70 ringnecks to his brother in Oregon who released them in that state's Willamette River Valley where they thrived and became the basic stock for propagation in other areas of the United States. Just when the first pheasants were introduced to South Dakota is still a point of historical argument. It is known that N. L. Witcher of Sturgis proposed to import several pairs from Oregon in 1891 — but no record has been found to prove whether he did or not. In 1898 Doctor Arne Zetlitz of Sioux Falls acquired two male and four female ringnecks and succeeded in raising about two dozen young which he released in Minnehaha County. By 1902 several of the birds were seen as far away as Yankton County, and in the following year

Doctor Zetlitz released another hatching which gave evidence of surviving east of Sioux Falls.

By 1908 — the year Henry Ford's famed Model T first appeared on South Dakota roads — other private citizens copied the doctor's example. Spink County farmers A. E. Cooper and E. L. Ebbert introduced pheasants south of Doland. A. C. Johnson released 25 birds on his ranch near Frankfort, and at Redfield a nide of the alien birds was turned loose on H. A. Hagman's farm in the James River Valley. After that the Redfield Chamber of Commerce sponsored a large-scale planting followed in 1911 by an additional 48 pairs released in Spink County by the Department of Game and Fish.

It was from this somewhat uncoordinated and experimental beginning that nature cooperated to develop for South Dakota a major sports industry and its official state bird. In 1941 Game Director J. W. Cluett was able to issue a booklet titled "50 Million Pheasants in South Dakota" which boasted in part: "It has been estimated that since the first open season in 1919 approximately 20,000,000 pheasants have been *legally* killed in South Dakota, the equivalent of more than 3,000 cars of beef steers. The average bag for the past dozen years has been 1,500,000 pheasants each season."

Next to buffalo, the Chinese ringneck pheasant had the greatest effect on the South Dakota economy of all wildlife species. Introduced to the state shortly before the turn of the century, the colorful game bird thrived so well that local and visiting hunters began harvesting considerably more than a million a year after the first open season was authorized in 1919. (South Dakota State Historical Society)

The legislature of 1905 finally approved the sale of public lands granted to the state to pay for the construction of a permanent capitol. The allotted 85,000 acres of western rangeland covered only a fraction of the cost, but the project moved forward, and the new building was dedicated in 1910. As indicated in the lower photo, it was erected adjacent to the earlier wooden hall. (South Dakota State Historical Society)

Peter Norbeck: The New Progressivism

On June 30, 1910, a new state capitol building — modeled generally after the federal edifice — was dedicated in Pierre. South Dakota had been granted 85,000 acres of public domain to finance construction, but because the land was in the central and western portions of the state, it produced only a small fraction of the million dollar cost. Besides giving the commonwealth much-needed office and meeting space, the domed structure was a welcome symbol of permanency.

Governor Vessey was succeeded by Frank M. Byrne of Faulkton, another progressive Republican. The election of Woodrow Wilson to the presidency, coupled with the continued intra-party squabbles among the Republicans, permitted the Democrats to make notable gains within the state, culminated in 1916 by the victory of Edwin S. Johnson, a Yankton County farmer, in the United States senatorial race.

Meanwhile, South Dakota — like the rest of the nation — was experiencing the accelerated transition into the automotive age. Massive steam tractors had proved that the mechanization of

One of the state's most colorful and exuberant public officials was Peter Norbeck, a progressive Republican who became the first South Dakota-born governor in 1916. Later, as a United States senator, he was instrumental in the creation of Custer State Park and the Rushmore Memorial. (South Dakota State Historical Society)

E. S. Callihan came to Sanborn County in 1880 in a covered wagon and three years later introduced motor-power transportation to Dakota Territory with his three-wheeled, steam-driven "autocycle." It was photographed with its inventor in Woonsocket in 1884 where it frightened horses and enthralled youngsters almost a dozen years before Henry Ford unveiled his first experimental vehicle in Detroit. (Minnesota Historical Society)

agriculture was not only possible but inevitable. Motor cars of varying designs and power sources — from Sears high-wheelers to 12-cylinder Nationals — appeared on country roads throughout the state as livery stables were converted to garages and gasoline became more important as a transportation fuel than oats.

In 1884 — 12 years before Henry Ford unveiled his famed Quadricycle in Detroit — E. S. Callihan of Woonsocket had introduced a steam-driven three-wheeler which startled his fellow citizens in the tiny Sanborn County village. In the late 1890s Louis Greenough and Harry Adams of Pierre adapted a two-cylinder gas engine to an Elkhart wagon and the resultant machine worked well enough to carry as many as eight passengers. The two men hoped to get their investment back by charging for rides at fairs and exhibitions, but they were a little ahead of their time. At Mitchell they were refused permission to bring their vehicles inside the town limits, and the *Yankton Press & Dakotan* warned editorially: "It is a dead moral certainty that the infernal machine will frighten horses and endanger the lives of men, women and children."

As late as 1910, Abraham L. Van Osdel, who had been the Populist candidate for governor 18 years earlier, lashed out at the motor car in *The Historian,* a magazine he published at Mission Hill: "The automobile is a plaything for idle minds and hands. It is also a very successful contrivance for killing people." Though prophetic, Van Osdel was a voice crying ineffectively from a prairie blufftop.

More realistically, Ransom E. Olds — the automotive pioneer who gave his name to the Oldsmobile and REO — had explained in simple terms why the motor car would eventually replace the horse: "It never kicks or bites, never tires on long runs, and never sweats in hot weather. It does not require care in the stable and only eats while on the road."

Progress on the roads and in the fields was matched by activities in the political arena. In 1916 the state's voters elected their first South Dakota-born governor, Peter Norbeck. Son of a Lutheran minister, Norbeck was born in the cellar of a crude frontier home near Vermillion in 1870. Before his entry into politics, he had been a successful artesian well-driller, operating as many as 50 rigs in North and South Dakota at a time when water was desperately needed by homesteaders. Though he was an avowed progressive Republican, he had the personality and leadership qualities to restore a semblance of harmony to his party, thus keeping it in power in the state despite a second consecutive Democrat administration at the national level.

The persistent Women's Christian Temperance Union and the Anti-Saloon League managed — in the election of 1916 — to get prohibition restored to the state constitution. While decried by the liquor interests as a retrogressive action, the South Dakota measure preceded by almost four years the ratification of the Eighteenth Amendment to the United States Constitution which gave Congress power to prohibit the manufacture and sale of intoxicating beverages.

While the prohibition issue gained many of the headlines and generated much of the heat, Governor Norbeck moved forward

Advertised as America's first four-door automobile, the Fawick Flyer was manufactured in Sioux Falls by Thomas O. Fawick, who started building motor cars as a teenager. Theodore Roosevelt, 26th President of the United States, greeted potential voters from the rear seat of the South Dakota-made auto during a campaign visit. (South Dakota State Historical Society)

The automobile came to South Dakota as it did to all other states, and its increased use started a gradual change in shopping, farm marketing and general living patterns. The importance of the railroads began to diminish, and small towns — like Volin, above — ultimately experienced declining business activity as improved roads and greater speed permitted farmers to travel to larger population centers. (Jorgen Bruget collection)

quickly and vigorously to obtain the progressive legislation he had championed in campaign speeches. Under steady pressure from him, the legislature approved a dozen constitutional amendments for submission to the people, many of them related to business activities in which the state could (in Norbeck's estimation) serve the people more fairly than they were being treated by private or corporate operations.

Among his proposals were numerous enterprises which he believed the state might operate for the mutual good of the citizenry: a coal mine, a cement plant, grain elevators, flour mills, stockyards, packing plants, a hydroelectric development and a hail insurance company. He backed a wildlife conservation program, workmen's compensation, a mothers' pension and especially a rural credits plan to permit the state to make loans to farmers. Conservatives called him radical, but when Norbeck was challenged by the Nonpartisan League — which moved in from North Dakota to promote state socialism — Republicans and Democrats alike joined forces to re-elect him and repudiate the League which they considered to be an undesirable "outside influence on internal affairs."

Governor Norbeck and his fellow progressives believed it was a proper function of government to attack monopolies which charged exorbitant prices, to seek cheap credit for the state's citizens, to eliminate marketing and shipping abuses and to develop natural resources for the benefit of all. Their program — not fully tested in application — was well underway when a national emergency suddenly rearranged all the priorities.

World War I: Fervent Patriotism Sometimes Misguided

On March 9, 1916, Francisco (Pancho) Villa led a force of Mexican irregulars across the border in an attack on Columbus, New Mexico, killing 17 Americans. This episode had repercussions which were felt in South Dakota on the following June 18 when President Wilson ordered the mobilization of the South Dakota National Guard. Within a week the regiment was assembled at Redfield and thereafter moved to San Benito near the southernmost tip of Texas.

For seven months the South Dakotans served along the Rio Grande River on guard duty and in training maneuvers. In early March the unit was sent home, but less than six weeks later — on April 6, 1917 — the official declaration of war against Germany was proclaimed and the regiment was again called up. Beginning with the assassination of Archduke Franz Ferdinand at Sarajevo in June of 1914, there had been a gradual buildup to the seemingly inevitable world conflict, so the American people were not taken completely by surprise. However, when the war actually came, South Dakotans were, like other citizens throughout the nation, caught up in a burst of patriotic fervor which at times was carried to extremes.

The state's National Guard contingent was given a flag-waving send-off, but it did not serve for long as a separate unit. Several companies were assigned to the 147th Field Artillery which was informally called "South Dakota's Own," and the remaining members were widely dispersed to fill the organizational needs of the national army. In addition to the National Guard regiment, many young men and women — including Indians and non-Indians — volunteered or were drafted until more than 32,000 South Dakotans (almost six percent of the total population) were in uniform. Those who stayed behind, meanwhile, felt duty-bound to profess their hatred for the German Kaiser and to participate in the war effort in every way possible.

Governor Norbeck appointed a State Council of Defense which was given broad emergency powers by the legislature convened in special session. The lawmakers also passed measures requiring instruction in patriotism in educational institutions, prohibiting the teaching of all foreign languages in common schools, establishing a home guard and enforcing compulsory labor by idle or unemployed people. Those who didn't don a uniform, buy bonds, contribute to the Red Cross, work to produce food or otherwise become involved in the war effort were branded as "slackers" and in some cases had their houses daubed with yellow paint.

South Dakota, of course, had many citizens of German derivation who had migrated directly from the Old Country or from southern Russia. Not all of them understood all the ramifications of the conflict and were trapped between their respect for the Fatherland as they remembered it and a growing love for their new nation. Others, like the Hutterites in particular, had left Russia because of the pacifist tenets of their religion. Over-zealous patriots seized Hutterite cattle and sheep which were sold to buy Liberty Bonds. Young Hutterians who refused to bear arms were sent to prison, and in Beadle County a court action was brought to dissolve the corporation under which the colonies operated.

In Bon Homme County a rumor was spread that the Hutterite mill which produced flour for the community at large was grinding glass with the wheat as an act of sabotage. It finally took a government investigation to absolve the colony of the charge. In time the pressure became too burdensome and all the communes — except the oldest one at Bon Homme — sold out at depressed prices and moved to Canada, victims of the same intolerance they had sought to escape by leaving Russia.

Elsewhere around the state German books, dishes and even valuable heirlooms were burned in public displays. In Yankton the name of the historic Rhine Creek was changed to the Marne, the old designation having German connotations, the new French. Restaurateurs even revised their menus to eliminate German-fried potatoes and everything else with a Teutonic sound. German-language newspapers in Aberdeen and Sioux Falls were suspended

With the completion of a permanent capitol building, Pierre citizens were hopeful that the battles to retain the seat of government were at an end. A vintage airplane signalled the beginning of a new era for the small Missouri River city whose influence was to grow as the state itself developed. (South Dakota State Historical Society)

and their editors jailed. Anyone caught speaking German was suspected of treason, and only after strong appeals had been made were ministers in German churches — who were forced to preach in English — permitted to give a brief resume of the sermons in the tongue their congregations understood.

Members of the Nonpartisan League with its socialist beliefs were villified and attacked. Local defense councils broke up their meetings and drove recruiters out of town. Similar if not stronger action was taken against the Industrial Workers of the World, a socialistic labor union whose card-carriers (called "wobblies") came into the region primarily as harvest hands. Grain elevators, bridges and other strategic sites were protected by home guards against possible sabotage by the workers, and vigilante groups were set up to drive them out of town.

When the war finally ended on November 11, 1918, it was determined that 210 South Dakotans were killed in action in Europe and about half that many died later from the effects of wounds. At home there were scars which would take a long time to heal. Even ex-Senator Pettigrew had been indicted under the Sedition Law for making remarks about the foolishness of the war. The case was dropped following the Armistice, but the animosity lingered on. Undoubtedly the war-time experience with the I.W.W. left a bitter attitude toward all labor unions in the minds of many of the state's citizens, a condition which was to persist long after the "wobblies" disappeared.

Intense patriotism marked the World War I era in South Dakota as it did elsewhere in the nation. Bond rallies, recruitment drives, Red Cross activities, a Patriots' Day in Yankton (below) were examples of homefront involvement. Less commendable were the burning of German-language books, confiscation of Hutterite livestock and the daubing of yellow paint on the homes of so-called "slackers." (Frank B. Karolevitz collection)

While the injustices and super-patriotic actions must be accepted as historical fact, it should also be recognized that the vast majority of South Dakotans — like Americans elsewhere — were committed to the war with a full sense of national pride, an intense desire to win, a willingness to accept uncommon sacrifice and an unadmitted trace of fear. Their extreme spirit of dedication caused them to do what they did — good and bad — and when it was all over, they were entitled to enjoy the great celebration which followed.

Aftermath of War: The Silk Shirt Era

Among the saddest memories of the "war to end all wars" were epidemics of influenza which hit the state during 1918 and 1919. The official report of the State Board of Health recorded 1,093 deaths out of 65,839 known cases during the two years, three times the number of South Dakota's combat casualties in France. There were an additional 846 deaths attributed to pneumonia which often followed a flu attack. Schools, churches, theaters, lodges and even pool halls were closed to the public. Funerals for the victims of Spanish Influenza (as the disease was known) had to be held outdoors with only relatives and those already exposed to the contagion in attendance. It was a time of mixed emotions as many families which celebrated the Armistice went home to houses draped in black crepe.

By 1920, however, the worst was over, and South Dakotans were anxious to heed what President Warren G. Harding called "the return to normalcy". But just as every succeeding generation learns, it was not possible to go back to the "good old days". Thirty-two thousand of the state's young people had experienced new places and new things. They had served "to make the world safe for democracy", they believed, and they wanted to enjoy the freedom and the good life which their victory signified. Unfortunately, the economic and political realities did not permit an extended period of euphoria. For a time young men bought silk shirts and new "flivers" (as sporty automobiles were called) and tried to get around the restrictions of the prohibition laws by patronizing bootleggers and speakeasies (illegal liquor traffickers and night clubs, respectively). Conditions began to change rather quickly, however.

Prices of agricultural products — always a primary barometer of well-being in South Dakota — dropped sharply after the war-time demands eased off. Farmers who had invested heavily in more acreage at inflated land values found themselves with mortgages on property worth only a fraction of what they owed. Small banks began to fail (nine in 1922, 36 in 1923) when loans went unpaid. Fortunately, there was adequate moisture in most areas and the general morale held up, but symptoms of deeper problems started to appear — although few people recognized them at the time.

Gladys Pyle, shown at her desk in Washington, D.C., when she was a short-term United States Senator following the death of Peter Norbeck, broke the barrier for women in politics in South Dakota with her election to the state house of representatives in 1922. The Huron Republican later became the first female constitutional officer, serving two terms as secretary of state beginning in 1926. (Pyle collection)

Election of Gladys Pyle: Women's Suffrage at Last

The strong role played by women in World War I finally broke down the last of the barriers which had kept them from the ballot box. The 19th Amendment to the Constitution was approved by Congress in June of 1919 and submitted to the state legislatures for the required ratification by three-fourths of them. Because the women wanted to vote in the presidential election of 1920, rapid action was necessary.

In South Dakota suffragettes urged Governor Norbeck to call a special session, but he turned down the request because the war effort had required an extra call-up during the same biennium and there was no money left to pay for a second. The women were not to be denied, however. It was agreed that if they could get a quorum assembled in Pierre at the legislators' own expense, a special session would be authorized. Despite the additional complication of a blizzard, enough senators and representatives came to the capital where — on December 4, 1919 — they approved the amendment. The legislators convened just before midnight on the 3rd and adjourned shortly after midnight on the 5th to fulfill the legal requirement specifying that a special session must last for a minimum of three days. Tennessee later became the 36th state to ratify the suffrage measure, and on August 20, 1920, the amendment was officially validated.

One of the leaders of the movement to achieve ratification was Mrs. John L. Pyle of Huron, widow of South Dakota's fourth attorney general who died in office of typhoid fever at the age of 42. She and her husband had been involved in combining the defunct Pierre University and the faltering Scotland Academy (both Presbyterian institutions) into a new school called Huron College. After his death in 1902, she succeeded him on the college's board of trustees and later became active in the W.C.T.U. and the State Equal Suffrage Association which she served as president. When South Dakota's women voted for the first time in 1920, Mrs. Pyle became the state's initial female presidential elector, while Doctor Helen Peabody, head of All Saints Girls' School in Sioux Falls, was elected a delegate to the national Republican convention, the first woman in the United States so honored.

Youngest of John and Mamie Pyle's four children was a daughter, Gladys, born in Huron on October 4, 1890. Graduate of the college her parents had been instrumental in establishing, Miss Pyle became a teacher, served as a volunteer worker when the flu epidemic in Huron required conversion of the Episcopal parish house and Elks Lodge into emergency hospitals, and lectured for the new South Dakota League of Women Voters of which her mother was first president.

In 1922 Gladys Pyle decided to run for the state legislature, something no woman had done before. In the Republican primary she was defeated by a small margin, but she asked for a recount which resulted in her nomination by a 53-vote margin. In November she was elected one of Beadle County's three representatives, leading the ticket and becoming an historic symbol of the emergence of women in South Dakota politics. Later she was to score other firsts, being elected secretary of state for two terms beginning in 1926 and United States senator in 1938. With Miss Pyle's victory in 1922, total equality for women was by no means achieved, but a giant stride was taken down the long, long road.

The "Roaring Twenties": A Gas War

Despite the edgy financial condition in the state, South Dakotans were swept up in a wave of social and individual freedom being expressed in various ways by the "under 30" men and women of the nation. It was the era of "bathtub gin" (homemade intoxicants), "flappers" (gum-chewing girls in short dresses and bobbed hair) and two popular dances called the "shimmy" and the Charleston. Women were seen smoking cigarettes in public (a previously brazen rarity), and a criminal element emerged as the result of the huge profits which could be made in the illegal liquor trade.

Meanwhile, in the state political arena Peter Norbeck had won a United States Senate seat and was succeeded by Governor William H. McMaster, who had been a banker in Gayville before moving to Yankton. McMaster subscribed to his predecessor's progressive philosophies and as a result became involved in an unusual and controversial governmental action relating to the sale of gasoline. In two decades the automobile had evolved from a strange novelty to an economic necessity, all of which required new emphasis on supply facilities and road networks. Gravel finally was applied to some of the state's rutted country lanes in 1921, and in 1923 Sioux Falls and Dell Rapids were linked by South Dakota's first concrete highway. That same year the price of motor fuel topped 26 cents, and the governor immediately expressed his displeasure.

Under the provisions of the constitutional amendments permitting state involvement in business, McMaster ordered the South Dakota Highway Department (which had been created in 1916 to take advantage of federal road-building funds) to begin selling gas at all of its district headquarters for 16 cents a gallon. Oil companies were furious, of course, but the motorists were delighted as the "governor's gas war" succeeded in forcing the price down at commercial pumps. After that, every time the private firms started to raise their rates, McMaster responded with another state sale. The legislature backed the chief executive with a specific law, but then the United States Supreme Court stepped in and ruled that the retail gasoline business was not a proper venture for government.

The influence of the automobile was reflected further with the completion of a million dollar bridge across the Missouri River at Yankton, an important link in the widely promoted Canada-to-Mexico Meridian Highway (later designated United States Highway 81). That same year the state cement plant near Rapid City began production, and Yankton's high school basketball champions almost won the national title in Chicago, beating teams from Chattanooga, Tennessee; Dallas, Texas; Emporia, Kansas; and Detroit, Michigan, before losing in the finals to an even smaller-town entrant, Windsor, Colorado.

Less publicized but of major significance was another 1924 achievement which affected many of South Dakota's Indian residents. In 1888 Congress had granted citizenship to Indian women married to white Americans and later to other natives who had fulfilled various requirements of the allotment acts. In 1919 all honorably discharged veterans of World War I were so rewarded, and five years later President Harding signed a bill to make citizens of *all* Indians not previously endowed.

Like the matter of equality for women, all the problems of the conflicting cultures were not solved by that belated act, but at least the Dakotas were no longer aliens in their own land.

BOOK NINE

THE CHALLENGE
OF
THE DIRTY THIRTIES

The grasshopper said:
"It would not be absurd
For you to name me
Your official state bird."
— *Anonymous*

Just four days before the state's fortieth birthday, an historical event known as Black Friday occurred half a continent away at the New York Stock Exchange. The collapse of the Wall Street market on October 29, 1929, heralded the beginning of the Great Depression, and during the decade which followed, South Dakota was to feel the effects of the economic disaster as much or more than any other section of the country.

The prelude to the crash gave little indication that such a severe jolt would strike the country so suddenly and last for so long. The United States had weathered numerous recessions and so-called panics in the past, but usually they lasted only a year or two and required little more than brief belt-tightening and a few adjustments in financial circles.

The administration of President Calvin Coolidge — who, as Vice-President, succeeded President Harding when the latter died in office in 1923 and was elected in his own right the following year — was rather tranquil and without surface problems of major consequence. The most newsworthy achievement during the period was Charles O. Lindbergh's solo flight across the Atlantic Ocean in a small monoplane during May of 1927. On August 2 that year Coolidge, who was noted for his brevity of speech, was in the Black Hills when he made the succinct, much-quoted announcement that he would not seek reelection. He said simply: "I do not choose to run for President in 1928" — and let it go at that. Previously he had established the summer White House at the Game Lodge in Custer State Park, undoubtedly at the urging of Senator Norbeck who had been instrumental in the creation of the 127,000-acre recreational area. The presence of the President of the United States in the park and at his working offices in Rapid City high school focused national attention on the Hills. In effect, the emergence of the state's vital tourist industry can be traced to that historic visitation.
(Clyde Goin collection)

In Pierre Governor McMaster was followed in office by Carl Gunderson, who like Peter Norbeck had been born on a homestead near Vermillion. Unfortunately for the new chief executive, the progressive programs of his predecessors began to exhibit the fiscal deficiencies the conservatives had predicted for them, and Gunderson was virtually powerless to head off the impending crisis.

Rural Credit: A Massive Debt and Scandal, Too

Among the state's liberal statutes were the bank depositors' guaranty and rural credits laws, each of which involved the government intimately in private financial affairs. The former offered insurance to individual savers against bank failure, while the latter was a farm loan program. Beginning early in the 1920s when the first small banks began to close their doors because of mortgage defaults, the guaranty fund was put under heavy pressure. By the time Governor Gunderson was inaugurated, depositors of 175 insolvent institutions had wiped out the available money and certificates of indebtedness were issued to those who came later. By the end of 1926 the fund was in arrears by 43 million dollars.

That first crisis was resolved (but not happily) when the legislature amended the law and the Supreme Court, in effect, declared the guaranty fund bankrupt. Private citizens were left holding almost 40 million dollars in worthless certificates, a condition which did not inspire confidence in governmental agencies.

The problems of the guaranty fund also caused the legislature to become concerned about the rural credits system, and it ordered a special investigation of the program's operation. It was discovered rather quickly that funds from the sale of the loan organization's bonds were invested in banks which had suspended operation, the largest amount being in a Pierre depository managed by A. W. Ewert, who just happened to be the treasurer of the rural credits board. Ewert, was convicted of embezzlement and sentenced to eleven years in the penitentiary.

The financial scandal — the second in South Dakota's short history — rocked the state and added to the distrust building up among the citizenry. Gunderson and his friends blamed Norbeck and McMaster for the terrible state of affairs (and not without some justification since they had championed the progressive measures so devotedly). But in the election of 1926 Gunderson fell victim to the circumstances and was defeated by William J. Bulow of Beresford, South Dakota's first Democrat governor. The popular Senator Norbeck rode out the criticism with little problem and was re-elected to the United States senate with a large majority.

The rural credits system was like a millstone around the neck of the state government for more than a quarter of a century. Almost 12,000 farm loans were made for a total of 45 million dollars. As farmers failed because of seriously reduced commodity prices, the state received title to almost two million acres of land through foreclosures. The value of the property had also dropped drastically, too, so the rural credits agency found itself with farms worth only a quarter of the original loan figure. Besides that, the Supreme Court ruled that the state had to pay taxes on the land it had acquired. Before the final payment on the debt was made in 1954, the grand progressive experiment — which sounded so good in theory — had cost South Dakota an estimated 57 million dollars.

Governor Bulow, in his first term, was so insistent upon a balanced budget that he vetoed the state appropriations bill when the legislators approved a deficit spending measure. His veto was upheld, and when the Republican majority refused to pass a new bill, the Supreme Court backed the governor who then convened a special session in which a satisfactory solution was achieved.

Bulow was re-elected with little difficulty in 1928. Throughout the nation there was a general feeling of prosperity as the price of stocks rose to record levels. South Dakotans were not particularly bad off, but the effects of the rural credits and guaranty fund fiascoes, plus continued bank failures and depressed prices for farm

During the Great Depression many South Dakotans found employment in various New Deal programs, primarily the Works Progress Administration and the Civilian Conservation Corps. A few of the more independent citizens turned to the tiny streams of the Black Hills with gold pans and sluicing equipment to try to eke out a few dollars a day to tide their families over the hard times. (Clyde Goin collection)

commodities, made the state's situation a little edgier than that of other areas where local problems were not present to compound the national calamity which struck in full force in 1930.

As dust and tumbleweeds reclaimed once fertile fields and abandoned farms, the historic reference to the Dakota prairies as the Great American Desert was revived by writers and historians. The challenge of a wrathful nature was too great for thousands of South Dakotans, many of whom packed what belongings they had and headed for the West Coast. (United States Department of Agriculture)

A Double Blow: Drouth and Depression

The stock market crash in late 1929 triggered a rapid reaction which swept across the country. Within a month owners of stock saw their paper holdings reduced in value by 30 billion dollars. Banks and businesses failed. Factories closed and mines shut down, and soon the unemployment lines in the cities began to grow longer and longer. It was a strange phenomenon which historians and economists have been trying to dissect and explain ever since; but directly faced with the problem at the time was President Herbert Hoover, whose international reputation for feeding the hungry of the world was challenged to the extreme by the sudden wave of poverty which swept over his own country.

In South Dakota — which had a population of 692,894 in 1930 (its all-time high decennial total through the 1970 census) — the situation was further aggravated by the extended period of depressed farm commodity prices which had wiped out what little savings rural residents might have accumulated. It also reduced their purchasing power, an unhappy fact which was soon felt by town merchants. Warren E. Green, a Hamlin County Republican, replaced Governor Bulow in Pierre, while the latter defeated United States Senator William McMaster in his bid for re-election. Economy became the watchword at the state capital as the obligations arising from the rural credits venture added to the internal problem. To make matters worse, a third major scandal broke into the headlines.

M. Q. Sharpe, the attorney general, uncovered serious irregularities in the state's banking department, and when the investigation was completed, Superintendent Fred R. Smith was arrested and confessed to embezzling more than a million dollars he had transferred to a Platte bank in which he had an interest. A dazed public could hardly believe what the news stories revealed; and just when it seemed that no further ills could be inflicted on the state, an unprecedented natural disaster administered the crowning blow.

In July of 1930 temperatures soared above the 100 degree mark and persisted until crops shriveled in the fields. The intense heat began to take its toll of fat hogs and cattle, too, so farmers rushed them to market in a shipping flurry which forced prices downward an additional notch. That was the beginning of a drouth cycle which was to plague South Dakota for the greater part of a wearying decade which came to be known as the "Dirty Thirties." The uncomplimentary title made reference to another clout from nature which the *Yankton Press & Dakotan* reported in its edition of April 18, 1931:

> One of the worst dust storms in many years visited Yankton and surrounding territory yesterday. Old-timers here failed to recall as severe a storm of the kind as far back as 35 or 40 years . . . The thick dust filled the air and obscured the sun, and many motorists used the lights on their cars as a precaution.

Unfortunately, the first of the "black blizzards" was to be followed by many more in the years to follow. The parching effect of torrid temperatures on over-farmed land not properly covered by vegetation created an ideal condition for wind erosion. It was largely a delayed repercussion from the intensified tillage of World War I when the government appealed for full-scale food production with patriotic slogans: "If you Can't Fight, Farm!" "Plow to the Fence for National Defense."

When the resultant storms rose on the horizon, housewives who packed towels and other materials around window sills and door thresholds didn't know whether they were keeping out the topsoil of North Dakota, South Dakota, Oklahoma or Saskatchewan. In time the repeated summertime gales piled the silt along fence rows like snow drifts until only the tops of posts could be seen. Unlike snow, however, the dust did not melt and disappear.

In 1931 the drouth and the depression did not crack the spirit of most hardy South Dakotans. They read about breadlines and soup kitchens being formed to feed the hungry in eastern cities, and they listened to news reports on their battery-powered radios. Editors within the state tended to write in optimistic tones, so much so that their editorials could almost be interpreted as whistling in the dark to keep their courage up.

There was no denying the reality of "hard times," however. The great hope, of course, was that the problem would go away as quickly as it had come. Unfortunately, that was not to be the case.

Democrats in Control: A New Deal

During the first seven decades of territorial and state government — from 1861 through 1930 — the Republican Party maintained almost complete control of the major elective offices. Of the 11 delegates to congress, only J. B. S. Todd and Moses K. Armstrong were Democrats. Louis K. Church was the lone Democrat among 11 territorial governors. In the statehood period there were 12 governors, 16 United States representatives and 10 United States senators, all members of the Grand Old Party except Governor William J. Bulow, Representatives Harry L. Gandy (who had been publisher of the *Wasta Gazette*) and Senator Edwin S. Johnson. With 54 of 60 winners in key positions, there was no question why South Dakota — in its early years — earned the reputation as a solid Republican state.

The expensive deficiencies of progressive Republican legislation, the much publicized financial scandals and the strength of Franklin D. Roosevelt as he wrested the presidency from Herbert Hoover gave South Dakota politics a new perspective in 1932. Only Senator Norbeck was able to buck the Democratic tide, as Tom Berry, a Belvidere rancher, became governor while his party took control of both houses of the legislature for the first time.

By inaugural day in 1933, the nation's economic condition deteriorated so badly that drastic action was necessary. President Roosevelt, in an effort to boost public morale, made his historic pronouncement that "the only thing we have to fear is fear itself" — and then he called Congress into special session to seek hard-hitting solutions to the country's plight.

The New Deal, promised by Roosevelt in a campaign speech, was put into effect through a series of measures aimed at the various national ills. The President himself was granted broad powers to implement programs and policies he and his advisers considered imperative. Many of the remedies were experimental and without precedent, but the Great Depression was without precedent, too, so old elixirs for earlier panics were deemed inappropriate. The Federal Emergency Relief Administration, the Agricultural Adjustment Administration, National Recovery Administration (with its Blue Eagle symbol), Public Works Administration, Works Progress Administration, Federal Housing Adminstration and numerous other agencies were created. All were known by simple abbreviations such as the FERA, AAA, NRA, PWA, WPA and FHA, with President Roosevelt being pictured by cartoonists as "chief cook of an alphabet soup" recovery program.

Governor Berry in South Dakota called for rigid economy in government as tax delinquencies mounted, more banks failed and mortgage foreclosures increased. The state got out of the hail insurance business and sold its unprofitable coal mine. Of all the state-owned ventures envisioned by the earlier progressives, only the cement plant proved to be a sound investment. After a modest small

Tom Berry, a working rancher from Belvidere (on lead pony), became the state's second Democratic governor in the election of 1932 when, for the first time, that party also took control of both houses of the legislature. Liaison with the federal administration was an important governmental activity as numerous New Deal programs — many of them experimental — were introduced in the concerted effort to turn the economic tide. (Clyde Goin collection)

grain and hay crop in 1932, the drouth returned with intensified fury in 1933 and 1934, and South Dakota became part of the great Dust Bowl of middle America. The so-called "Okie" migration to California began, and many South Dakotans joined the exodus and headed for the West Coast.

In the meantime, the majority of the citizens gritted their teeth and did what they could to hang on. Many farmers had become involved in the Farm Holiday movement, which was no holiday at all but a militant effort to stop mortgage foreclosures and to reverse the disastrous price trend. Even before President Roosevelt was inaugurated, angry farmers established picketlines on roads with the intent of stopping all livestock, grain and dairy products from going to market. Such a withholding action, they felt, would force prices up when commodities grew scarce. The rural strikers pulled the pockets of their bib-overalls inside out to indicate their financial straits, and they blocked highways with planks full of sharp spikes to keep trucks from passing. The greatest activity of this type occurred in the southeastern section of the state, and it came to a head on February 4, 1933, near Jefferson when a milk producer from Elk Point was shot to death while trying to run the blockade. The Farm Holiday, which did little more than stir up animosities, began to fade shortly after that when new federal programs started to offer hope for improvement.

As it was, commodity prices had dipped so low that farmers who shipped hogs and cattle to market when they could no longer afford to feed them did not receive enough in return to pay the trucker and the selling fees. With farmers having no money to spend, the depression spread quickly to the towns and cities, too, and by the end of 1934 the number of South Dakotans on relief rolls reached 39 percent of the total population, the highest figure for any of the 48 states. By then the depths had been reached, and there was nowhere to go but up.

Glistening Gold: A Lonely Bright Spot

Among the various readjustments being made in the United States was the repeal of national prohibition on December 5, 1933, when Utah became the 36th state to ratify the substitute 21st Amendment. From the beginning, the anti-liquor measure was unpopular, controversial, difficult to enforce and conducive to underworld involvement. South Dakota, too, had its share of illegal alcohol stills and bootleggers. During the summer of 1933 Governor Berry had jumped the gun somewhat by calling the legislature into special session to pass a law legalizing the sale of beer in the state. This was done not merely to make the beverage available to parched South Dakotans, but because it offered a new source of tax revenue to provide matching funds necessary for the state to get relief grants under the Federal Emergency Relief Administration.

The exodus from America's Dust Bowl states constituted one of the most dramatic and tragic episodes in the nation's history. This photograph, taken in central South Dakota and released by the Works Progress Administration, depicted an unstaged reality often repeated. Indians on the west-river reservations were particularly hard hit and had less opportunity to escape. (Clyde Goin collection)

Ratification of the repeal amendment came just in time for a big celebration in the Black Hills. On January 30, 1934, the Gold Reserve Act was passed, establishing the price of the precious metal at $35 a troy ounce; earlier the nation had gone off the gold standard by executive order of the President, which meant that gold could no longer be used as a medium of exchange. The ensuing complex economic maneuvers which affected national and international finance could be reduced to a simple, promising fact in South Dakota: it meant that the production of the Homestake Mining Company would be purchased by the government at a guaranteed premium price.

Contradictorily, while the rest of the state was struggling through the bleak period, the situation at Lead and elsewhere in the vicinity of the mines was strangely reversed. An air of prosperity prevailed as the work force was expanded at the Homestake. In 1934 the company sold sixteen and a half million dollars worth of gold, and its corporate stock reached $430 a share from a pre-depression level of $50.

It was an incongruous circumstance. With the economy so seriously depressed everywhere else, the legislature turned to the most potential source of tax revenue, the underground wealth of the Black Hills' most productive lode. In 1935 a four percent ore tax was levied, and the $750,000 collected from the Homestake provided a third of the state's operating budget. All other mines were excluded by tonnage exceptions. By 1936 the company's stock had climbed to $544 a share, after which its tax burden was raised to six percent. As a result, all South Dakotans benefitted indirectly from the gold output as the Homestake assumed an even greater portion of the state's financing.

In addition to changes of direction relating to prohibition and gold, the Indian Reorganization Act was passed on June 18, 1934. By its terms the much abused land allocation program (in effect for 47 years) was terminated, and the practice of de-Indianization was reversed. Surplus land was returned to tribal control, and a system of government for the reservations was outlined. Because of dire conditions imposed by the weather and the general depression, however, the milestone policy reversal did not have the elating impact it might have had under different circumstances. Many white ranchers leasing land were wiped out financially and left the area, while the limited numbers of Indian cattle failed to survive the drouth and the local needs for food.

The reorganization law — like most Indian policy legislation — satisfied some and disturbed others. In general, however, tribal governments were strengthened by the measure and were promised greater authority in the management of their own affairs, a condition

Explorer II, with a 3,700,000 cubic foot gas capacity, was held to the floor of the Black Hills Stratosphere Bowl with mooring ropes payed out by soldiers as the massive bag was filled with helium. At dawn on November 11, 1935, the balloon was released to begin its 13-mile climb to an altitude record which was unchallenged for 21 years. (©National Geographic Society)

which did not totally occur in practice in ensuing years. Unfortunately, because the Indian standard of living was already so low before the Great Depression struck, conditions on the reservations were doubly difficult. Red Cross aid, private philanthropy and finally direct federal assistance under various New Deal programs maintained a survival existence for most families.

The Civilian Conservation Corps — a work-relief program for young men between the ages of 17 and 24 — was a particular boon to many Indians, not only because it provided employment but because of the work accomplished in tribal communities. The CCC, incidentally, employed more than 25,000 enrollees and supervisory personnel during its existence in South Dakota. Its workers made numerous improvements within parks and other recreational areas, planted thousands of trees, built dams and wildlife refuges and battled the depleting effects of soil erosion.

Distribution of government commodities — reminiscent of the old treaty ration days — helped alleviate hunger on the reservations. Unlike the past, however, many non-Indian fellow South Dakotans were also standing in line to receive oranges, powdered milk, preserved meats and other surplus products which were more vital to health than many of the recipients cared to admit.

Prelude to the Space Age: The Stratosphere Bowl

During the mid-'30s, South Dakotans needed all the diversion they could get to take their minds off their troubles, and in the Black Hills a natural sunken amphitheater became the site of three such attention-grabbing events. The National Geographic Society and the United States Army Air Corps teamed up to attempt explorations of the stratosphere by balloon, and the unique crater-like bowl — some 425 feet from rim to bottom — was selected as a logical launching arena.

The first ascension took place on July 28, 1934, and after the massive bag of helium had reached an altitude of 60,000 feet, the fabric began to rip and the balloon and gondola crashed in a field near Holdredge, Nebraska, after the men aboard had parachuted to safety. The exciting drama caught the fancy of Americans everywhere and focused favorable attention on South Dakota. Interest in a second flight was high, but after the long preparatory work, the balloon split open an hour before takeoff and the mission was cancelled.

A third try was scheduled for late 1935, and again the nation's press — also looking for brighter news — highlighted the activities at the remote Stratosphere Bowl. The following graphic description of the ascent was included in *A South Dakota Guide,* a WPA project to give employment to writers and researchers in the state:

Captains Orvil A. Anderson, pilot, and Albert W. Stevens, scientist, wore football helmets to protect themselves on their descent in Explorer II, the balloon sponsored jointly by the National Geographic Society and the United States Army Air Corps. Fortunately, they landed without problem near White Lake, South Dakota, after an eight-hour flight in November of 1935. (© National Geographic Society)

. . . for weeks scientists, balloonists and Army troops toiled day and night in preparation for the flight. Finally, on November 10, the long-awaited high pressure area drifted in from the west, indicating the weather would be ideal for a flight the next day. All guests were barred from the bowl; truck loads of soldiers arrived from Fort Meade to hold the balloon in leash while the helium gas flowed into it. At night a huge battery of floodlights, placed in a circle around the floor of the basin, were [sic] turned on, lighting the bowl so brightly that it was possible to read a newspaper at any time during the night.

Mooring ropes were attached to each of the points in the scalloped edge of a girdle encircling the balloon near the top, and these ropes were payed out by the soldiers as the balloon filled with gas. Soon after inflation began, some gas formed a pocket in the fabric underneath and caused a 17-foot tear, resulting in more than an hour's delay while it was being mended. As the first streak of dawn was seen above the cliffs, the important task of fastening the gondola to the balloon was completed . . . The 40 bags of lead dust, the emergency parachute and heavy scientific equipment . . . could be seen hanging from the gondola's sides as the craft was maneuvered to take advantage of favorable air currents. Inside were Captain Albert W. Stevens, scientist, and Captain Orvil A. Anderson, pilot, making last preparations. At 7:01 a.m. word was given to cast off, and the giant balloon, clearing the rim of the bowl by only 50 feet, floated upward.

Explorer II, then the world's largest balloon, was made of two and two-thirds acres of cloth and weighed 15,000 pounds including gondola, instruments and crew. Its height at takeoff was 316 feet

The grasshopper invasions of the Dirty Thirties — like the dust storms of the same period — almost had to be experienced to be believed. In addition to devouring drought-diminished crops, the voracious insects nibbled house paint, piled up under store windows and street lights and literally made railroad tracks and hardtop roads slippery with their crushed bodies. (South Dakota State Historical Society)

In an almost futile effort to overcome the grasshopper menace, farmers scattered poison bait by hand, and agricultural engineers devised mechanical contraptions to speed up the process. Old hay rakes (bottom) were redesigned as 'hopper-catchers in the desperate struggle to save what crops the searing sun did not destroy. (Cooperative Extension Service, South Dakota State University)

from ground to bag-top. In the cumbersome craft, Anderson and Stevens soared to an altitude of 72,395 feet (13.71 miles above sea level), at that time man's highest ascent above the earth. For an hour and a half the two men made observations and collected data, and on their way down they achieved a radio hookup with the commander of a seaplane (the China Clipper) flying over the Pacific Ocean and with an editor in London. The historic eight-hour flight ended with a perfect landing in an open field near White Lake, South Dakota, 240 miles east of the landing site.

A Final Blast: The Crisis Passes

Almost predictably, the extended drouth was accompanied by another natural enemy of agriculture: the grasshopper. The voracious insect — which had helped chase many of the region's earliest homesteaders back to the security of less challenging eastern states — took advantage of the good hatching weather and undisturbed egg deposits in abandoned fields to build up its numbers to destructive proportions. On many farms what crops the sun didn't burn up, the grasshoppers devoured.

Huge swarms migrated across the state; and in addition to the effects of their insatiable appetites, they became one more distasteful, morale-cracking symbol of an unhappy era. In cities and towns they piled up against store windows and under street lamps. They landed in such quantities that they made highways and railroad tracks slippery with their squashed remains. Entomologists worked hard to find effective controls, but one of the earliest — a poisoned bran spread at the ends of corn rows and other strategic locations — took a toll of songbirds, pheasants and other wildlife along with the intended victims.

Like the crisis stage of a burning fever, all the natural calamities seemed to reach a live-or-die peak in 1936 when a summer heat wave of stifling intensity engulfed the region. In June and July there were at least 32 days in which temperatures topped 100 degrees; on July 18 the mercury reached the 116-degree mark as concrete streets buckled at the seams and asphalt roadways melted. More black blizzards, grasshoppers and an infestation of caterpillars in the southeastern portion of the state added to the miseries. People prayed for rain — privately and publicly — and then on July 27 a heat-relieving shower fell on some of the counties.

New Deal programs such as the Works Progress Administration provided the dual advantages of employment and community betterment. A town hall at Wilmot, a museum at Rapid City, a jail in Canton, a new courthouse for Aurora County in Plankinton, a swimming pool in Lemmon, numerous bridges, roads (like the one below at Long Lake) and other worthwhile projects were completed despite the fact that a certain amount of political boondoggling was involved. (Clyde Goin collection)

"Before" (above) and "after" views of the same Beadle County farm illustrated the rapid and dramatic recovery made in some areas of the state even before the end of the 1930s. New agricultural techniques and crops played an important role in the turn-around, but rain was the most vital ingredient. (United States Department of Agriculture)

No one knew it at the time, but with that welcome moisture, the weather cycle which created and characterized the Dirty Thirties, began slowly to change for the better. There was still a long way to go, however, because the improvement was almost imperceptively gradual. Migrations from the state continued to run high. New Deal relief measures were still necessary to keep families warm, fed and clothed (many rural residents wore matching shirts and dresses sewn from printed cotton feed bags). Attempts were made to utilize the region's extensive lignite coal resources, but even with cheap depression labor the results were not economically feasible. Farm prices — which had started to rise slightly because of political efforts and successive years of poor yields — remained well below favorable recovery levels.

In Mitchell the Corn Palace decorators brought in evergreen boughs from the Black Hills to supplement the meager supply of fancy corn and small grain normally used for the design work. On the open prairie, the ubiquitous Russian thistles — seeds of which were reputedly brought over inadvertently from the Old Country in the clothing or baggage of immigrants — continued to tumble across the silt-covered fence rows to accentuate the fact that the land, as well as the economy, faced a long period of revitalization.

Governor Tom Berry attempted to overcome tradition and was defeated in his third-term bid by Leslie Jensen of Hot Springs, former collector of internal revenue for South Dakota and independent phone company executive. At the same time the Republicans recaptured the state senate by the slim margin of a single vote. Some analysts interpreted the trend back to customary Republican domination as a general concensus that the worst was over and that voters were responding normally again. On the other hand, President Roosevelt's wide plurality over Alfred M. Landon in South Dakota was apparently something else again.

While the Great Depression may be considered as a somewhat brief and isolated segment of the state's history, that narrow view does not take into account the scars and deep-seated attitudes which survivors — young and old — carried over into later decades. Memories of the crash, the cropless years, the dust, the poverty and all the other limitations of the era governed the thinking of parents of teenagers in the 1950s and 1960s. Youngsters could not grasp the severity of life in the Dirty Thirties in their own age of television, autos and affluence; to some degree the so-called "generation gap" of the later time period had its spawning amid the "hard knocks" of the past.

BOOK TEN

THE CHALLENGE OF A CHANGING LAND

> *"Come all ye weary and heavy laden*
> *and renew your youth without the*
> *aid of goat glands or Lydia Pink-*
> *ham's compound, and bless this hap-*
> *py, youthful, growing state with*
> *your presence, for all that South*
> *Dakota lacks is folks."*
>
> — *Will A. Wells*
> *Webster Journal, 1927*

The federal census of 1940 gave South Dakota a population of 642,961 which was 49,888 less than the previous count ten years earlier. Not only had the Great Depression affected the well being of individuals who lasted out the struggle, but it disrupted the gradual growth pattern of the state as a whole. A people shortage was not particularly noticeable on November 3, 1938, when an estimated 125,000 spectators were in attendance at the national cornpicking contest on a farm south of Sioux Falls. More significant, of course, was the fact that South Dakota fields were again producing sufficient yields to warrant consideration of the state for such a prestigious event.

That year Harlan J. Bushfield, an attorney from Miller was elected governor to succeed Leslie Jensen, who tried for the Senate seat made vacant by the death of Peter Norbeck in 1936. The Republicans won a complete victory in 1938, but Jensen's bid was thwarted in the primary by J. Chandler Gurney of Yankton, who went on to defeat Tom Berry in November for the regular six-year senatorial term. Governor Berry had appointed Herbert Hitchcock to fill Norbeck's position until the 1938 election in which Gladys Pyle won the two-month "short term," giving her another first in state politics.

Chan Gurney was a pioneer of the radio industry in South Dakota, having been manager of WNAX in Yankton when those call letters were familiar from Canada to Mexico among early-day listeners who bought trees, hog tonic and other products from the Gurney Seed and Nursery Company which owned the station. It was Gurney who introduced a North Dakota farmboy accordionist named Lawrence Welk to broadcasting which, in turn, led to the musician's career as a nationally prominent television entertainer. The new senator had become popular himself as the announcer of the state high school basketball tournament at a time when some fans were still using homemade crystal sets for reception.

(South Dakota Department of Tourism and Economic Development)

In 1927 only Borglum's work shacks and initial stone removal (top) altered the natural appearance of the massive granite promontory in the Black Hills selected for the Shrine of Democracy. As he was "first in the hearts of his countrymen," George Washington (bottom) was also first on the mountain. (South Dakota State Historical Society)

In 1939 South Dakota celebrated its fiftieth birthday in an atmosphere of optimism. The value of farm crops for the year exceeded $75 million, no bank failures were recorded and a potential new source of revenue — the tourist industry — seemingly blossomed overnight as Americans everywhere indicated their intention to make up for the unlamented stay-at-home years. An estimated one million auto travelers came to the state, with their primary destination being the Black Hills and a phenomenal attraction called the Rushmore Memorial.

A showman as well as an artist, Gutzon Borglum (in knee pants) received the ceremonial drill bits from President Calvin Coolidge in a much-publicized inaugural program on August 10, 1927. Directly behind the President was Governor William J. Bulow, the first Democrat to hold that office in the state. With only a veiled promise of federal support from Coolidge, Borglum nonetheless tackled with great enthusiasm the monstrous task to which the remainder of his life would be devoted. (National Park Service)

Gutzon Borglum: Man Against a Mountain

Charles E. Rushmore was a young New York attorney representing eastern interests of the tin-and-mica Etta Mine near Harney Peak in the heart of the Black Hills. According to tradition, in 1885 he was returning from a visit to the diggings when the small party with which he was traveling passed an impressive granite formation which caused the lawyer to inquire about the promontory's name. Someone in the group (the honor is generally attributed to William W. Challis, a prospector and guide) supposedly said in jest: "Never had any, but it has now — we'll call the damn thing Rushmore." Whether the quotation is exact or not, whatever flippant remark was made ultimately gave title to one of South Dakota's most prominent landmarks. [The United States Board of Geographic Names officially recognized the title in 1930.]

Almost 40 years after Rushmore's visit to the Hills, State Historian Doane Robinson — in the early 1920s — began to espouse the carving of a gigantic Old West epic scene into one of the granite peaks of the *Paha Sapa*. The trail led him to Idaho-born Gutzon Borglum, then in his mid-50s, who had gained national prominence for a Confederate memorial he was creating on Stone Mountain in Georgia. With Senator Norbeck lending his influence, Borglum was

The scaffolding and rigging problems on the Shrine of Democracy project were enormous. Borglum maintained careful supervision over his employees — many of them unemployed miners available during the Great Depression — as the faces began to appear in the granite. Transfer of design dimensions from a scale model (see left of Lincoln's mouth) demanded mathematical precision. (South Dakota State Historical Society)

lured to South Dakota to discuss a possible project. Subsequently, when the already renowned sculptor broke off with his Altanta sponsors after a bitter quarrel, he returned to the Black Hills to pursue the idea of a mammoth statuary unequaled anywhere in the world.

Borglum rejected the concept of a western heritage theme, insisting that a work so gargantuan should be national in scope. In August of 1925 during a reconnaissance on horseback, he was shown the 6,040-foot Mount Rushmore with its bald outcropping of smooth-grained granite. His search was over; he accepted a $250 check from the Rapid City Commercial Club; and less than two months later — on October 1 — he and his confident friends held a public dedication of the unfunded project with more than 3,000 curious spectators in attendance. By then the artist was too enamored with the proposal to let fiscal obstacles delay him. He moved his family to Keystone, a tiny mining village near the site, and began the preparatory work. When President Coolidge established the Summer White House in Custer State Park in 1927, Borglum was ready for a second dedication and the baptismal drilling on the 60-foot-high head of George

Idaho-born Gutzon Borglum was in his mid-50s when he accepted the commission to carve the Shrine of Democracy on Mount Rushmore. Ironically, while he toiled at the project during the 1930s, South Dakota was experiencing one of the most trying periods in the state's history. Then, in 1939 when the gargantuan sculpture was officially dedicated, the long years of drouth and depression also came to an unlamented end. (South Dakota State Historical Society)

Washington, the first of four United States Presidents to be memorialized on the mountain.

[Of the money the sculptor had received to get to that point, $5,000 had come from Charles Rushmore, then an elderly man who may or may not have realized he was on the threshold of immortality.]

On August 10, Coolidge arrived at the scene on horseback, bedecked in cowboy boots and a ten-gallon hat. In his usual terse manner, he announced: "We have come here to dedicate a cornerstone that was laid by the hand of the Almighty." Then he spoke the magic words that Borglum and the other promoters had hoped for — that the monument deserved the support of the national government.

From that point on, the story of Borglum's mountain masterpiece became a saga of unrelenting persistence against geological, financial and political obstacles. A partially completed head of Thomas Jefferson had to be "erased" when a fault in the granite was discovered. Democrats in Congress threatened to withhold funding if Woodrow Wilson's image did not replace that of Theodore Roosevelt; later a congresswoman demanded the addition of Susan B. Anthony to the lineup. South Dakota school children contributed their pennies to the project in the heart of the depression. Senator Norbeck, in addition to maintaining continual leverage for fiscal aid at the federal level, became personally involved in the development of the famed Iron Mountain Road with its pigtails, switchbacks and tunnels, the latter designed to point directly toward the Borglum creation in the distance. Unemployed miners, who had no artistic experience or training, had to be schooled by the temperamental sculptor whose career goals were reshaped to pursue the single-purpose objective of carving a monument which, in his words, would be "so inspiring that people from all over America will be drawn to come and look and go home better citizens."

Altogether 450,000 tons of rock had to be blasted and chipped away from Mt. Rushmore before the task was completed. On July 4, 1930, President Hoover was present for George Washington's unveiling. On August 23, 1936, President Roosevelt attended the Jefferson commemoration. Always a showman, Borglum had another flamboyant ceremony to reveal Lincoln's features as part of the 150th anniversary celebration of the adoption of the Constitution in 1937; and on July 2, 1939, all four majestic faces were officially dedicated as a highlight of South Dakota's 50th year of statehood.

Borglum had more refining and retouching work to do, of course, but the dozen years of incessant labor — plus the strain of confrontation with politicians, members of the Memorial Commission and other governmental agencies — had taken its toll. On March 6, 1941, the 74-year-old sculptor (who from 1925 had averaged only about $10,000 a year in personal return for his creative genius and other contributions) died unexpectedly of a heart attack in Chicago. Thereafter, his son Lincoln was given the assignment of

The original idea for a massive carving on one of the Black Hills' granite formations has been credited to Doane Robinson (right), long-time secretary of the South Dakota State Historical Society. After Borglum's masterpiece on the mountain was dedicated in 1939, Robinson and Governor Harlan J. Bushfield posed with a blowup of a *Saturday Evening Post* cover, an example of the new, favorable publicity which Mount Rushmore began to obtain for the state. (South Dakota State Historical Society)

finishing the project. On October 31 that same year the final drilling was completed, and then the precipitous entry of the United States into World War II precluded another ostentatious ritual. Borglum before his death had expressed his satisfaction with the work and his confidence in the immortality of the colossal achievement:

> My dream has come true . . . There, on the mountain top, as near to Heaven as we could make it, we have carved portraits of our leaders, that posterity and civilization may see hundreds of thousands of years hence what manner of men our leaders were, with a prayer and a belief that there among the clouds they may stand forever, where wind and rain alone shall wear them away.

Not only did the Shrine of Democracy fulfill the artist's hopes as a patriotic mecca for all Americans, but it became an encompassing symbol of South Dakota's historic response to challenge against any and all odds.

Pearl Harbor: Repercussions on the Prairie

South Dakota was well on the way to economic recovery when Japanese warplanes attacked Pearl Harbor in the Hawaiian Islands on Sunday morning, December 7, 1941. While that particular event was a stunning surprise to the nation as a whole, the possibilities of an impending war had been considered in the United States for at least half a decade. As a matter of fact, when the bombs fell on the Oahu naval base almost half a world away, South Dakota's 147th Field Artillery Regiment — the first state National Guard unit to be federalized under a new defense-strengthening policy — was already on the Pacific Ocean enroute to the Philippines where another generation of volunteer soldiers from the prairies had fought more than 40 years earlier.

Additional South Dakota National Guard organizations — including the 132nd Engineer Regiment, the 34th Signal Company, the 109th Quartermaster Regiment and the 109th Engineer Regiment —

The wife of Governor Harlan J. Bushfield christened the hull of the *U.S.S. South Dakota* on June 7, 1941, exactly six months before the Pearl Harbor attack. Mrs. Bushfield later was appointed to succeed her husband as United States senator, the state's second woman to fill a short-term vacancy in the Upper House of Congress. With her for the launching ceremony was Secretary of the Navy Frank Knox. (Evans Nord collection)

had been activated prior to Pearl Harbor. In the four years to follow, fully one-tenth of the state's population donned military uniforms in response to the all-out national emergency.

Involvement of the nation in both European and Pacific war theaters generated a massive unified effort in all 48 states, each participating according to its own unique abilities as well as in the overall needs of personnel, finances, rationing, price controls and conservation. In South Dakota, of course, that meant a concentration on agricultural production. Despite manpower shortages and farm equipment badly in need of repair or replacement after the skimping depression years, the citizenry responded quickly and generously.

Students and townsfolk volunteered to do farm work. School children collected vitally important scrap materials and pods from the wild milkweed (the floss from which was used to fill life jackets for pilots and sailors). In Lead the War Production Board curtailed

The *U.S.S. South Dakota*, known as "Battleship X" and "Old Nameless" because of security restrictions, won 13 battle stars during World War II action in the Pacific, a total unsurpassed by any other naval vessel. After the Japanese surrender the *South Dakota* was relegated to the "mothball fleet" at Philadelphia, and in 1962 the Navy decided to scrap the once majestic flagship of the United States Third Fleet. Fortunately, interested citizens were able to preserve selected portions of the 680-foot dreadnought battleship, in a permanent memorial at Sioux Falls. (Evans Nord collection)

While the emphasis on mining in South Dakota has always been on gold, non-metallic minerals have also been produced in commercial quantities, especially during World War II when the demands for bentonite, feldspar and mica from the Black Hills were intensified. The glass, pottery and enamel industries particularly required feldspar; and deposits (like the one shown above near Keystone) were tapped and utilized. (Clyde Goin collection)

the gold operation so that employees could be shifted to strategic metal mines. The Homestake Company converted its machine shops to war requirements, manufacturing — among other things — airplane parts and hand grenades.

Unlike the experience of 1917-18, World War II in South Dakota did not generate the strong anti-German reactions on the home front so prevalent in the earlier conflict. This was due largely to the fact that the German-Russians and direct emigrants from the Fatherland were by then two and three generations removed from European ties.

Correspondingly, since few Japanese had ever lived in the state, the area was spared involvement in the confinement of Japanese-Americans in relocation camps, an ill-advised policy which was to be greatly lamented in ensuing years. Though there were some hoarders, profiteers, draft-dodgers and ration-stamp connivers, the general war-time attitude was one of subdued emotionalism and almost stoic dedication to the cause.

Army Air Corps installations of varying size and importance were located at Pierre, Mitchell, Watertown, Rapid City and Sioux Falls, the latter being a technical training base. The Rapid City field ultimately was enlarged to handle mammoth B-36 bombers and became a major permanent component of the Strategic Air Command, named Ellsworth Air Force Base in 1953 to honor its late commandant, Brigadier General Richard E. Ellsworth, who was killed in a plane crash that year.

In Fall River County near Provo the Igloo Ordnance Depot was established as part of the nation's arsenal. The state's colleges — with enrollment depleted — adapted courses and facilities to the needs of the war. Throughout South Dakota, War Bond rallies were held; Red Cross volunteers knitted sweaters and wrapped bandages; "victory gardens" were planted; women rode tractors and learned to

Joe Foss (right) was the leading combat pilot for United States forces in World War II, as the Marine major shot down 26 Japanese planes and won the Congressional Medal of Honor. He was elected governor of South Dakota in 1954. Francis H. Case (pictured with him) served the state as a United States representative and senator. (South Dakota State University)

weld; and, sadly enough, tears were shed in more than 2,000 households where loved ones were lost in combat or died of other war-related causes.

The state had an ample share of military heroes, of course, typified by three combat pilots with outstanding records: Marine Major Joseph Jacob Foss, a native of rural Minnehaha County who shot down 26 Japanese airplanes and won the Congressional Medal of Honor; Lieutenant Cecil E. Harris of Cresbard, who destroyed 24 enemy aircraft in the air and four on the ground; and First Lieutenant George Stanley McGovern, a native of Avon, who flew a B-24 Liberator appropriately named the *Dakota Queen* on 35 bombing missions over Europe and won the Distinguished Flying Cross in the process. In later years Foss and McGovern were to face one another as contestants in the political arena.

Dr. Ernest O. Lawrence, native of Canton, was awarded a Nobel Prize in 1939 for his invention of the cyclotron which, in turn, made possible the atom bomb. The brilliant scientist, who died in 1958, had the unique distinction of having lawrencium, the 103rd known chemical element, named for him. (Sioux Falls Argus Leader)

Meanwhile, another native of the state — Ernest Orlando Lawrence, born at Canton and with a doctorate from Yale University — was to play a vital role in the climactic finale of the global struggle. In 1939 Lawrence had received the Nobel prize in physics for his invention of the cyclotron, a device which was a key factor in the development of the atomic bomb.

On May 6, 1945, Germany had surrendered unconditionally, less than a month after President Roosevelt had died. He was succeeded by his Vice President, Harry S. Truman, who was soon faced with one of the momentous military decisions of all time. Doctor Lawrence and other scientists had perfected the nuclear warhead, and the President reluctantly approved its use. Consequently, on August 6 the world heard the startling news of the first atomic explosion at Hiroshima, Japan. On August 9 a second blast leveled much of Nagasaki; and, as a direct result, five days later the long, costly war was brought to an abrupt close.

Never proud of his part in the adaptation of his cyclotron to the creation of destructive force, Doctor Lawrence died on August 27, 1958, at Palo Alto, California, an avowed proponent of the peaceful use of atomic energy. Element 103, lawrencium, is named for him. His brother, John H. Lawrence, was graduated from Harvard Medical School and became renowned for his research in medicine, especially in the application of atomic energy to surgery. Their father, Carl G. Lawrence, served as president of Southern Normal (University of South Dakota/Springfield) and Northern Normal and Industrial School (Northern State College) Aberdeen.

South Dakotans celebrated the end of the worldwide conflict with as much enthusiasm as other Americans. There was an intense desire to return to the relatively uncomplicated existence of the past (drouth and dust storms excluded, of course) — but such yearnings were to become mostly wishful dreams. As it turned out, the extended effects of the war — over and above the international military engagements — were so widespread and diverse that life in South Dakota (or any other state, for that matter) would never be the same again.

Post-War Boom: Prosperity at Last!

Throughout its struggling evolvement as a territory and state, South Dakota moved from crisis to crisis in the continuing quest for well-being. Grasshoppers, drouth, floods, financial scandals, blizzards, wars, dust storms, depressions and other natural and man-made setbacks came along with such regularity that the state seemed destined to unending challenge and frustration. As a result of out-migration for military service and jobs in vital industries, the census of 1945 showed a further population drop to 589,702, less than 6,000 above the 1910 level. From that war-time nadir, however, a rebirthing took place which started South Dakota on a long-awaited upward plane.

In the political arena, the Republicans had re-established dominant control in 1942. Harlan Bushfield moved to the United States Senate and was replaced in the governor's chair by M. Q. Sharpe, Kennebec attorney who seldom used his given name, Merrell Quentin. Two years later, with the Allies on the offensive in Europe and the South Pacific, the G.O.P. scored a landslide victory, re-electing Governor Sharpe and winning every seat in the state senate and all but three in the house. Even Franklin Roosevelt, who had out-polled Republican candidates in South Dakota during the depression, showed poorly in the state balloting, though he won his fourth term nationally over Thomas E. Dewey. A wave of conservatism following the New Deal relegated the state's Democrats to an almost powerless position from which loyal party die-hards could only watch and wait for a political resurrection at some later date.

The Homestake Mining Company at Lead grew from a prospector's claim into one of the world's most valuable gold-producing properties. From shafts extended more than a mile below the earth's surface, the historic mine has continued to extract precious metal from low-grade ore in quantities sufficient to make South Dakota the leading gold-producing state in the Union. During World War II mining activities were severely curtailed and the Homestake firm manufactured hand grenades and other requirements of battle. (Public Relations Department, Homestake Mining Company)

More important economically was the fact that South Dakota's rainfall during the war years and immediately after was sufficiently adequate to deliver bountiful crop yields when the nation needed them most. Despite labor shortages and restrictions imposed by the national emergency, the state's farmers in 1944 produced almost 310 million bushels of grain and tended more than seven million head of cattle, hogs and sheep (a record number at that time). The following year was even better; and when peace was finally restored, the South Dakota economy was riding a crest of prosperity.

In many ways 1945 became a line of demarcation separating two historical eras. The scope of the war just ended; the extensive technological developments it fostered; the threat of nuclear destruction in any future military involvement; ever-widening chinks in age-old economic, social, political and religious foundations — all began to affect the traditional American living pattern. A far more mobile society grew out of a seemingly universal obsession of returning service people to own a new automobile as a symbol of self-freedom. Young veterans who had been exposed to the far reaches of the globe could not all be held in their native South Dakota; they were replaced, on the other hand, by out-of-staters who had appreciated the "elbow room" and rural lifestyle observed during service assignments in Sioux Falls, Rapid City, Provo and elsewhere. These changes are emphasized, of course, because in the aftermath of war, South Dakota would no longer be a semi-isolated, mid-continental island "off the beaten path." Air transport, interstate freeways and television were to hasten the erosion of parochialism in the years to follow.

The elimination of governmental controls made gasoline, automobiles and shotgun shells available for a revived invasion of tourists and pheasant hunters. Good crops and favorable prices made it possible for farmers to pay off past indebtedness at an accelerated rate. The Rural Electrification Administration — created in 1935 as a New Deal program — stepped up its campaign to wire farms and ranches in a state where kerosene lamps, windchargers and battery radios persisted longer than horses.

Concurrently, miners returned to the Homestake from widely scattered defense jobs, and gold production began anew. In 1947 company employees in Lead voted more than four to one against the United Mine Workers as a bargaining agent; and statewide, strong statutes limiting union activity were passed to supplement a so-called "right-to-work" amendment to the state constitution approved overwhelmingly by the electorate. In simplistic terms, the "right-to-work" law guaranteed that employment could not be denied any individual for failure to join a union, but labor leaders, on the other hand, insisted that the amendment prevented achievement of full membership and the resultant ability to bargain effectively with management. The controversial issue was to flare up again as interest in industrial development began to grow in the state.

Governor Sharpe attempted to buck the conservative attitude of the citizenry by seeking a third term in 1946 as Tom Berry had tried ten years earlier. Tradition prevailed and he was defeated in the Republican primary by George T. Mickelson. The Selby attorney easily won the general election in another sweeping G.O.P. victory in which only four Democrats went to the state legislature. Thereafter, the law-makers promptly passed a measure banning a third successive term for governors.

Mickelson was an avid supporter of a bonus for World War II veterans, and following his re-election in 1948, a $28 million appropriation was approved and dispensed, satisfying the state's self-imposed obligation and bringing a belated close to the historic war-time era.

Following Senator Bushfield's death in 1948, his widow — Vera Cahalan Bushfield, a native of Miller — was appointed to fill the short-term vacancy, serving from October 6 to December 26 of that year, reminiscent of the similarly brief tenure of Gladys Pyle in the Upper House ten years earlier.

Harnessing the Missouri: A Challenge Met

From territorial days, far-sighted Dakotans had viewed the meandering Missouri, not as a giant to be feared, but as a workhorse to be corraled and utilized. Under control, it would provide tremendous irrigation potential and electrical generating capacity. Furthermore, a series of dams on the river would relieve — if not eliminate — the disastrous flood which came, usually with the springtime ice breakup, to destroy property, drown livestock and cut new channels into fertile farm land.

For decades men talked about development of the stream; some thought in terms of dams, and others championed channelization for restoration of the once profitable shipping business. Always, however, the enormous cost was prohibitive, and countless meetings through the years ended in dreams but not construction. During the Dirty Thirties, Will G. Robinson, as president of the Upper Missouri River Development Association, traveled the state in behalf of that organization's ambitious plan. It called for 21 locks and dams between Sioux City and the mouth of the Yellowstone, with a nine-foot navigation channel between Yankton and the Iowa border city. To some, the proposal sounded far-fetched and unachievable, but others continued to keep the vision alive in spite of the seemingly insurmountable obstacles — physical, financial and political.

Somewhat ironically, when World War II was raging in both major theaters of operation, the United States Congress passed the Flood Control Act of 1944 on December 22 of that year. Thus, in the midst of a great national emergency, South Dakota received the grandest Christmas present in its 55-year history. Involved were two separate proposals — one credited to Lieutenant General Lewis A. Pick of the Corps of Engineers and the other to W. G. Sloan of the

Bureau of Reclamation — meshed under congressional direction into a single multi-purpose concept for the Missouri Basin which came to be known as the Pick-Sloan Plan.

The overall program — which was to be modified considerably through the years — was immense and complex, involving a

Harnessing the Missouri River required a combination of technical genius and enormous financial resources. The four dams within the South Dakota borders included Oahe near Pierre (top) and Gavins Point at Yankton (bottom), the southernmost of the Pick-Sloan barriers. Lake Oahe was created by the largest of the dams, and the Gavins Point backwater became known as Lewis and Clark Lake. (United States Army Corps of Engineers)

minimum of 100 dams and reservoirs on the Missouri and its tributaries. Of primary importance to South Dakota, however, was the fact that four of the five major dams proposed would be within the state's borders.

With the cessation of hostilities, work was scheduled first on the Fort Randall project some six miles south of Lake Andes. In 1946 a construction community appropriately named Pickstown sprang up on the river bank, and the long and expensive task of checking Old Muddy's capricious, destructive habits was underway. Not only would the resultant lakes change the face of the state itself, the recreational interests of its citizens, certain agricultural techniques, tourist patterns and — to some degree — the climate, but the basic work force and subcontractual activity added immeasureably to South Dakota's post-war economy.

When it was apparent that proposed dams on the Missouri would flood historic sites of both white and Indian cultures, research efforts by various universities, The Smithsonian Institution and other agencies were intensified. Archaeological diggings revealed additional clues about pre-Sioux inhabitants, and then the reservoir waters covered the Arikara village locations, Lewis and Clark camps and other points of interest, probably for all time. (United States Army Corps of Engineers)

In the order of building starts, Fort Randall Dam was followed by the Oahe project, begun in 1950 near Pierre; Gavins Point, west of Yankton in 1952; and Big Bend, at Chamberlain in 1960, with United States Senator Lyndon B. Johnson as speaker for the ground-breaking ceremonies. Because the impounded waters of the four dams would flood many historical sites — early trading posts, ghost towns, Lewis and Clark camp stops, Indian villages and other

Snagging of paddlefish became a unique South Dakota-Nebraska recreational feature following impoundment of the Missouri River. Prehistoric in its biological characteristics, the strange specimen has a duck-like bill and a spine of cartilege rather than bone. Undoubtedly paddlefish have been in the stream for centuries, but they were seldom caught except by accident prior to the dams which caused the fish to congregate at the spillways. Despite a cavernous mouth, the "spoonbill catfish" (as the species has been erroneously called) does not take bait, but feeds on minute plankton strained from the river water. (United States Army Corps of Engineers)

noteworthy locations — much archaeological research paralleled the construction work. With the completion of the Big Bend barrier in 1966, the once "water poor" region entered a new era in which the state would be the recipient of both short-term and long-range benefits from the harnessed Missouri. Flood control, electric power generation and multiple recreational advantages were felt almost immediately. The four reservoirs came to be known as the Great Lakes of South Dakota. Dreams of giant irrigation projects and

Electric power, flood control, irrigation and recreation were major benefits derived from the dams erected on the Missouri during the two decades from 1946 to 1966. The first to be completed was Fort Randall (top), and the last of the four in South Dakota was Big Bend (bottom). The Fort Randall reservoir was named Lake Francis Case for the United States senator from Custer who served the state during much of the construction period, while the Big Bend backwater was designated Lake Sharpe for Governor M. Q. Sharpe. (United States Army Corps of Engineers)

pipelines of fresh water to towns and cities with supply problems generated increasing interest. In Fall River and Custer counties, the Angustora Dam on the Cheyenne River gave evidence that the Pick-Sloan Plan had more to offer than the main stem facilities. The ultimate impact of the waterway development cannot be measured or predicted in entirety, however, because it is a continuing application of imagination, technology and political decision.

While the dams were being built, South Dakotans carried on in a business-as-usual routine. Dame Nature proved that she would always be a challenge, despite the engineering and scientific genius of men, when severe blizzards in 1949 and 1952 required Governor Mickelson (and his successor, Sigurd Anderson) to take emergency action to supply stranded communities and to deliver feed to starving livestock and pheasants. In 1952, United States Air Force planes participated in a unique hay-drop to reach isolated cattle herds.

In his second term Governor Anderson (the second Norway-born chief executive and the first to poll over 200,000 votes) had the privilege of serving when the lingering and crippling Rural Credit obligations were finally paid off. At that time — in 1953 — the state became one of eight which could boast of being debt-free. That same year the first commercial oil well began producing in Harding County, adding a new dimension to the economy. In the meantime, another generation of young men and women had put on uniforms to serve the nation in an undeclared but full-scale war in Korea, and Governor Joe Foss, hero of an earlier conflict, signed a bonus bill in 1955 which resulted in payments to more than 26,000 veterans.

George T. Mickelson, governor from 1947 to 1951, unfurled the state flag authorized by the legislature of 1909. The banner features the Great Seal against a blue background. The state motto — "Under God the People Rule" — appears within the seal. (South Dakota State Historical Society)

Foss had been elected to his first term in 1954, was re-elected in 1956 and two years later made a bid to unseat United States Representative George McGovern, who in 1956 had become the first Democrat in 20 years to win a major office in South Dakota, ousting incumbent Harold O. Lovre when he and the G.O.P. apparently disregarded their opponent as a 34-year-old upstart until it was too late to head off the disaster. McGovern, son of an ex-baseball professional turned Methodist preacher, had considered the ministry himself before becoming a $4,500-a-year history professor at his alma mater, Dakota Wesleyan University in Mitchell. He later left his faculty position to serve as executive secretary of the Democratic Party, and from that assignment he launched his own political career. In the 1958 balloting — along with McGovern's victory over Foss — the Democrats elected Ralph Herseth, a Houghton area rancher and implement dealer, to the governorship, the third member of their party to achieve the goal in the state's history.

Two years later — in 1960 — the minority party pitted the popular McGovern against United States Senator Karl E. Mundt, who, like his opponent, had also been an educator before he was first elected to Congress in 1938. Mundt, who had gained national notoriety as acting chairman of the House Un-American Activities Committee during its hearings in 1948 on the case of Alger Hiss, turned back his younger challenger, who promptly was thrust into a

Ralph and Lorna Buntrock Herseth — both from pioneer Brown County families — were a husband-and-wife political team. He served as South Dakota's 21st governor; and following his death, she was elected secretary of state. (Herseth collection)

role of greater prominence and publicity when President John F. Kennedy appointed him head of the Food for Peace program being implemented at that time. Coincidentally, Mundt's cohort in the investigation activities was a California Congressman named Richard M. Nixon, who also was to become a political adversary of McGovern almost a quarter of a century later. In addition to Mundt's re-election in 1960, the Republican resurgence that year also resulted in the defeat of Governor Herseth by Archie Gubberud, a farmer from Alcester.

Getting ahead of the story somewhat, McGovern returned to the state from his federal post in 1962 to try again for the Senate, this time against incumbent Francis H. Case, former Black Hills newspaperman and — coincidentally enough — like McGovern, the son of a minister, graduate of Dakota Wesleyan and possessor of a graduate degree from Northwestern University. Case, unfortunately, died of a heart attack in the spring of the year, and the Republican central committee — on the twentieth ballot — selected as its candidate Lieutenant Governor Joseph H. Bottum, an attorney originally from Faulkton, over such prominent contenders as ex-governors Foss and Anderson in a field of seven. After a bitter campaign, McGovern emerged the apparent winner by a mere 100 votes out of more than a quarter of a million ballots cast. As it turned out, a recount — dramatic in its closeness — finally assured him of victory by a margin of just 597.

Meanwhile, on September 8, 1959 — with the temperature at 96 degrees in the Black Hills — a forest fire suddenly broke out between Lead and Deadwood. Started by a windblown piece of burning trash which ignited the tinder-dry grass, the flames roared through the trees, threatening both cities with destruction as hundreds of firefighters battled the blaze through the day and night. A change in wind direction caused the temperature to drop almost 70 degrees as the frantic effort to control the holocaust went on. As the men took turns eating at soup kitchens and catching a brief rest, they were badly chilled by the unseasonal weather. Like pioneer Dakotans who had opposed prairie fires in earlier days, they could not let up despite physical exhaustion, and by the end of the second day, they had saved both historic cities with the help of courageous pilots who dropped bentonite slurry on the advancing flames. It took an entire week to stamp out the periodic flareups, and then the sprawling acres of charred forests became a frightening reminder of a dreadful episode which could have been ever so much worse.

The following summer brought drouth conditions to many of the counties, but through the years the hardy South Dakotans had learned to expect the ups and downs of nature. Though the effects were sorely felt, the citizenry no longer pulled up stakes as they had in the pioneer period; the state, at long last, had matured and developed sufficiently to withstand such discouraging but endurable blows.

The previously mentioned election of 1960 in which Karl Mundt defeated George McGovern for the Senate seat featured another race which to South Dakota had even more historical importance. In the First Congressional District, Republican Ben Reifel out-polled Ray Fitzgerald 120,033 to 103,755.

The significance, of course, was that Reifel had been born of a Brule Sioux Indian mother and a German-American father in a log cabin at Parmalee on the Rosebud Reservation on September 19, 1906. He was graduated from South Dakota State College in 1932, served during the depression as an agricultural extension agent and an administrator for the Bureau of Indian Affairs, after which he became a United States Army officer in World War II. In 1952 he earned his doctorate in public administration at Harvard University.

The election of Reifel to the United States House of Representatives in 1960 — just one year prior to the 100th anniversary of the creation of Dakota Territory — was a milestone event. By no means did it imply that the differences between Indians and non-Indians

Ben Reifel (center) became the first Sioux Indian to hold a major political office in South Dakota when he was elected United States representative in 1960. He was returned to office on four additional occasions before he retired voluntarily. Beginning in 1938, Karl Mundt (right) served five terms in the House of Representatives and four in the Senate, the longest tenure in Congress by any South Dakotan. He was incapacitated by a stroke in 1969 and died in 1974. (Karl E. Mundt Archives, Dakota State College)

had been resolved, but it pointed out clearly that a majority of whites, blacks, reds and yellows would not hesitate to choose a South Dakotan of Sioux derivation and ample qualification to represent them in the halls of Congress. Not only did Representative Reifel win in 1960, he was re-elected by substantial margins four more times before he voluntarily retired in 1970. It was an achievement which even the militant old Sitting Bull might have appreciated: to see a fellow Teton popularly chosen to a vital leadership role affecting *all* peoples.

Sitting Bull himself — born and ultimately killed in the traditional Teton domain of South Dakota — had been re-introduced into the state's heritage in a rather flamboyant manner, which also might have pleased the proud and loquacious Hunkpapa showman.

Following his death at the hands of Indian policemen on December 15, 1890, the lifeless Sitting Bull had been removed to Fort Yates where, according to the reports of Agent James McLaughlin, he was buried two days later in a canvas shroud in a remote corner of the post's military cemetery. Afterwards, when a decision was made to abandon the particular burial grounds and move the occupants' remains to Keokuk, Iowa, Indians learned of the plan and were successful in their appeal to government authorities to have Sitting Bull's bones — already exhumed — reinterred where they were.

For many years the Hunkpapa leader lay alone in the neglected graveyard until a coterie of history-conscious individuals — Indian and white — decided that the famed medicine man deserved better treatment in death. Clarence Greyeagle of Bullhead, South Dakota, a nephew of Sitting Bull, contacted the three living granddaughters and obtained powers of attorney from them to have their grandfather reburied in a small park overlooking the Missouri River near Mobridge.

Officials of the federal government, the governors of North and South Dakota and other prominent political figures were involved in the long negotiations before it was decided to yield to the wishes of the descendants. There was still concern, however, that citizens of Fort Yates might attempt to thwart the removal, so an elaborate, military-type plan was devised for a secret, night-time invasion of the old cemetery. Author Harold Shunk — himself of Sioux derivation, who in his long career served as superintendent of four Indian agencies and later as president of the South Dakota State Historical Society — described the dramatic episode in a serialized feature in the *Hill City Prevailer* titled "The Story of Sitting Bull":

> The strategists . . . arranged for a heavy truck with a hoist for removing the concrete slab which topped the grave, for a gang of brawny shovel-wielders, for a neat but strong box to hold the bones, and for a heavy steel vault of best quality which they had purchased from an undertaker who agreed to officiate. They also lined up three cars with depend-

A bust of Sitting Bull was sculpted by Korczak Ziolkowski to mark the site of the Hunkpapa medicine man's final resting place overlooking the Missouri River west of Mobridge in Corson County. The Indian leader, who was killed on December 15, 1890, during the course of his arrest, was first buried at Fort Yates, North Dakota. In 1953 his bones were removed to South Dakota after a dramatic raid on the untended plot where they had lain for 63 years. (South Dakota Department of Economic and Tourism Development)

able drivers, each with space in the luggage compartment for the box with the remains. They also engaged a light plane to land near the grave at dawn with accommodations for the much desired cargo.

When all had been carefully planned and the date selected [the night of April 8,1953], one car was sent to Bullhead to pick up Greyeagle, who had the powers of attorney from the Sitting Bull heirs. The Indian agent at Fort Yates was alerted and asked to be present . . . Furthermore, the intrepid group of history-makers did not want any delay in reburial after the remains had been obtained. They, therefore, arranged to have a power shovel on hand . . . so that a grave could be dug in a matter of minutes. They also wanted the remains so buried that they would be secure against attempts at recovery or disturbance. For this purpose they arranged to have 20 tons of ready-mixed concrete on hand to be poured around the steel vault in the new grave.

The night selected for the venture was raw and cold, with a nasty east wind spitting wet snow. By two in the morning the party was underway, and in a couple of hours all were at the grave . . . the power hoist on the truck quickly moved the concrete slab and the shovel men took over. The sandy soil made digging easy, and careful shovel work soon exposed what was unmistakably most of the bones of a human skeleton . . . After the remains had been placed in the homemade casket with a quantity of earth from where the bones had rested, the party began to scan the sky to the south for the air taxi which was to arrive at dawn. [The plane, unfortunately, had been grounded by the weather.]

With all convenient speed, the signal for return to South Dakota was given, and as visibility increased with coming daylight, a watcher was placed in each of the cars to keep a sharp lookout for possible pursuers. The casket was placed in one of the cars, and all three started back, but each by a different road. The car with the remains was to take a little-used shortcut by way of Kenel. The truck with the steel vault fully exposed was to proceed on still another road . . . Fortune favored the strange expeditionary force and it crossed the South Dakota line unnoticed.

When the performers in the historic coup arrived at Memorial Park, the power shovel rapidly dug a grave ten feet deep. The ready-mixed concrete dispenser then dumped in concrete to the depth of two feet. The wooden box containing the remains of Sitting Bull was then placed in the steel vault which was lowered into the wet concrete. The grave was then filled on the top with the mixture. The remains of the dead chief are embedded in a solid block of concrete weighing over 20 tons.

The unique foray — like a Hollywood script in its unfolding — received national and international news coverage, the first story breaking when the bearers of Sitting Bull's mortal relics were able to contact the Associated Press from Wakpala by telephone. Despite its promotional overtones, in many ways the raid was a romantic gesture to cap the life of the controversial Hunkpapa who played a messiah-type role among his people, and, as a result, earned an important niche in the history of South Dakota. Korczak Ziolkowski — who, much like Gutzon Borglum, responded to an obsession to carve a monumental replica of Chief Crazy Horse in Black Hills granite — sculpted a memorial bust of Sitting Bull to adorn the grave site in Corson County.

From his eternal vantage point on the west bluffs of the once free-flowing Missouri, Sitting Bull lies in spirit as a symbol of the challenging past, not only for his people, but for all who struggled to make a home — permanent or nomadic — on the land which came to be known as South Dakota.

AN EPILOGUE

THE CHALLENGE OF THE FUTURE

*It never is verboten for any South Dakotan
To laugh and talk as freely as he votes,
And if they haven't riches to carry in their britches,
They always carry laughter in their throats.*
— *Badger Clark*

Day by day, the continuing story of South Dakota pushes into the future, leaving in its wake an ever-lengthening heritage of development and achievement. That wake, of course, has at various times been glassy smooth and volcanicly turbulent — and undoubtedly there will be ups and downs for new generations as there have been for the old.

The passage of time has proved on numerous occasions that the promising visions of one decade can quickly become the failures and disappointments of the next. In the early 1870s, for instance, the dreams of great fleets of river steamers on the Missouri were exciting to young entrepreneurs; within ten years almost all of the boats were gone. The "boomers" of the 1880s were confident that great cities would blossom on the prairies along rail lines of invaluable worth; instead, scores of the potential "new Chicagos" have faded or disappeared completely, while hundreds of miles of track have been torn up.

(Travel Division South Dakota Department of Highways)

297

The promotional cry of the 1890s boasted that an "endless" artesian water bonanza would generate expansive industrial development in South Dakota and free farmers forever of their dependency upon rain; but like the buffalo and other natural resources, the supply proved no match for greed and conservancy ignorance. Despite glowing predictions, periodic discoveries of coal, tin and petroleum in the past have failed to live up to expectations. The progressive schemes of the 1920s — especially the Rural Credits program to protect South Dakotans from lending agencies and giant corporations — were gaudy and expensive balloons which burst and left greater problems than they were originally meant to solve.

There were the reverse examples, too. No South Dakotan at the turn of the century would have imagined the ultimate impact of the Chinese ringneck pheasant on the state. The same was true of the Rushmore Memorial as a tourist attraction, the Homestake Mine as a persistent economic factor and — in a different vein — the adaptability of a relatively new crop called soybeans. While the Missouri River dams delivered almost immediate benefits, the various other phases and modifications of the Pick-Sloan Plan became subject to the inexorable test of time. So also did a seemingly mysterious Space Age facility in Minnehaha County known as EROS, for Earth Resource Observation Systems, developed as a data center for information sent down from satellites orbiting above the globe more than 40 times higher than the record-breaking balloon flight from the

The EROS project, Earth Resource Observation Systems, near Baltic brought the Space Age pointedly to South Dakota, as the data center began recording and disseminating information received from orbiting satellites. A Remote Sensing Institute at South Dakota State University was also established to make practical use of the scientific imagery collected by EROS. (South Dakota Department of Economic and Tourism Development)

Governor Richard F. Kneip dedicated the Lewis and Clark Memorial Bridge over the Missouri at Chamberlain in July of 1974 as a further link in the two interstate highway systems crossing the state (I-29 and I-90). That same year Kneip became South Dakota's first third-term governor and the first to be elected under a constitutional revision authorizing a four-year stay in office. (South Dakota Department of Economic and Tourism Development)

Stratosphere Bowl in 1935. Even the traditional agricultural practices faced re-evaluation because of changing markets, economic pressures, new techniques and equipment and the erosion of the small family farm.

In two successive national elections, native sons of South Dakota were selected by the Democratic Party as presidential candidates. Born at Wallace, Hubert H. Humphrey (right) spent part of his boyhood in Doland and Huron. He became Vice President of the United States in 1964 and opposed Richard M. Nixon four years later. The birthplace of George S. McGovern was Avon in Bon Homme County. A former professor at Dakota Wesleyan University, he became a United States senator in traditionally Republican South Dakota before being nominated to challenge President Nixon's re-election bid in 1972. (McGovern collection)

As the state moved slowly toward its 100th birthday, the challenges continued. On June 9, 1972, torrential rains in the Black Hills resulted in a tragic flood which claimed the lives of 238 people in Rapid City, Keystone, Box Elder, Black Hawk and elsewhere along the courses of Rapid and Box Elder creeks. The dollar value of damages, disaster relief, cleanup operations and restoration amounted to more than the original payment to France for the entire Louisiana Territory.

Less than a year later, South Dakota made national headlines again when approximately 150 armed representatives of the American Indian Movement (AIM) took over the historic village of Wounded Knee on the Pine Ridge Reservation and precipitated an eleven-day confrontation with local, state and federal authorities. The incident — which came to be known as Wounded Knee II — settled little, but it emphasized clearly that the age-old conflict of cultures was not over.

Politically, the two-party system reasserted itself when Democrat Richard F. Kneip, former state legislator and agricultural equipment dealer from Salem, upset the re-election bid of Governor Frank L. Farrar. Farrar, a Britton attorney, had succeeded Nils Boe, a native of Baltic, as South Dakota's 24th chief executive, 21 of them Republicans. Meanwhile, a constitutional revision extending the term

The South Dakota State School of Mines in Rapid City (shown as it appeared in the 1930s) was established by law in 1885. Eastern State Normal School at Madison — oldest of four such colleges — was founded in 1881, Spearfish in 1883, Southern at Springfield in 1897 (though it had been authorized 16 years earlier) and Northern at Aberdeen in 1902. (Clyde Goin collection)

Casey Tibbs of Fort Pierre, an international rodeo champion, exhibited his skill and tenacity aboard "Nugget" at the Great Western Livestock Rodeo in Los Angeles. Earlier Dakota cowboys went through many of the same gyrations to break wild horses — but without audiences or prize money. (South Dakota Department of Economic and Tourism Development)

United States Marine Corps officer, William "Billy" Mills, a Teton Sioux from Pine Ridge, won a gold medal for the United States in the 10,000 meter run in the 1964 Olympic Games, one of the most notable athletic achievements by a South Dakotan. Prowess contests of all kinds were an important part of Indian culture, and white pioneers were equally sports conscious. Baseball was played on the Dakota prairies almost as soon as the Territory was formed, and in 1925 the American Legion Junior Baseball program had its birthing at Milbank. (South Dakota State Historical Society)

of the office from two to four years resulted in Governor Kneip's tenure becoming the longest in the state's history.

The tax structure; the fate of the government-owned cement plant; the ability of the people to support the seven public institutions of higher learning at Vermillion, Brookings, Springfield, Madison, Aberdeen, Rapid City and Spearfish; out-migration of youth; Indian jurisdictional and treaty matters; and multiple concerns relating to conservation of natural resources became nagging problems of the future as they had been nagging problems of the past.

Two South Dakota-born political figures played unique roles on the national scene. Hubert H. Humphrey, whose birthplace was at Wallace in Codington County, had achieved the second highest office in the land as Vice President during the administration of President Lyndon B. Johnson. In 1968 Humphrey was chosen the Democratic candidate for the Presidency and was defeated by Richard M. Nixon by slightly more than a half million votes in the popular balloting.

Four years later, George McGovern — the second successive native of the state to become the standard-bearer for his party — was beaten by the same Republican opponent. It was ironic, of course, that the two South Dakotans who achieved the unique distinction were both Democrats from a traditionally Republican stronghold; and though neither was able to carry the state in the presidential voting, they gave ample evidence that philosophical beliefs on the prairies were undergoing transformation, too.

Accenting that change in 1972 was the election of Democrat James Abourezk to the United States Senate to succeed Karl Mundt, who retired after being incapacitated by a stroke. It was the first time that South Dakota did not have a Republican in the Upper House. James Abdnor, a Kennebec rancher, won Abourezk's House seat to become the only G.O.P. member of the state's delegation in Washington, D.C., as Democrat Frank Denholm, a former Day County sheriff, was re-elected in the First District.

In August of 1974 Mundt died of a heart ailment after having served in the United States Congress for 34 years, five terms in the House and four in the Senate (more than any other South Dakotan). Once a speech teacher at Eastern Normal College in Madison, he would be remembered appropriately as author of the legislation creating the Voice of America. In the year of his death, Republicans regained both House seats when Abdnor was re-elected and 32-year-old Larry Pressler, a former Rhodes Scholar from the University of South Dakota, upset Denholm. Pressler conducted his campaign from his family home near Humboldt, the same Minnehaha County town where Karl Mundt had been born 74 years earlier. As further evidence that South Dakota's politics had evolved from old-time Norwegian and German dominance, Senator Abourezk and Representative Abdnor were both sons of Lebanese immigrants who had been ranch-to-ranch itinerant merchants in the state's west-river country.

The federal census of 1970 listed 14 cities in the United States with populations greater than that of South Dakota. There are those who insist that the lack of people is a short-coming of serious proportions; others will argue just as vehemently that the open spaces are a major asset in an age of "urban sprawl" elsewhere. Some say that South Dakotans have an inferiority complex about their homeland; others contend that a state with the Rushmore Memorial, the nation's foremost source of gold and farm receipts totaling more than a billion dollars annually does not have to take a back seat to anyone.

Partly — because of the small census count and the local attitude that "everyone knows everyone else," South Dakotans are not particularly hero-conscious — at least not demonstratively so. They will acknowledge with some pride that Frank Baum, author of "The Wizard of Oz" once operated a variety store and published a newspaper in Aberdeen; that Mentor Graham, Abraham Lincoln's teacher, spent his final years in Blunt; that James Earle Fraser, designer of the buffalo nickel and creater of the famed "End of the Trail" sculpture, grew up on a ranch near Mitchell; and that Charles Partlow "Chic" Sale — who gained national recognition as a homespun humorist and whose name became synonymous with the outdoor plumbing he regularly lampooned — was born in Huron in 1885, son of Doctor F. O. Sale, an organizer of the territorial dental association.

The state's citizens are appreciative of the talents of actress Mamie Van Doren, born Joan Olander at Rowena; national television personalities Tom Brokaw, a network newsman, and Myron Floren, an accordionist, both born in Webster; Joe Robbie, a Sisseton native and graduate of the University of South Dakota law school, who became managing partner of the Miami Dolphins professional football franchise (with guidance from Joe Foss, who was named commissioner of the American Football League following his retirement from politics); another professional football star and coach, Norm Van Brocklin, who was born at the tiny village of Parade in Dewey County; novelist Cameron Hawley, who wrote — among other titles — "Executive Suite" and "Cash McCall" and whose birthplace was Howard; artist Oscar Howe, a full-blooded Sioux born on the Crow Creek Reservation; Billy Mills, a Teton from Pine Ridge who won a gold medal for the United States in the 10,000 meter run at the Olympic Games in Tokyo in 1964; and Casey Tibbs, international rodeo champion from Fort Pierre.

More provincially, however, each year since 1912 (when Huron College sponsored the first state basketball tournament won by Redfield over Lake Preston), the residents — Indian and non-Indian — have honored their high school hoop champions with seemingly greater enthusiasm than they have extended to national celebrities. The phenomenon has caused one historian to note that "South Dakotans would rather battle other South Dakotans than unite and tackle mutual problems within and beyond the state."

Be that as it may, South Dakota and her people — by individual and mutual effort — have survived a timbre-testing past and have faced the future with the optimistic spirit of later-day homesteaders. The land of unknown Asiatic wanderers, mysterious Mound Builders, Manuel Lisa, Sitting Bull, Annie Tallent, Crazy Horse, Arthur Mellette, Peter Norbeck, Gladys Pyle, Niels Hansen, Ernest Lawrence, Ben Reifel, George McGovern and the long parade of citizens of all creeds, colors and callings has earned the proud title of *The Challenge State!*

ACKNOWLEDGMENTS

This book is a printed reality primarily because of the interest and enthusiasm of two men: Don Barnhart, former State Superintendent of Public Instruction, and Les Helgeland, chairman of the South Dakota Bicentennial Commission. Their recognition of the need in the schools — and understanding of the scope of the research and writing task involved — culminated in a realistic sponsorship arrangement between the Division of Elementary and Secondary Education and the Bicentennial Commission which made the project feasible.

Once the first step was taken, many others participated in the fulfillment of the mission. Publisher Donald P. Mackintosh and Editor N. Jane Hunt of Brevet Press guided the manuscript through the production process, offering appropriate contributions to enhance the final product. Robert R. Speltz and F. R. Wanek, in administrative roles for the Division of Elementary and Secondary Education, cooperated generously in facilitating the necessary governmental contracts and clearances. So, too, did Arnie Stenseth of the Bicentennial Commission.

In the area of research, Dayton W. Canaday, director of the State Historical Resource Center, responded quickly and positively to all requests for assistance, as did Bonnie Gardner, picture curator. Jan Dykshorn, Janice Fleming, Janet Lounsberry and Barton Voigt of the staff were equally helpful. From the first announcement of the project, the Executive Board of the State Historical Society offered encouragement and support, while individual members Bob Lee (Sturgis), James B. Dunn (Lead), R. B. Swanberg (Sisseton) and Harold W. Shunk (Rapid City) provided specific materials and counsel for the book.

Special thanks are extended to Doctor Herbert S. Schell of the University of South Dakota; to Florence Kribell and Dennis L. Nelson (Yankton), Ardis Ruark (Mitchell), Helen J. Bergh (Aberdeen) and R. B. Williams (Sturgis), who — along with other educators — sent outlines and suggestions to guide the book's development for practical application in the classroom; to Martha Schaer, Irene Kolar and many other librarians in anonymity; to George B. German, Donald G. Brekke, C. B. Gunderson, Richard Blair, Clyde Goin and Jan Rasmussen, who made special publications and other materials available to me; and to daughter Jill Karolevitz for research legwork.

In addition, there were literally hundreds of friends, teachers, associates and some strangers who, through the years, have abetted this work directly and indirectly: in lecture halls of the past, libraries, newspaper morgues, museums, history conferences and a few coffee houses. Other writers — such as history columnist Ellen Tobin of the *Yankton Daily Press & Dakotan* — were of great help because of the ideas they generated.

For a variety of reasons, I owe an appreciative nod to Chuck Cecil and Doctor Paul E. Collins, South Dakota State University; Paul Sampson, National Geographic Society; June Sampson, W. H. Over Museum; Gloria C. Hanson, Division of Elementary and Secondary Education; Lee Sudlow, South Dakota Cooperative Extension Service; William Honerkamp and Steve Nelson, State Department of Economic and Tourism Development; Larry K. Tennyson, State Department of Agriculture; Harold D. Moore, Buechel Memorial Sioux Museum; and Pearl Hein, archivist, Karl E. Mundt Library.

Lastly, I am unceasingly grateful to my wife, Phyllis, who for the fourteenth time in less than ten years has assisted in many, many ways to pull me through another book deadline.

To all those benefactors I have remembered — and any I may have inadvertently overlooked — I offer my sincere thanks.

— R.F.K.

Special Contributors to the First Printing

The following individuals and organizations participated with the South Dakota Division of Elementary and Secondary Education and the State Bicentennial Commission in sponsorship of the first printing: South Dakota Sheriffs and Police Officers Association; South Dakota Girls' State; Daughters of the American Revolution, South Dakota Chapter; South Dakota Hairdressers and Cosmetologists Association; Veterans of Foreign Wars, Department of South Dakota; V.F.W. Auxiliary; First State Bank, Roscoe; State Bank of Waubay; South Dakota Lung Association; The Farmers' State Bank, Estelline; Tabor Chamber of Commerce; American State Bank, Yankton; Burke State Bank; Veblen Community Ruritan; Ray Plowman, Armour; South Dakota Chiropractic Auxiliary; Bank of Cresbard; Citizens' State Bank, Arlington; Northern Oahe Historical Society; Ella Bachman, Isabel; Lawrence County Historical Society; South Dakota Library Association; South Dakota State Firefighters' Auxiliary; John E. Bergh, Volga; South Dakota Civil Preparedness Association.

— R.F.K.

BIBLIOGRAPHY

Vital to the production of this book, in addition to the titles listed below, were the microfilms of the *Yankton Daily Press & Dakotan*, which span almost the entire existence of the Territory and State; the various publications of the South Dakota State Historical Society, especially the discontinued monthly bulletin, *The Wi-Iyohi;* the collections of the Yankton County Historical Society; and literally hundreds of miscellaneous periodicals, theses, clippings and personal records too numerous to be included here.

Allen, Albert H. *Dakota Imprints, 1858-1889.* New York: R. R. Bowker, 1947.

Anson, Robert Sam. *McGovern: A Biography.* New York: Holt, Rinehart and Winston, 1972.

Armstrong, Moses K. *The Early Empire Builders of the Great West.* St. Paul: E. W. Porter, 1901.

Athearn, Robert G. *Forts of the Upper Missouri.* Englewood Cliffs, N. J.: Prentice-Hall, 1967.

Bailey, Dana R. *History of Minnehaha County, South Dakota.* Sioux Falls, S.D.: Brown & Saenger, 1899.

Barton, Winifred. *John P. Williamson, A Brother of the Sioux.* New York: Revell, 1919.

Beadle, William H. H. *Dakota: Its Geography, History and Resources.* St. Paul: D. D. Merrill, 1888.

Bennett, Estelline. *Old Deadwood Days.* New York: J. H. Sears, 1928.

Black Hills Flood of June 9, 1972. Rapid City, S.D.: Midwest Research Publishers, 1972.

Blasingame, Ike. *Dakota Cowboy: My Life in the Old Days.* New York: G. P. Putnam's Sons, 1958.

Bourke, John G. *On the Border with Crook.* New York: Charles Scribner, 1891.

Boyles, Kate and Virgil. *The Homesteaders.* Chicago: A. C. McClurg & Co., 1907.

Bragstad, R. E. *Sioux Falls in Retrospect.* Sioux Falls, S.D.: privately printed, 1967.

Branch, E. Douglas. *The Hunting of the Buffalo.* New York: D. Appleton and Company, 1929.

Brown, Jesse and Willard, A. M. *The Black Hills Trails.* Rapid City, S.D.: Rapid City Journal, 1924.

Bryde, John. *Modern Indians.* Vermillion, S.D.: University of South Dakota, 1969.

Burdick, Usher L. *The Last Days of Sitting Bull, Sioux Medicine Chief.* Baltimore: Wirth Brothers, 1941.

Casey, Robert J. *The Black Hills and Their Incredible Characters.* Indianapolis: The Bobbs-Merrill Company, Inc., 1949.

_____ and Borglum, Mary. *Give the Man Room.* Indianapolis: The Bobbs-Merrill Company, Inc., 1952.

_____ and Douglas, W. A. S. *Pioneer Railroad: The Story of the Chicago and North Western System.* New York: Whittlesey House, 1948.

Cash, Joseph H. "A History of Lead, South Dakota 1876-1900," *South Dakota Historical Collections.* Vol. XXXIV. Pierre, S.D.: South Dakota State Historical Society, 1968.

Chittenden, Hiram M. *History of Early Steamboat Navigation on the Missouri River.* New York: Francis P. Harper, 1903.

_____. *History of the American Fur Trade of the Far West.* (2 vols.) New York: Press of the Pioneers, 1935.

Clem, Alan L. *South Dakota Political Almanac.* (Second edition) Vermillion, S.D.: The Dakota Press, 1969.

Clowser, Don C. *Dakota Indian Treaties.* Deadwood, S.D.: privately printed, 1974.

Cooke, David Coxe. *Fighting Indians of the West*. New York: Dodd, Mead & Company, 1954.

Coursey, Oscar W. *A Complete Biographical Sketch of General William Henry Harrison Beadle*. Mitchell, S.D.: Educator Supply Co., 1916.

_____. *A History of Dakota Wesleyan University for Fifty Years, 1885-1935*. Mitchell, S.D.: Dakota Wesleyan University, 1935.

_____. *Beautiful Black Hills*. Mitchell, S.D.: Educator Supply Co., 1926.

_____. *Biography of Senator Alfred Beard Kittredge, His Complete Life Work*. Mitchell, S.D.: Educator Supply Co., 1915.

_____. *Literature of South Dakota*. Mitchell, S.D.: Educator Supply Co., 1916.

Cropp, Richard. *The Coyotes: A History of the South Dakota National Guard*. Mitchell, S.D.: Educator Supply Co., 1962.

Crouse, Nellis M. *La Verendrye: Fur Trader and Explorer*. Ithaca, N.Y.: Cornell University Press, 1956.

Custer, Elizabeth B. *Boots and Saddle, or Life in Dakota with General Custer*. New York: Harper and Bros., 1885. (Reprinted Norman, Okla.: University of Oklahoma Press, 1962).

Dalthorp, Charles, editor. *South Dakota's Governors*. Sioux Falls, S.D.: Midwest-Beach Co., 1953.

Deloria, Vine, Jr. *Custer Died for Your Sins: An Indian Manifesto*. New York: Macmillan Company, 1969.

Derleth, August. *The Milwaukee Road: Its First Hundred Years*. New York: Creative Age Press, 1948.

Dick, Everett. *The Sod-House Frontier, 1854-1890*. Lincoln, Neb.: Johnsen Publishing Co., 1954.

Douglas, Walter B. *Manuel Lisa*. New York: Argosy-Antiquarian, Ltd., 1964.

Durand, George H. *Joseph Ward of Dakota*. Boston: Pilgrim Press, 1913.

Duratschek, Sr. M. Claudia, O.S.B. *Crusading Along Sioux Trails: A History of the Catholic Missions of South Dakota*. Yankton, S.D.: Benedictine Convent of the Sacred Heart, 1947.

_____. *The Beginnings of Catholicism in South Dakota*. Washington, D.C.: The Catholic University of America Press, 1943.

_____. *Under the Shadow of His Wings*. Aberdeen, S.D.: North Plains Press, 1971.

Eastman, Charles A. *From the Deep Woods to Civilization*. Boston; Little, Brown and Company, 1916.

_____. *Indian Heroes and Great Chieftains*. Boston: Little, Brown and Company, 1926.

_____. *Old Indian Days*. Garden City, N.Y.: Doubleday & Company, Inc., 1907.

Eastman, Elaine Goodale. *Indian Legends Retold*. Boston: Little, Brown and Company, 1919.

Fielder, Mildred. *Railroads of the Black Hills*. Seattle: Superior Publishing Company, 1964.

_____. *The Treasure of Homestake Gold*. Aberdeen, S.D.: North Plains Press, 1970.

_____. *Wild Bill and Deadwood*. Seattle: Superior Publishing Company, 1965.

Finerty, John F. *War-Path and Bivouac, or The Conquest of the Sioux*. Chicago: Donohue, 1890.

Fite, Gilbert C. *Mount Rushmore*. Norman, Okla.: University of Oklahoma Press, 1952.

Garland, Hamlin. *A Son of the Middle Border*. New York: Macmillan Company, 1917.

_____. *Book of the American Indian*. New York: Harper and Bros., 1923.

Hanson, Joseph Mills. *South Dakota in the World War 1917-19*. Pierre, S.D.: South Dakota State Historical Society, 1940.

_____. *The Conquest of the Missouri*. Chicago: A. C. McClurg & Co., 1909.

Hebard, Grace R. *Sacajawea*. Glendale, Calif.: A. H. Clark Co., 1933.

History of the Hutterite Mennonites. Freeman, S.D.: Pine Hill Press, 1974.

History of the Sisseton-Wahpeton Sioux Tribe. Sisseton, S.D.: Sisseton-Wahpeton Sioux Tribe, Inc., 1972.

History of Southeastern Dakota: Its Settlement and Growth. Sioux City, Ia.: Western Publishing Company, 1881.

Holley, Frances C. *Once Their Home, or Our Legacy from the Dakotahs.* Chicago: Donohue & Henneberry, 1892.

Howe, M.A. DeWolfe. *Life and Labors of Bishop Hare, Apostle to the Sioux.* New York: Sturgis and Walton, 1911.

Hunkins, Ralph V. and Lindsey, John C. *South Dakota: Its Past, Present and Future.* New York: Macmillan Company, 1932.

Hunt, N. Jane, editor. *Brevet's South Dakota Historical Markers.* Sioux Falls, S.D.: Brevet Press, 1974.

Hurt, Wesley R. and Lass, William E. *Frontier Photographer: Stanley J. Morrow's Dakota Years.* Lincoln, Neb.: University of Nebraska Press, 1956.

Hyde, George E. *A Sioux Chronicle.* Norman, Okla.: University of Oklahoma Press, 1956.

_____. *Red Cloud's Folk.* Norman, Okla.: University of Oklahoma Press, 1937.

_____. *Spotted Tail's Folk: A History of the Brule Sioux.* Norman, Okla.: University of Oklahoma Press, 1961.

Hyde, William J. *Dig or Die, Brother Hyde.* New York: Harper and Bros., 1954.

Jennewein, J. Leonard. *Calamity Jane.* Huron, S.D.: privately printed, 1952.

_____ and Boorman, Jane, editors. *Dakota Panorama.* Sioux Falls, S.D.: Dakota Territorial Centennial Commission, 1961. (Reprinted Sioux Falls, S.D.: Brevet Press, 1974).

Johnson, Willis E. *South Dakota, A Republic of Friends.* Mitchell, S.D.: Educator Supply Co., 1923.

Josephy, Alvin M., Jr. *The Indian Heritage of America.* New York: Alfred A. Knopf, 1968.

Karolevitz, Robert F. *Newspapering in the Old West.* Seattle: Superior Publishing Company, 1965.

_____. *Pioneer Church in a Pioneer City.* Aberdeen, S.D.: North Plains Press, 1971.

_____. *Where Your Heart Is: The Story of Harvey Dunn, Artist.* Aberdeen, S.D.: North Plains Press, 1970.

_____. *Yankton: A Pioneer Past.* Aberdeen, S.D.: North Plains Press, 1972.

Kaufman, Fred S. *Custer Passed Our Way.* Aberdeen, S.D.: North Plains Press, 1971.

Kellar, Kenneth C. *Seth Bullock: Frontier Marshal.* Aberdeen, S.D.: North Plains Press, 1972.

Kingsbury, George W. *History of Dakota Territory.* (5 vols.) Chicago: The S. J. Clarke Publishing Company, 1915.

Kohl, Edith E. *Land of the Burnt Thigh.* New York: Funk and Wagnalls, 1938.

Krause, Herbert and Olson, Gary D. *Prelude to Glory.* Sioux Falls, S.D.: Brevet Press, 1974.

Lamar, Howard Roberts. *Dakota Territory 1861-1889: A Study of Frontier Politics.* New Haven, Conn.: Yale University Press, 1956.

Lass, William E. *A History of Steamboating on the Upper Missouri River.* Lincoln, Neb.: University of Nebraska Press, 1962.

Lee, Wayne C. *Scotty Philip, The Man Who Saved the Buffalo.* Caldwell, Idaho: The Caxton Printers, Ltd., 1975.

Lewis, Meriwether and Clark, William. *Original Journals of the Lewis and Clark Expedition, 1804-1806.* New York: Dodd, Mead & Company, 1904.

Lowe, Barrett. *Heroes and Hero Tales of South Dakota.* Minneapolis: Hale, 1931.

_____. *Twenty Million Acres: The Story of America's First Conservationist, William Henry Harrison Beadle.* Mitchell, S.D.: Educator Supply Co., 1937.

Lowie, Robert H. *Indians of the Plains.* New York: McGraw-Hill Book Company, 1954.

Luttig, John C. *Journal of a Fur-Trading Expedition on the Upper Missouri, 1812-1813.* St. Louis: Missouri Historical Society, 1920.

Martin, Cy. *The Saga of the Buffalo.* New York: Hart Publishing Company, Inc., 1973.

McGillicuddy, Julia B. *McGillycuddy, Agent.* Palo Alto, Calif.: Stanford University Press, 1941.

McGregor, James H. *The Wounded Knee Massacre, From the Viewpoint of the Sioux.* Minneapolis: Lund Press, 1940.

McLaughlin, James. *My Friend the Indian.* Boston: Houghton Mifflin Co., 1910.

Meadowcroft, Enid L. *The Story of Crazy Horse.* New York: Grossett and Dunlap, 1945.

Meyer, Roy W. *History of the Santee Sioux: United States Indian Policy on Trial.* Lincoln, Neb.: University of Nebraska Press, 1967.

Miles, Nelson A. *Personal Recollections.* Chicago: Werner Company, 1896.

Miller, David H. *Ghost Dance.* New York: Duell, Sloan and Pearce, 1959.

Miller, Margaret. *Hay County History.* Vermillion, S.D.: Broadcaster Press, Inc., 1972.

Neihardt, John G. *Black Elk Speaks.* New York: William Morrow & Co., 1932. (Reprinted Lincoln, Neb.: University of Nebraska Press, 1961).

————. *Song of Hugh Glass.* New York: Macmillan Company, 1915.

————. *The River and I.* New York: G. P. Putnam's Sons, 1910.

Nelson, Bruce. *Land of the Dakotahs.* Minneapolis: University of Minnesota Press, 1946.

Oehler, C. M. *The Great Sioux Uprising.* New York: Oxford University Press, 1959.

Parker, Watson. *Black Hills Ghost Towns.* Chicago: Swallow Press, 1974.

Peattie, Roderick, editor. *The Black Hills.* New York: Vanguard Press, Inc., 1952.

Reese, John B. *Some Pioneers and Pilgrims on the Prairies of Dakota.* Mitchell, S.D.: privately printed, 1920.

Riggs, Stephen Return. *Mary and I: Forty Years With the Sioux.* Chicago: W. G. Holmes, 1880.

Robinson, Doane. *Brief History of South Dakota.* New York: American Book Company, 1926.

————. *Encyclopedia of South Dakota.* Sioux Falls, S.D.: Will A. Beach Printing Co., 1925.

————. *History of the Dakota or Sioux Indians.* Aberdeen, S.D.: News Printing Co., 1904.

————. *History of South Dakota.* (2 vols.) Chicago: B. F. Bowen and Co., 1904.

————. *History of South Dakota.* (3 vols.) Chicago: The American Historical Society, Inc., 1930.

Rolvaag, O. E. *Giants in the Earth.* New York: Harper and Bros., 1924.

Rosen, Peter. *Pa-Ha-Sa-Pa, or The Black Hills of South Dakota.* St. Louis: Nixon-Jones Printing Co., 1895.

Salisbury, Albert P. and Jane. *Two Captains West.* Seattle: Superior Publishing Company, 1950.

Sampson, York, editor. *South Dakota: Fifty Years of Progress 1889-1936.* Sioux Falls, S.D.: S.D. Golden Anniversary Book Co., 1939.

Sandoz, Mari. *Cheyenne Autumn.* New York: Hastings House Publishers, 1953.

————. *Crazy Horse, The Strange Man of the Oglalas.* New York: Alfred A. Knopf, 1942.

Schell, Herbert S. *A History of South Dakota.* Lincoln, Neb.: University of Nebraska Press, 1961.

Shunk, Harold. "The Story of Sitting Bull." Serialized in 18 installments in *The Hill City (S.D.) Prevailer,* beginning January 1, 1974, and ending May 16, 1974.

Smith, George M. *South Dakota, Its History and Its People.* Chicago: The S. J. Clarke Publishing Company, 1915.

———— and Young, Clark M. *History and Government of South Dakota.* New York: American Book Company, 1904.

Sneve, Virginia Driving Hawk. *They Led a Nation.* Sioux Falls, S.D.: Brevet Press, Inc., 1975.

South Dakota Guide. Federal Writers' Project, Works Progress Administration. Pierre, S.D.: State Publishing Co., 1938.

South Dakota Historical Collections. (38 vols.) Pierre, S.D.: South Dakota State Historical Society, 1905-74.

South Dakota Place Names. South Dakota Writers' Project, Works Progress Administration. Vermillion, S.D.: University of South Dakota, 1941. (Reprinted Sioux Falls, S.D.: Brevet Press, 1973).

Spindler, Will H. *Tragedy Strikes at Wounded Knee.* Gordon, Neb.: Gordon Publishing Co., 1955.

Spring, Agnes Wright. *The Cheyenne & Black Hills Stage and Express Routes.* Lincoln, Neb.: University of Nebraska Press, 1948.

Standing Bear, Luther. *Land of the Spotted Eagle.* Boston: Houghton Mifflin Co., 1933.

_____. *My People, The Sioux.* Boston: Houghton Mifflin Co., 1928.

Stutenroth, Stella Marie. *Daughters of Dakotah.* Mitchell, S.D.: Educator Supply Co., 1942.

Sully, Langdon. *No Tears for the General.* Palo Alto, Calif.: American West Publishing Co., 1974.

Swiss-Germans in South Dakota. Freeman, S.D.: Pine Hill Press, 1974.

Taber, Clarence W. *Breaking Sod on the Dakota Prairies.* New York: World Book Company, 1924.

Tallent, Annie D. *The Black Hills, or The Last Hunting Ground of the Dakotahs.* St. Louis: Nixon-Jones Printing Co., 1899. (Reprinted Sioux Falls, S.D.: Brevet Press, 1974).

Thorpe, Cleata B. *The John L. Pyle Family: Dakotans Extraordinary.* Huron, S.D.: Creative Printing Co., 1973.

Torrey, Edwin C. *Early Days in Dakota.* Minneapolis: Farnham Printing and Stationery, 1925.

Van Nuys, Laura Bower. *The Family Band.* Lincoln, Neb.: University of Nebraska Press, 1961.

Vestal, Stanley. *New Sources of Indian History, 1850-91.* Norman, Okla.: University of Oklahoma Press, 1934.

_____. *Sitting Bull, Champion of the Sioux.* New York: Houghton Mifflin Co., 1932.

_____. *The Missouri.* New York: Farrar and Rinehart, 1945.

_____. *Warpaths and Council Fire: The Plains Indians' Struggle for Survival in War and in Diplomacy.* New York: Random House, 1948.

Waldo, Edna LaMoore. *Dakota.* Caldwell, Ida.: Caxton Printers, 1936.

WarCloud, Paul. *Sioux Indian Dictionary.* Pierre, S.D.: State Publishing Co., 1968.

Wenzlaff, Gustav G. *Sketches and Legends of the West.* Pierre, S.D.: Capitol Supply Co., 1912.

White, Dale. *Steamboat Up the Missouri.* New York: Viking Press, Inc., 1958.

Wilder, Laura Ingalls. *Little Town on the Prairie.* New York: Harper and Bros., 1941.

_____. *The Long Winter.* New York: Harper and Bros., 1940.

Wissler, Clark. *Indians of the United States.* Garden City, N.Y.: Doubleday & Company, Inc., 1953.

INDEX

James River (Jacques, Dakota) - 8, 12, 28, 34, 49, 51, 68, 82, 88, 91, 131, 133, 137-138, 219, 221, 237.
Jamestown Alert - 149.
Jamestown, N.D. - 219.
Jay Cooke and Company - 96.
Jayne, William - 53-56, 60, 64, 67-69, 72, 78, 88.
Jefferson (Adelescat) - 89, 125-126, 258.
Jefferson, Pres. Thomas - 21-22, 274.
Jenney, Walter P. - 109-110.
Jensen, Leslie - 267, 269.
Jewel Cave - 5.
John Morrell and Company - 232, 234.
Johnson, A. C. - 237.
Johnson, Pres. Andrew - 77, 80, 101.
Johnson, Edwin S. - 239, 256.
Johnson, Pres. Lyndon B. - 287, 302.
Jones County - 224.
Josie L. K. (ferryboat) - 133.
"Judge Brookings" (locomotive) - 84.

Kadoka - 1.
Kenel - 295.
Kennebec - 282, 302.
Kennedy, Pres. John F. - 291.
Keokuk, Ia. - 293.
Keystone - 273, 278, 300.
Kidder, Jefferson P. - 51.
Kills Game and Comes Home - 66.
Kimball - 134, 143.
Kind, Ezra - 103.
Kingsbury County - 33, 150.
Kingsbury, George W. - 45, 56, 72, 87, 128, 137, 174.
Kiowa Indians - 11-12.
Kittaning, Pa. - 54, 80.
Kittredge, Alfred B. - 221, 231.
Kneip, Richard F. - 1, 299-300, 302.
Knights of Labor - 209.
Knox, Frank - 276.
Ku Klux Klan - 157, 159.
Kyle, James H. - 210, 221.

La Beau - 225, 231.
Lake Andes (town) - 286.
Lake Francis Case - 288.
Lake Herman - 42.
Lake Kampeska - 47.
Lake Madison Chautauqua Association - 210.
Lake Mitchell - 8.
Lake Oahe - 285.
Lakeport - 89.
Lake Preston (town) - 303.
Lake Sharpe - 288.
Lake Superior - 11.
Lake Traverse - 40.
La Londette, Edouard - 17.
Lamar, Howard Roberts - 80.
Landon, Alfred M. - 267.
La Verendrye brothers - 1, 18, 21, 23, 34, 75, 232.

La Verendrye, Francois - 17-19.
La Verendrye, Louis Joseph - 17-19.
La Verendrye, Pierre - 18.
Lawrence, Carl G. - 281.
Lawrence County - 130, 172.
Lawrence, Ernest O. - 280-281, 304.
Lawrence, John H. - 281.
Lead - 1, 111, 114, 159-160, 162-163, 182, 216, 218, 259, 277, 282-283, 291.
Leavenworth, Henry - 28, 30-31.
LeBeau, J. B. - 163.
Lee, Andrew E. - 214-215, 217.
Lee, Annie Chappell - 214.
Lee, Robert E. - 77.
LeMars, Ia. - 84.
Lemmon - 32, 104, 224, 231, 265.
Lemmon, G. E. - 224.
Leola - 157, 221.
Lesterville - 158.
Le Sueur, Charles Pierre - 17.
Lewis and Clark - 20, 22-26, 30, 32, 39, 45, 76, 286-287.
Lewis and Clark Lake - 285.
Lewis and Clark Memorial Bridge - 299.
Lewis, Meriwether - 22.
Lincoln, Pres. Abraham - 43, 52-53, 72, 77-78, 272, 274, 303.
Lincoln, Mary Todd - 45, 53-54, 78.
Lincoln, Neb. - 91.
Lindbergh, Charles O. - 251.
Lisa, Manuel - 23, 25-26, 28, 304.
Litchfield, Minn. - 63-64.
Little Big Horn River - 30, 97, 117, 119-120, 186.
Little Crow - 63.
Livingston (ferryboat) - 139.
Livingston, Robert R. - 21.
Loisel, Registre - 21, 23.
Long Lake - 265.
Lookout Mountain - 103.
Los Angeles, Calif. - 301.
Loucks, Henry L. - 209.
Lounsberry, Clement A. - 99-100.
Louisiana Territory (Purchase) - 5, 19, 21-22, 30, 34, 300.
Love Dog - 15.
Love, Nat - 114.
Lovre, Harold O. - 290.
Lower Brule Agency - 193, 230.
Luttig, John C. -26.

MacKenzie, Murdo - 224.
Mad Bear - 66.
Madison - 147, 168, 178-179, 300, 302.
Maine (battleship) - 217.
Maloney, Chris - 62.
Mammoth Springs - 211.
Mandan Indians - 10-11, 20, 24, 34.
Mandan, N.D. - 149.
Manhattan Island, N.Y. - 36.
Mankato, Minn. - 64, 68.
Manuel, Fred - 113, 162-163.
Manuel, Moses - 113, 162-163.

Manypenny, George W. - 120, 122.
Marion Junction - 133.
Marriott, A. D. - 224.
Marsh, Grant - 118-119.
Marshalltown, Ia. - 70.
Marty, Bishop Martin - 186, 189.
Matador Ranch - 224.
Mazakutamani, Paul - 42.
McBride, John - 62.
McCall, Jack - 113-114.
McCook, Edwin S. - 95-96, 106.
McGillicuddy, Valentine T. - 201, 203.
McGovern, George S. - 217, 280, 290-292, 299, 302, 304.
McKay, William T. - 104.
McKenzie, Alexander - 146-150.
McKinley, Pres. William - 220, 222, 228.
McLaughlin, James A. - 194, 199, 293.
McMaster, William H. - 249, 252, 255.
McPherson County - 150, 157.
Mdewankanton Indians - 1, 9, 12, 40.
Meade, George C. - 105.
Meckling - 141.
Medary - 1, 41, 51, 99.
Medicine Creek - 131.
Mellette, Arthur C. - 1, 165, 172, 174-175, 177-181, 198, 205, 209-210, 215, 304.
Mellette County - 231.
Mendota, Minn. - 40.
Meridian Highway (U.S. 81) - 249.
Meyer, Carl W. - 130.
Miami Dolphins - 303.
Mickelson, George T. - 284, 289.
Midway County - 51.
Milbank - 134, 181, 301.
Milbank, Jeremiah - 134.
Miles, Nelson A. - 199, 206.
Miller - 269, 284.
Mills, Anson - 120, 121.
Mills, William - 301, 303.
Milltown - 138.
Miner County - 138, 179.
Minneconjou Indians - 1, 9, 12, 79, 200, 203.
Minnehaha County - 99, 171, 173, 236, 280, 298, 302.
Minnesota River - 27, 40, 63.
Mission Hill - 240.
Mississippi River - 11, 17-18, 21, 27, 30, 39, 75.
Missouri Fur Company - 20-21, 28.
Missouri River - 3, 10-12, 14, 17-23, 25-28, 30-33, 39-40, 43-47, 49-50, 52, 54, 64, 68-69, 72-73, 75-77, 79, 81-83, 85-88, 90-91, 100-102, 107-108, 110, 119, 125-131, 133-134, 137-140, 142, 144, 160-161, 181, 187, 194, 206, 221-222, 224-225, 227, 231, 244, 249, 284-288, 293-294, 297-299.
Missouri River Transportation Company (Coulson Packet Line) - 85, 118-119, 142.

Mitchell - 133, 138, 143, 149, 226-228, 240, 267, 279, 290, 303.
Mitchell, Alexander - 131, 134.
Mobridge - 66, 222, 225, 231, 293-294.
Mohawk Indians - 36.
Montana City (gold camp) - 111.
Moody County - 207.
Moody, Gideon C. - 172, 177-178, 211.
Moreau River - 1.
Morrow, Stanley J. - 94, 113, 121.
Mound Builders - 8, 10-11, 304.
Mundt, Karl E. - 290-292, 302.
Murdo - 224.
Murray, Alexander H. - 65.

Nairn, John - 68.
Narcelle, Edward - 223.
Narcelle, Narcisse - 223.
Narcelle, Paul - 223.
National (auto) - 240.
National Geographic Society - 261-262.
National Recovery Administration - 257.
National Woman Suffrage Association - 174.
Nauvoo, Ill. - 39.
Neihardt, John G. - 75-76.
Nellie Peck (steamboat) - 139.
New Holland - 158.
New Orleans, La. - 18, 21.
New York Stock Exchange - 251.
Nicollet, Joseph N. - 32.
Niobrara River - 44, 126.
Nixon, Pres. Richard M. - 291, 299, 302.
Nonpartisan League - 242, 245.
Norbeck, Peter - 238-239, 241-243, 247, 249, 251-252, 256, 269, 272, 274, 304.
Northern Pacific Railroad - 99, 126, 146, 150, 212, 219.
Northern State College (Northern Normal and Industrial School) - 281, 300.
North Platte River - 102, 117.
Northwest Company - 20.
Northwestern Independent - 58.
Northwestern University - 291.
Northwest Ordinance of 1787 - 36.
Nuttall, Thomas - 31.

Oahe Dam - 1, 285, 287.
Oahe Mission - 186.
Oelrichs - 166.
O'Fallon, Benjamin - 30.
Oglala Boarding School - 193.
Oglala Indians - 1, 9, 12, 30, 79, 100, 110, 120, 122, 187, 191-192, 197, 204.
Ohio River - 11.
Oldsmobile - 241.
Olds, Ransom E. - 241.
Omaha Indians - 20.
Omohundro, J. B. (Texas Jack) - 113, 116.

Rowena - 173, 303.
Royer, Daniel F. - 198-199, 206.
Running Water - 133.
Rural Electrification Administration - 283.
Rushmore, Charles E. - 272, 274.
Rushmore Memorial (Shrine of Democracy) - 239, 270-275, 298, 303.
Russell, Thomas H. - 106-108.

Sacajawea - 23-24.
St. James, Neb. - 68.
St. Louis Fur Company - 26.
St. Louis, Mo. - 18, 20-21, 24, 26, 31, 43, 45, 53, 76-77, 83, 85-86.
St. Paul, Minn. - 41, 95, 206.
St. Paul Press - 65.
St. Peter (steamboat) - 32.
Sale, Charles P. (Chic) - 303.
Sale, F. O. - 303.
Salem - 300.
Salmon River - 72.
San Benito, Tex. - 243.
Sanborn County - 240.
Sand Lake - 34.
San Francisco, Calif. - 218-219.
Sans Arc Indians - 1, 9, 12, 79.
Santee Indians - 9, 12, 40-41, 47, 63-70, 82, 87, 201, 203-204, 207.
Saturday Evening Post - 275.
Schell, Herbert S. - 72.
Scotland - 166.
Scotland Academy - 248.
Sears (auto) - 240.
Selby - 284.
Semipalatinsk, Siberia - 218.
Seventh Cavalry Regiment - 92-95, 100, 102-104, 117-120, 186, 200-202.
Shaffer, William - 54.
Shannon, George - 24.
Sharpe, M. Q. - 255, 282, 284, 288.
Sheidley Company - 224.
Sheldon, Charles H. - 211-215.
Sheldon, Rev. Stewart - 169.
Sherman, E. A. - 171.
Sherman, William T. - 100.
Shober, John H. - 50, 56.
Short Bull - 197, 200.
Shoshone Indians - 23.
Shunk, Harold - 293.
Sica (Sieche) Hollow - 1, 205.
Sidney, Neb. - 114, 162.
Sioux City and Black Hills Transportation Company - 127.
Sioux City Register - 62.
Sioux City, Ia. - 42, 50-51, 57, 64, 73, 81, 83-85, 89, 92, 107-108, 137, 148, 226, 284.
Sioux City Times - 107.
Sioux (Dakota) Indians - 1, 9, 11-12, 14-16, 18, 20-21, 26, 28, 30, 33, 39, 41-42, 45-47, 58, 64, 73, 75-76, 79, 88, 101, 103, 105, 109-110, 116-121, 129,

135, 156, 161, 185, 191-193, 195-198, 200, 203-205, 232, 292-293, 303.
Sioux Falls (Sioux Falls City) - 41-42, 50-51, 54, 57-58, 64, 66-67, 79, 82, 91, 99, 131, 135, 137, 145-146, 148, 166-167, 170-172, 174-177, 186, 209-210, 212, 216-217, 221, 232, 234, 236-237, 241, 244, 248-249, 269, 277, 279, 283.
Sioux Falls College (Dakota Collegiate Institute) - 170-171.
Sisseton - 181, 207, 303.
Sisseton Indians - 9, 12, 40, 185.
Sisseton-Wahpeton (Lake Traverse) Reservation - 198, 203, 205, 207.
Sitting Bear - 66.
Sitting Bull - 118, 120, 186, 189-191, 193-194, 199, 292-295, 304.
Slim Buttes - 120-121.
Sloan, W. G. - 284.
Smith, Fred R. - 255.
Smith, Harry W. (Preacher) - 113.
Smith, Jedediah - 32, 34.
Smithsonian Institution - 286.
Smutty Bear - 47-49.
Smutty Bear Bottom - 49.
Somers, Jim - 61.
Sounding Heavens - 42.
Sousa, John Philip - 226-228.
South Dakota Highway Department - 249.
South Dakota League of Women Voters - 248.
South Dakota National Guard - 243, 276.
South Dakota (Dakota) School of Mines - 161, 300.
South Dakota State Historical Society - 18, 275, 293.
South Dakota State University (Dakota, South Dakota Agricultural College) - 145, 147, 212, 214, 218, 221, 292, 298.
Southern Minnesota Railway - 134.
Southern Pacific Railroad - 99.
Spanish-American War - 216.
Spanish Influenza - 246.
Spearfish - 103, 114, 147, 300, 302.
Spencer - 216.
Spink County - 42, 237.
Spink County War - 180.
Spink, Solomon - 96.
Spirit Lake Massacre - 41.
Spirit Mound - 24.
Split Rock Creek - 82.
Spotted Tail - 109, 111, 122, 187-189, 200.
Springfield, Ill. - 53.
Springfield (Wanari) - 83, 91, 133, 138-139, 147, 300, 302.
Stanage, John - 62.
Stanage, Mrs. John - 51.
Standard, The - 140.
Standing Bear, Luther - 191.